Houghton Mifflin Mathematics

Authors

Lelon R. Capps   W.G. Quast   Mary Ann Haubner

William L. Cole   Leland Webb   Charles E. Allen

Coordinating Author

Ernest R. Duncan

Consultants

Diane Ashenberger
Teacher
Murrell Taylor Elementary School
Jacksonville, Arkansas

Mary S. Jackson
Teacher
Greenview Elementary School
Columbia, South Carolina

Pat Traylor
Teacher
Laurel Elementary School
San Mateo, California

Houghton Mifflin Company   BOSTON

Atlanta   Dallas   Geneva, Ill.   Lawrenceville, N.J.   Palo Alto   Toronto

CONTENTS

4 SUBTRACTION FACTS THROUGH 7 81

5 SUBTRACTION FACTS THROUGH 10 107

6 PLACE VALUE THROUGH 99 135

10 MEASUREMENT 249

11 ADDITION AND SUBTRACTION TWO DIGIT NUMBERS 279

12 GEOMETRY AND FRACTIONS 309

13 ADDITION AND SUBTRACTION FACTS THROUGH 18 337

1

Read with the children:

Count the number of pencils. Do you have more than 8?

NUMBERS THROUGH 10

ONE AND TWO

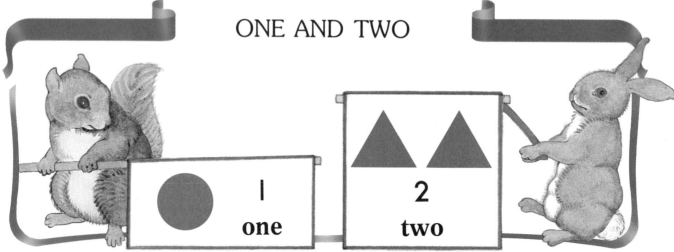

●	**1** one
▲▲	**2** two

Ring the number.

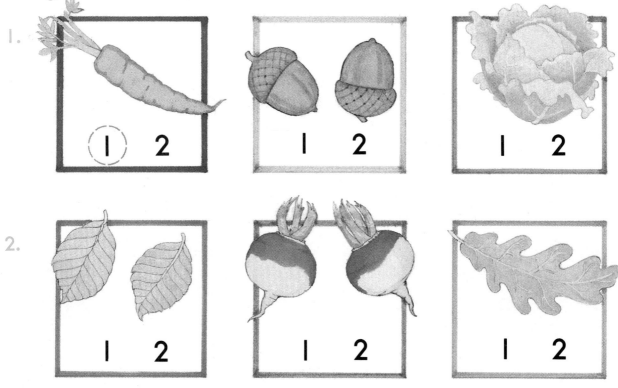

1.   ① 2   1 2   1 2

2.   1 2   1 2   1 2

Write 1 and 2.

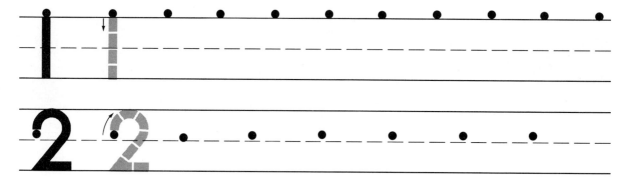

Identifying One and Two, Writing 1 and 2

THREE AND FOUR

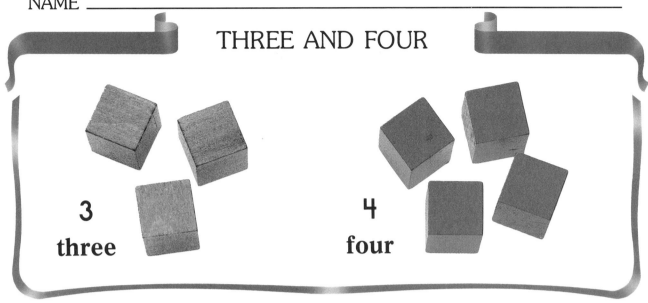

3
three

4
four

Ring the number.

1.   3   4   3   4   3   4

2.   3   4   3   4   3   4

3.   3   4   3   4   3   4

Identifying Three and Four   three   **3**

Write 3 and 4.

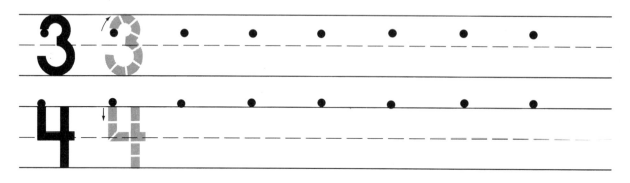

Write the number.

4.

‾3‾

‾ ‾ ‾

5.

‾ ‾ ‾

‾ ‾ ‾

6.

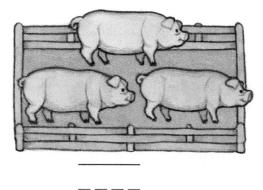

‾ ‾ ‾

‾ ‾ ‾

Writing 3 and 4

FIVE AND SIX

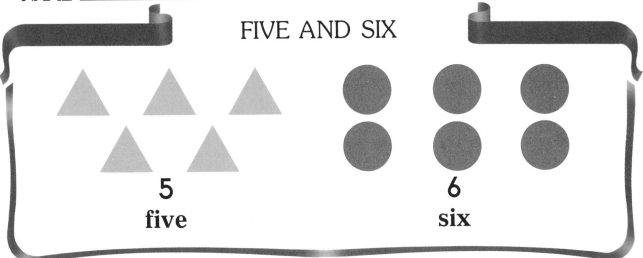

5
five

6
six

Ring the number.

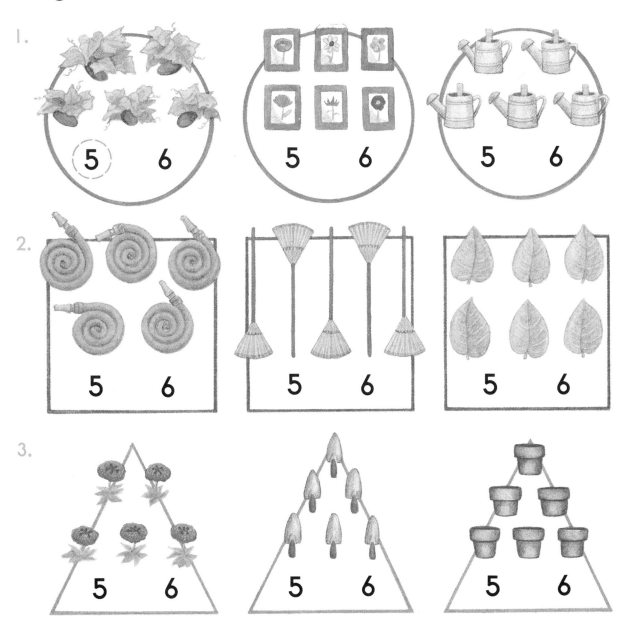

1.

| 5   6 | 5   6 | 5   6 |

2.

| 5   6 | 5   6 | 5   6 |

3.

| 5   6 | 5   6 | 5   6 |

Write **5** or **6**.

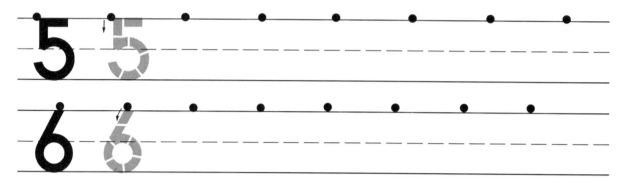

Write the number.

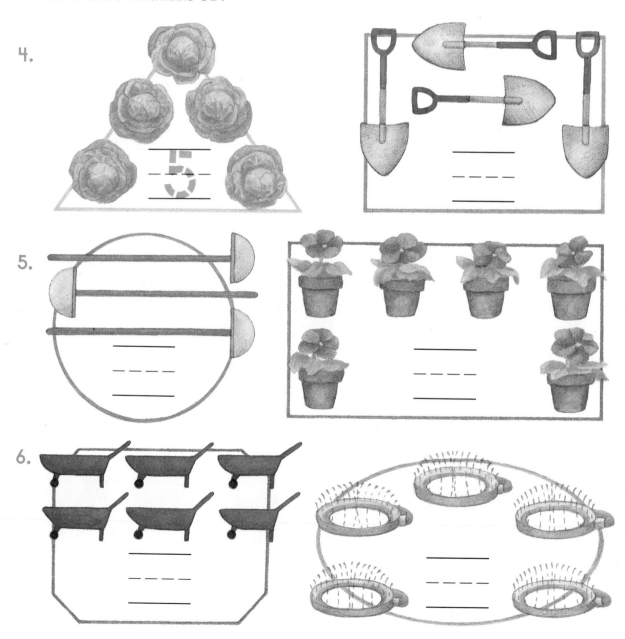

4.

5.

6.

PROBLEM SOLVING

Ring the 🚗 nearest the 🛑.

Ring the  nearest the .

7.

8.

9.

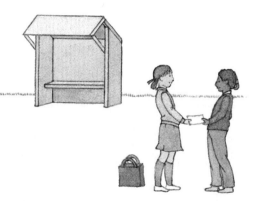

☆ Ring the red number
nearest the blue number.

10. 0   I   2   ③   4   5   6
_____

11. 0   I   2   3   4   5   6
_____

12. 0   I   2   3   4   5   6

Copyright © 1987 by Houghton Mifflin Company. All rights reserved. Printed in U.S.A.

Problem Solving

ZERO

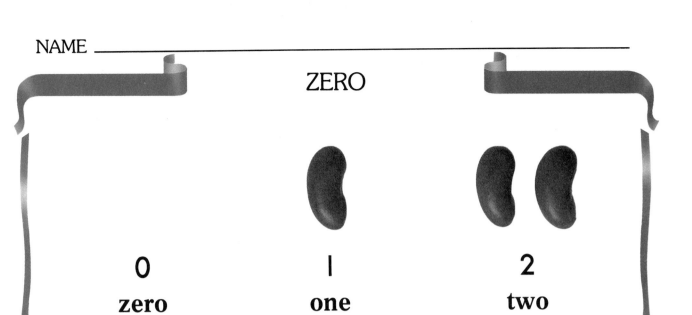

0	l	2
zero	**one**	**two**

Ring the number.

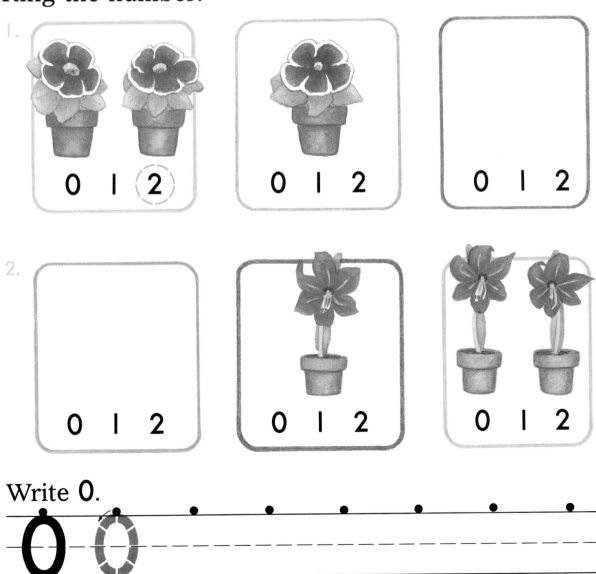

1.

0 l (2)

0 l 2

0 l 2

2.

0 l 2

0 l 2

0 l 2

Write 0.

0 0

Write the number.

3.

4.

(pages 1–10)

CHECKPOINT 1   Write the number.

1.

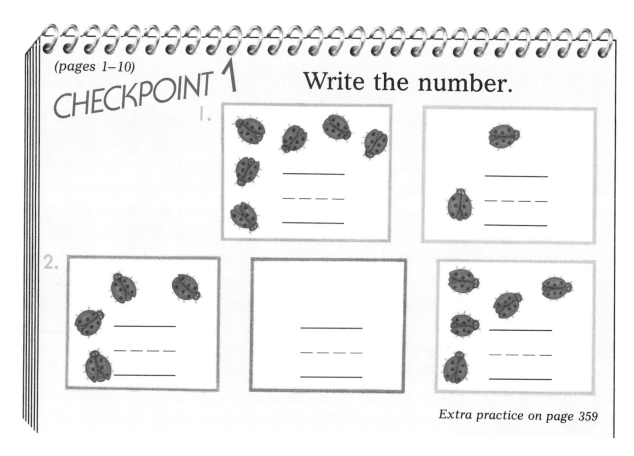

2.

Extra practice on page 359

SEVEN AND EIGHT

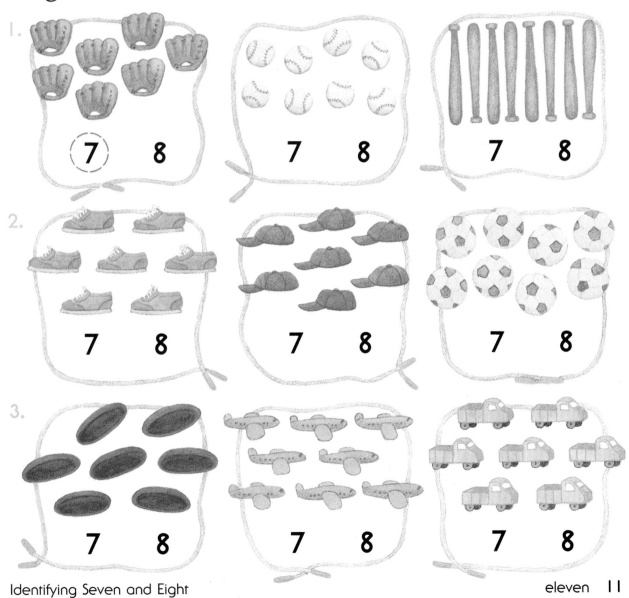

7
seven

8
eight

Ring the number.

1.
(7)   8

7   8

7   8

2.
7   8

7   8

7   8

3.
7   8

7   8

7   8

Identifying Seven and Eight

Write **7** and **8**.

7 7 • • • • • • •

8 8 • • • • • • •

Write the number.

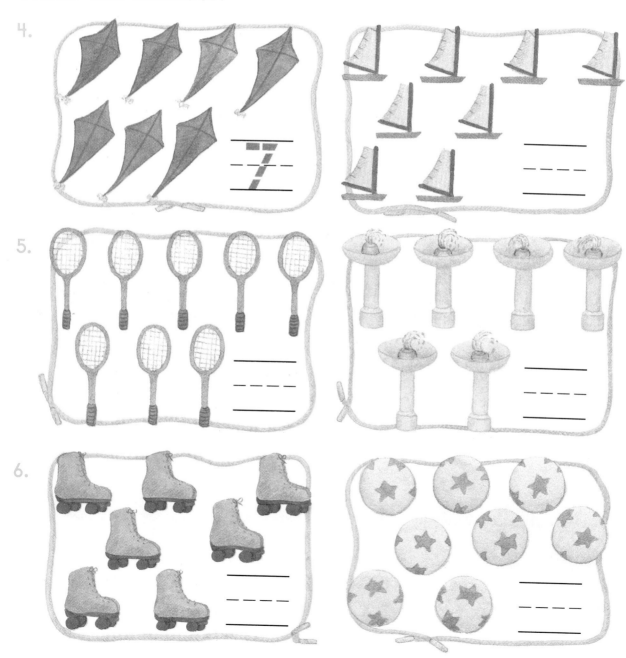

4. _7_

5.

6.

NINE AND TEN

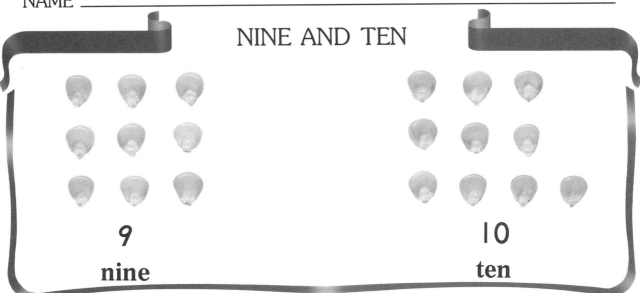

9

nine

10

ten

Ring the number.

1.

(9)   10

9   10

9   10

2.

9   10

9   10

9   10

3.

9   10

9   10

9   10

Write 9 and 10.

9 9 • • • • • •

10 10 • • • • • •

Write the number.

4. _____ 9 _____

_____ _____

5. _____ _____

_____ _____

6. _____ _____

_____ _____

Writing 9 and 10

PENNIES

1¢
penny

Write the number.

1.   __2__ ¢

2.   _____ ¢

3.   _____ ¢

4.   _____ ¢

5.
        _____ ¢

6.   _____ ¢

Ring enough pennies.

7. 3¢

8. 4¢

9. 6¢

10. 5¢

11. 7¢

12. 8¢

Identifying Value of Pennies to 10¢

ORDERING

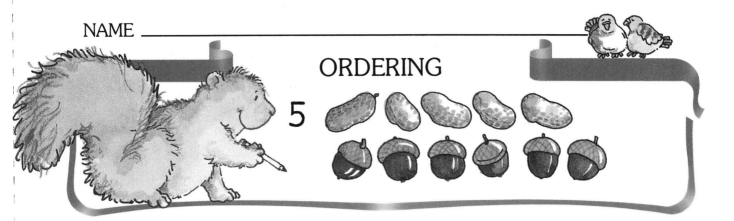

5

Write the number.

1. __0__

2. ____

3. ____

4. ____

5. ____

6. ____

7. ____

8. ____

9. ____

10. ____

11. ____

Write the missing numbers.

12.

| 0 | 1 | 2 | 3 | | | 6 | | | 9 | |

13.

| 0 | 1 | 2 | | | | | | | | 10 |

14.

| 0 | 1 | 2 | | | | | 8 | | |

15. Write the numbers in order.

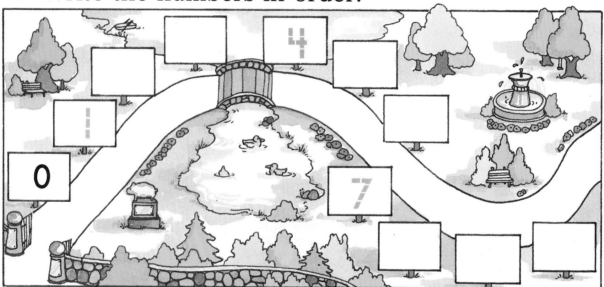

16. Join the dots in order.

Writing Numbers in Order, 0–10

PROBLEM SOLVING

2. ✓
    X
    Ring

(pages 11–20)

CHECKPOINT 2   Write the number.

1.

2.

I				5

3.

¢

4. Ring the 🍵 . ✓ the 🥛 .

Extra practice on page 359

Problem Solving

NAME _____

Ring the number.

1.
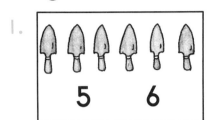 5 6

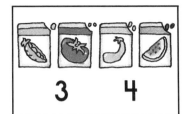 3 4

 1 2

Write the number.

2.
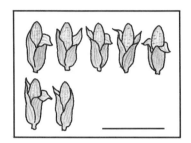 _____

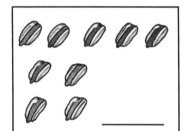 _____

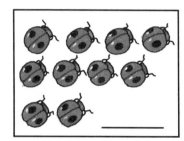 _____

Write the number.

3. 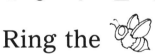 _____ ¢

Write the numbers in order.

4. **0 1 2 ___ ___ 5 6 ___ ___ ___ 10**

Ring the . ✔ the .

5.

MATHEMATICS and SOCIAL STUDIES

You can write or say numbers to **6** in different ways.

Write **1** through **6**.

1.

2.

3.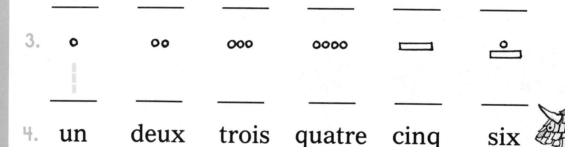

4. un   deux   trois   quatre   cinq   six

5. uno   dos   tres   cuatro   cinco   seis

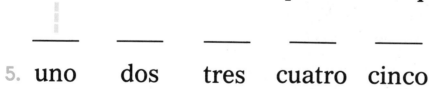

NAME _____

Enrichment

If **all** are , color them red.

If **some** are , color the blue.

1.
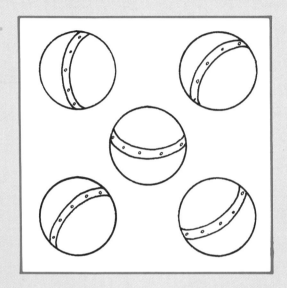

2.

3.
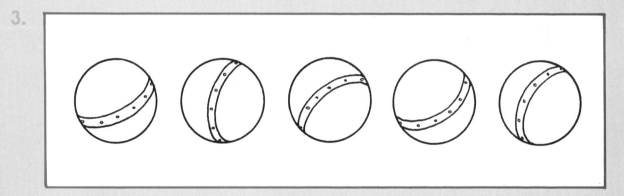

4.

5.
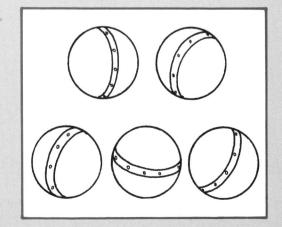

If **some** are dogs, color the dogs brown.
If **none** are dogs, do not color any.

6.

7.

8.

9.

10.

Enrichment: Logical Thinking

CUMULATIVE REVIEW

Fill in the ⬯ for the correct answer.

Which shows the number?

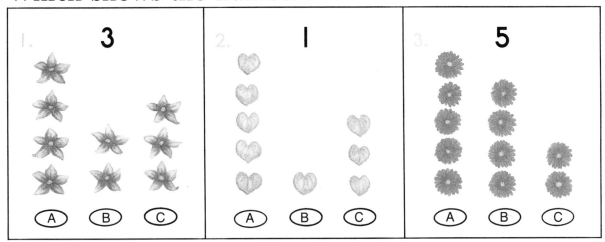

How many?

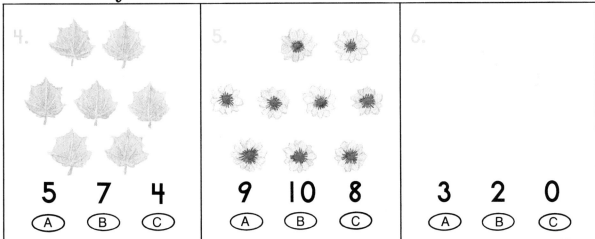

What number is missing?

7.	8.	9.
2, 3, __?__, 5	5, __?__, 7, 8	__?__, 1, 2, 3
4 1 0	3 6 9	4 5 0
(A) (B) (C)	(A) (B) (C)	(A) (B) (C)

How much?

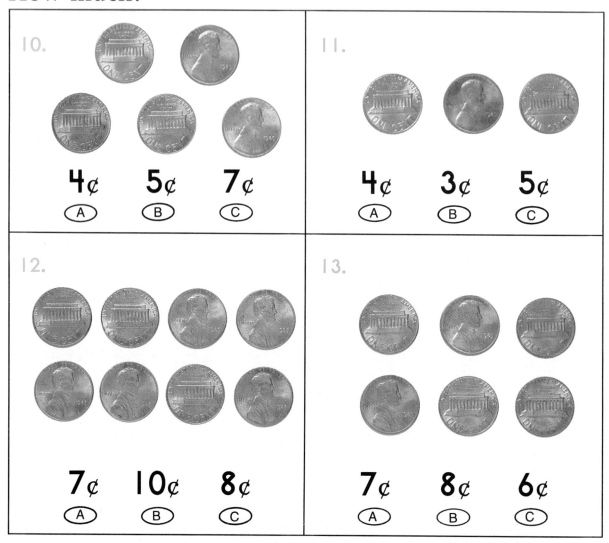

10.

4¢ (A)   5¢ (B)   7¢ (C)

11.

4¢ (A)   3¢ (B)   5¢ (C)

12.

7¢ (A)   10¢ (B)   8¢ (C)

13.

7¢ (A)   8¢ (B)   6¢ (C)

LANGUAGE and VOCABULARY REVIEW

Match. Draw a line from the number to the word.

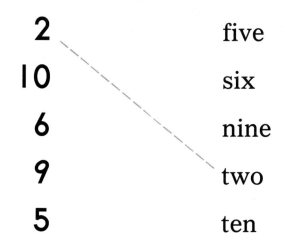

2   five

10   six

6   nine

9   two

5   ten

Read with the children:

Some people are
walking in the rain.
How many are children?
How many are adults?
How many are there in
all?

2

ADDITION
FACTS THROUGH 7

27

BEGINNING ADDITION

How many?

2

How many join?

+　**1**

How many in all?

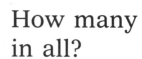

=　**3**

Write the number.

How many?　**How many join?**　**How many in all?**

1.

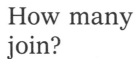

___1___ **+** ___2___ **=** ___3___

2.

___ **+** ___ **=** ___

3.

___ **+** ___ **=** ___

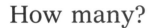

Beginning Addition

ADDING 1 OR 2

$3 + 2 = \underline{5}$ $2 + 2 = \underline{4}$

How many?

1.

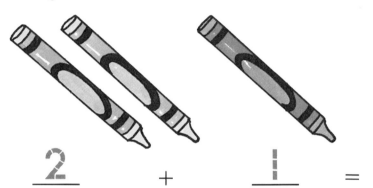

$\underline{2}$ + $\underline{1}$ =   _____

2.

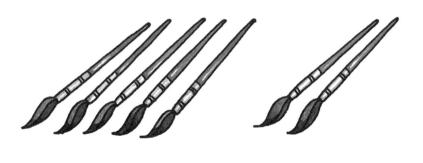

_____   +   _____   =   _____

3.

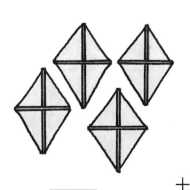

_____   +   _____   =   _____

Add.

4.

$1 + 2 = \underline{\hphantom{00}}$

5.

$5 + 2 = \underline{\hphantom{00}}$

6.

$4 + 2 = \underline{\hphantom{00}}$

7.

$2 + 2 = \underline{\hphantom{00}}$

Tell the story. Then add.

8.

$3 + 2 = \underline{\hphantom{00}}$

9.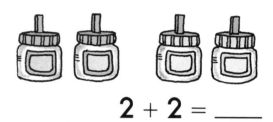

$4 + 1 = \underline{\hphantom{00}}$

10.

$6 + 1 = \underline{\hphantom{00}}$

11.

$3 + 1 = \underline{\hphantom{00}}$

Adding 1 or 2

ADDING 1, 2, OR 3

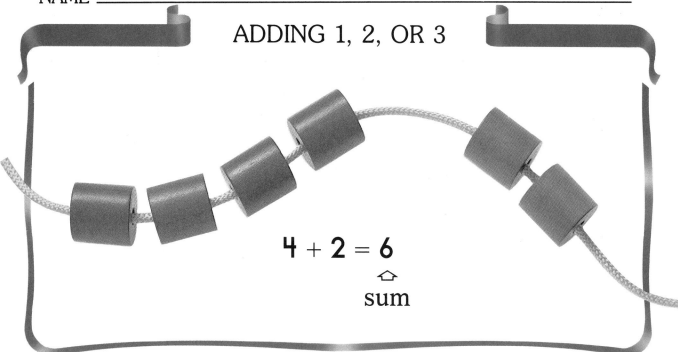

$$4 + 2 = 6$$

⇧
sum

Write the numbers. Ring the sum.

1.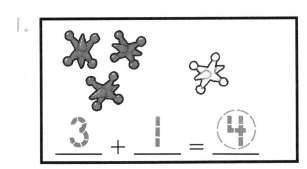

$\underline{3} + \underline{1} = \underline{4}$

2.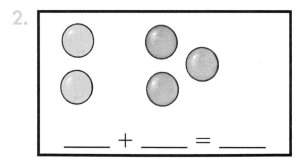

_____ + _____ = _____

3.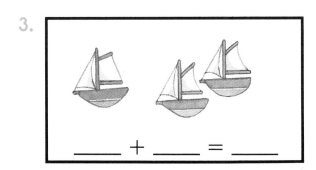

_____ + _____ = _____

4.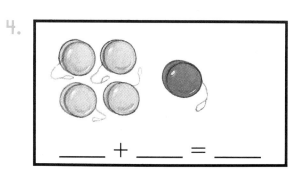

_____ + _____ = _____

5.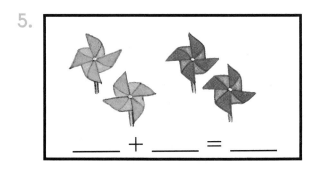

_____ + _____ = _____

6.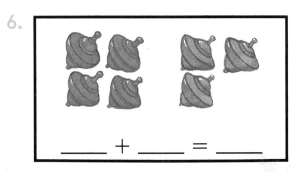

_____ + _____ = _____

Write the sum.

7. 1 + 1 = ____   3 + 2 = ____   4 + 1 = ____

8. 4 + 2 = ____   3 + 3 = ____   1 + 2 = ____

9. 6 + 1 = ____   2 + 2 = ____   1 + 3 = ____

10. 3 + 3 = ____   2 + 1 = ____   5 + 1 = ____

11. 2 + 3 = ____   3 + 1 = ____   4 + 2 = ____

12. 4 + 3 = ____   5 + 2 = ____   4 + 3 = ____

5 + 1 is **greater than** 5.

Think of the sum.
If greater than **5**, color 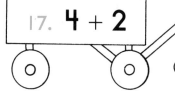 .

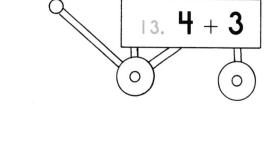

13. 4 + 3

14. 1 + 3

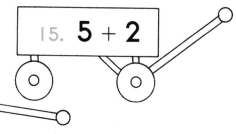

15. 5 + 2

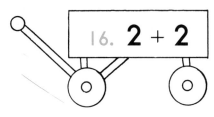

16. 2 + 2

17. 4 + 2

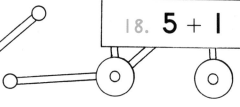

18. 5 + 1

Adding 1, 2, or 3

ADDING 1, 2, OR 3

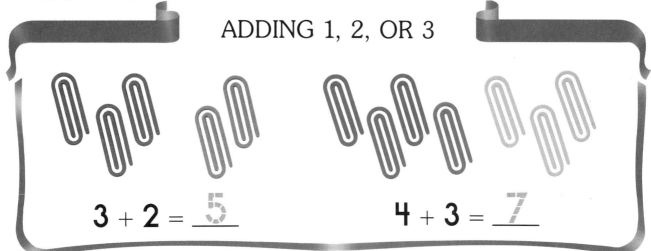

$3 + 2 = \underline{5}$ $4 + 3 = \underline{7}$

Add.

1.

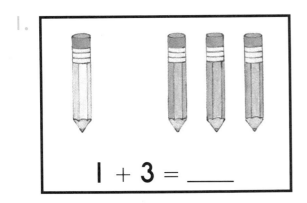

$1 + 3 = \underline{}$

2.

$2 + 2 = \underline{}$

3.

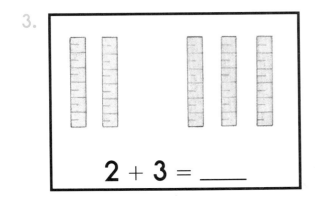

$2 + 3 = \underline{}$

4.

$1 + 1 = \underline{}$

5.

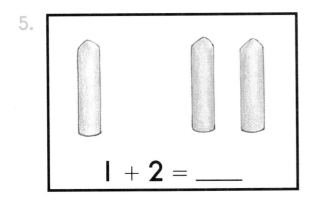

$1 + 2 = \underline{}$

6.

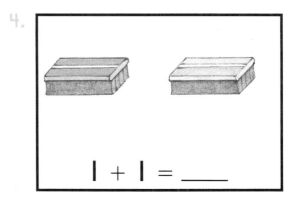

$4 + 2 = \underline{}$

Add.

7. $3 + 1 =$ _____ $2 + 3 =$ _____ $2 + 2 =$ _____

8. $2 + 1 =$ _____ $3 + 3 =$ _____ $5 + 2 =$ _____

9. $1 + 2 =$ _____ $5 + 1 =$ _____ $1 + 3 =$ _____

10. $2 + 1 =$ _____ $1 + 3 =$ _____ $6 + 1 =$ _____

11. $3 + 2 =$ _____ $4 + 1 =$ _____ $1 + 1 =$ _____

12. $3 + 3 =$ _____ $2 + 3 =$ _____ $2 + 1 =$ _____

13. $5 + 1 =$ _____ $1 + 3 =$ _____ $3 + 3 =$ _____

14. $4 + 3 =$ _____ $4 + 2 =$ _____ $4 + 3 =$ _____

(pages 27–34)

CHECKPOINT 1

Add.

1. $3 + 2 = \boxed{}$ $1 + 3 = \boxed{}$

2. $4 + 3 = \boxed{}$ $2 + 3 = \boxed{}$ $2 + 1 = \boxed{}$

3. $3 + 3 = \boxed{}$ $5 + 2 = \boxed{}$ $6 + 1 = \boxed{}$

Extra practice on page 361

PROBLEM SOLVING

1. Color the number of each you see in the picture.

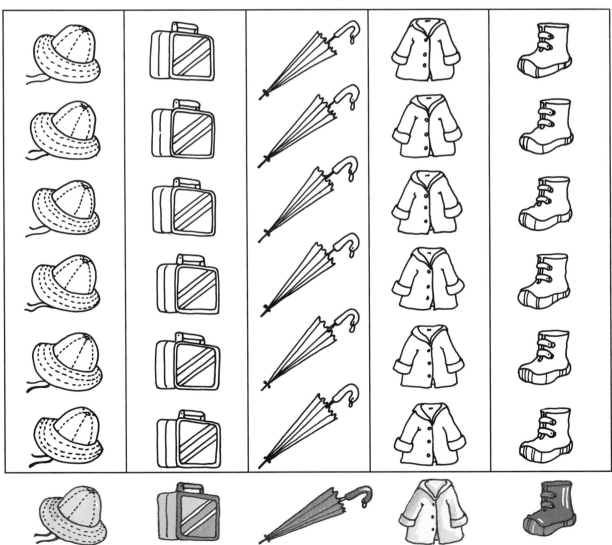

2. Color the number of each you see in the picture.

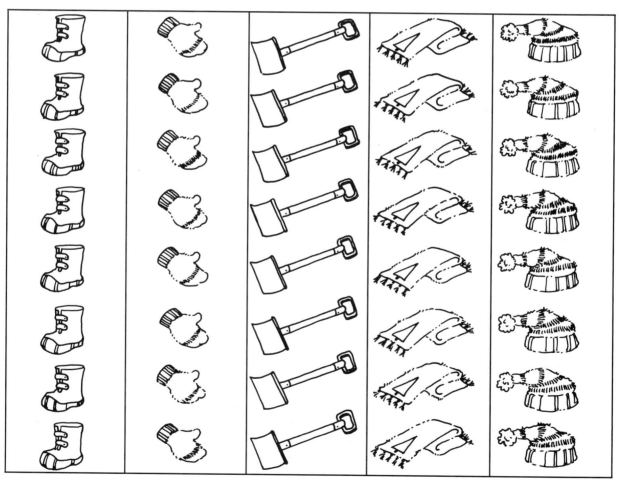

Problem Solving

ADDING WITH ZERO

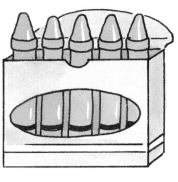
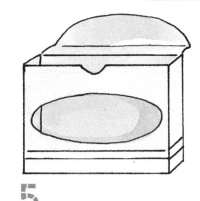

$$5 + 0 = \underline{5}$$

Add.

1.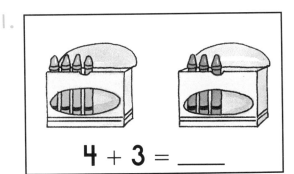

$$4 + 3 = \underline{}$$

2.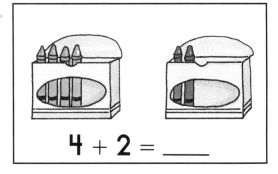

$$4 + 2 = \underline{}$$

3.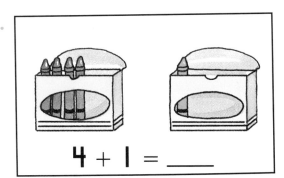

$$4 + 1 = \underline{}$$

4.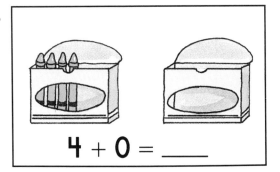

$$4 + 0 = \underline{}$$

5.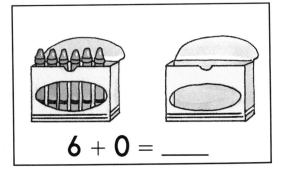

$$6 + 0 = \underline{}$$

6.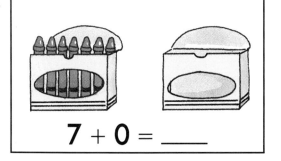

$$7 + 0 = \underline{}$$

Add.

7. $3 + 1 = \underline{\quad}$ $2 + 0 = \underline{\quad}$ $4 + 1 = \underline{\quad}$

8. $5 + 0 = \underline{\quad}$ $6 + 0 = \underline{\quad}$ $3 + 0 = \underline{\quad}$

9. $1 + 3 = \underline{\quad}$ $2 + 2 = \underline{\quad}$ $6 + 1 = \underline{\quad}$

10. $5 + 1 = \underline{\quad}$ $3 + 2 = \underline{\quad}$ $1 + 0 = \underline{\quad}$

11. $3 + 4 = \underline{\quad}$ $4 + 0 = \underline{\quad}$ $7 + 0 = \underline{\quad}$

12. $2 + 3 = \underline{\quad}$ $5 + 2 = \underline{\quad}$ $4 + 0 = \underline{\quad}$

13. $2 + 0 = \underline{\quad}$ $4 + 2 = \underline{\quad}$ $3 + 3 = \underline{\quad}$

14. $6 + 0 = \underline{\quad}$ $3 + 2 = \underline{\quad}$ $4 + 3 = \underline{\quad}$

Tell the story. Then add.

15.

$3 + 2 = \underline{\quad}$

16.

$2 + 2 = \underline{\quad}$

38 thirty-eight

Adding with Zero

NAME _____

ADDING IN ANY ORDER

If you know	Then you know

$$3 + 2 = \underline{5}$$ $$2 + 3 = \underline{5}$$

Write the number. Then add.

1.

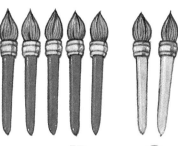   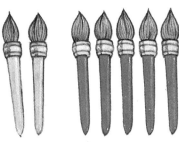

$$\underline{5} + \underline{2} = \underline{7} \qquad \underline{2} + \underline{5} = \underline{7}$$

2.

$$\underline{} + \underline{} = \underline{} \qquad \underline{} + \underline{} = \underline{}$$

3.

$$\underline{} + \underline{} = \underline{} \qquad \underline{} + \underline{} = \underline{}$$

Add.

4. $1 + 4 =$ _____   5. $4 + 3 =$ _____   6. $4 + 0 =$ _____

   $4 + 1 =$ _____ $3 + 4 =$ _____ $0 + 4 =$ _____

7. $6 + 1 =$ _____   8. $4 + 2 =$ _____   9. $2 + 3 =$ _____

   $1 + 6 =$ _____ $2 + 4 =$ _____ $3 + 2 =$ _____

10. $5 + 2 =$ _____   11. $6 + 0 =$ _____   12. $2 + 1 =$ _____

    $2 + 5 =$ _____ $0 + 6 =$ _____ $1 + 2 =$ _____

$2 + 1$ is **less than 5**.

Think of the sum.
If less than **5**, color  blue .

15. $3 + 1$

13. $2 + 2$

14. $3 + 4$

16. $5 + 2$

17. $0 + 4$

18. $1 + 2$

Order Property

NAME _____

ADDING ANOTHER WAY

$$
\begin{array}{r}
5 \\
+2 \\
\hline
7
\end{array}
$$

5 + 2 = __7__

Add.

1.  $\begin{array}{r} 3 \\ +1 \\ \hline \end{array}$

2.  $\begin{array}{r} 3 \\ +2 \\ \hline \end{array}$

3.  $\begin{array}{r} 2 \\ +1 \\ \hline \end{array}$

4.  $\begin{array}{r} 1 \\ +4 \\ \hline \end{array}$

5.  $\begin{array}{r} 2 \\ +2 \\ \hline \end{array}$

6.  $\begin{array}{r} 4 \\ +2 \\ \hline \end{array}$

7.  $\begin{array}{r} 4 \\ +2 \\ \hline \end{array}$

8.  $\begin{array}{r} 5 \\ +0 \\ \hline \end{array}$

9.  $\begin{array}{r} 2 \\ +3 \\ \hline \end{array}$

Add.

10.
$$\begin{array}{r} 2 \\ +0 \\ \hline \end{array}$$
$$\begin{array}{r} 1 \\ +4 \\ \hline \end{array}$$
$$\begin{array}{r} 0 \\ +3 \\ \hline \end{array}$$
$$\begin{array}{r} 4 \\ +2 \\ \hline \end{array}$$
$$\begin{array}{r} 1 \\ +5 \\ \hline \end{array}$$
$$\begin{array}{r} 4 \\ +3 \\ \hline \end{array}$$

11.
$$\begin{array}{r} 2 \\ +2 \\ \hline \end{array}$$
$$\begin{array}{r} 5 \\ +0 \\ \hline \end{array}$$
$$\begin{array}{r} 2 \\ +4 \\ \hline \end{array}$$
$$\begin{array}{r} 1 \\ +1 \\ \hline \end{array}$$
$$\begin{array}{r} 4 \\ +1 \\ \hline \end{array}$$
$$\begin{array}{r} 3 \\ +3 \\ \hline \end{array}$$

12.
$$\begin{array}{r} 1 \\ +1 \\ \hline \end{array}$$
$$\begin{array}{r} 4 \\ +1 \\ \hline \end{array}$$
$$\begin{array}{r} 3 \\ +3 \\ \hline \end{array}$$
$$\begin{array}{r} 6 \\ +0 \\ \hline \end{array}$$
$$\begin{array}{r} 5 \\ +1 \\ \hline \end{array}$$
$$\begin{array}{r} 2 \\ +5 \\ \hline \end{array}$$

13.
$$\begin{array}{r} 1 \\ +2 \\ \hline \end{array}$$
$$\begin{array}{r} 0 \\ +3 \\ \hline \end{array}$$
$$\begin{array}{r} 4 \\ +0 \\ \hline \end{array}$$
$$\begin{array}{r} 3 \\ +1 \\ \hline \end{array}$$
$$\begin{array}{r} 3 \\ +2 \\ \hline \end{array}$$
$$\begin{array}{r} 5 \\ +1 \\ \hline \end{array}$$

Tell the story. Then add.

14.

$$\begin{array}{r} 2 \\ +2 \\ \hline \end{array}$$

15.

$$\begin{array}{r} 4 \\ +1 \\ \hline \end{array}$$

Addition, Vertical Form

ADDING THROUGH 7

2	yellow	5	green
3	brown	6	red
4	orange	7	blue

Add. Then color.

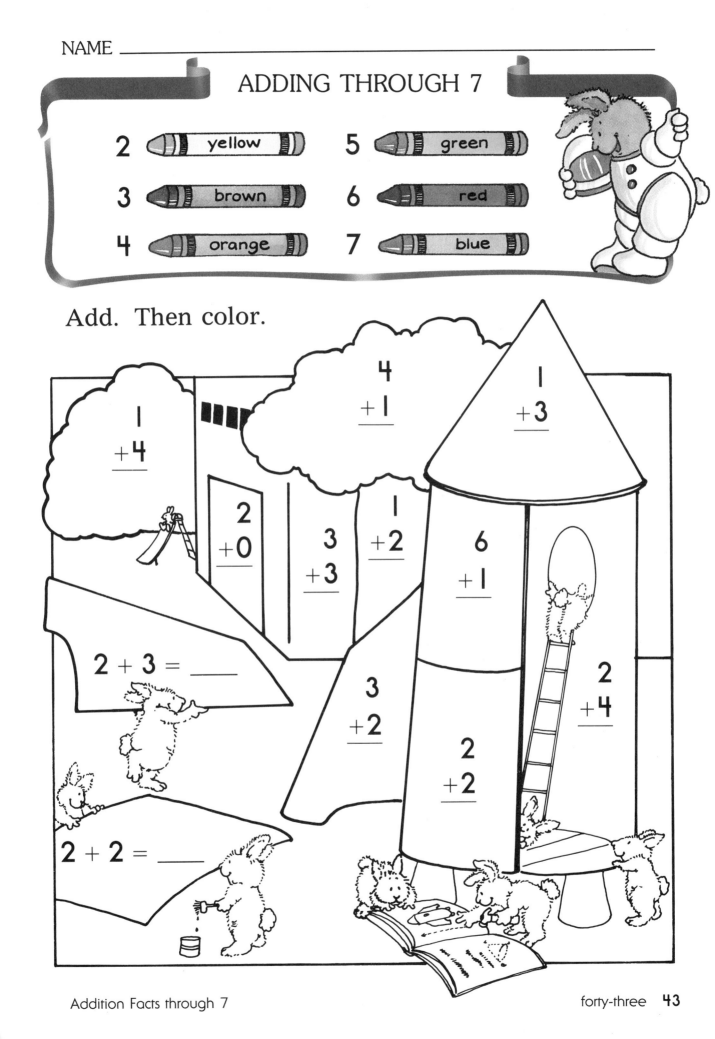

$$\begin{array}{r}1\\+4\\\hline\end{array}$$

$$\begin{array}{r}4\\+1\\\hline\end{array}$$

$$\begin{array}{r}1\\+3\\\hline\end{array}$$

$$\begin{array}{r}2\\+0\\\hline\end{array}$$

$$\begin{array}{r}3\\+3\\\hline\end{array}$$

$$\begin{array}{r}1\\+2\\\hline\end{array}$$

$$\begin{array}{r}6\\+1\\\hline\end{array}$$

$$\begin{array}{r}3\\+2\\\hline\end{array}$$

$$\begin{array}{r}2\\+2\\\hline\end{array}$$

$$\begin{array}{r}2\\+4\\\hline\end{array}$$

2 + 3 = ____

2 + 2 = ____

Add.

2.
$$\begin{array}{r} 2 \\ +0 \\ \hline \end{array}$$
$$\begin{array}{r} 1 \\ +4 \\ \hline \end{array}$$
$$\begin{array}{r} 0 \\ +0 \\ \hline \end{array}$$
$$\begin{array}{r} 4 \\ +2 \\ \hline \end{array}$$
$$\begin{array}{r} 1 \\ +5 \\ \hline \end{array}$$
$$\begin{array}{r} 2 \\ +2 \\ \hline \end{array}$$

3.
$$\begin{array}{r} 5 \\ +0 \\ \hline \end{array}$$
$$\begin{array}{r} 2 \\ +3 \\ \hline \end{array}$$
$$\begin{array}{r} 1 \\ +1 \\ \hline \end{array}$$
$$\begin{array}{r} 4 \\ +1 \\ \hline \end{array}$$
$$\begin{array}{r} 3 \\ +3 \\ \hline \end{array}$$
$$\begin{array}{r} 6 \\ +0 \\ \hline \end{array}$$

4.
$$\begin{array}{r} 5 \\ +1 \\ \hline \end{array}$$
$$\begin{array}{r} 1 \\ +2 \\ \hline \end{array}$$
$$\begin{array}{r} 0 \\ +3 \\ \hline \end{array}$$
$$\begin{array}{r} 4 \\ +0 \\ \hline \end{array}$$
$$\begin{array}{r} 3 \\ +1 \\ \hline \end{array}$$
$$\begin{array}{r} 3 \\ +2 \\ \hline \end{array}$$

☆ Add. Join the dots in order.

5.

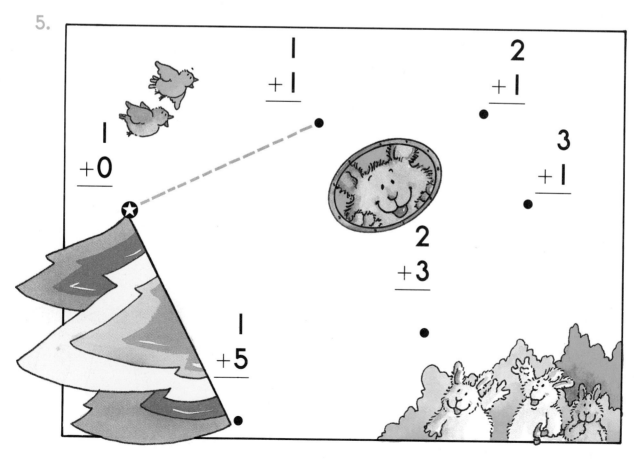

Addition Facts

PROBLEM SOLVING

Complete the number sentence.

1. ___3___ 🪟 + ___2___ 🪟 = ___5___ in all

2. ___ 🥤 + ___ 🥤 = ___ in all

3. ___ 🪑 + ___ 🪑 = ___ in all

4. ___ 🧰 + ___ 🧰 = ___ in all

Complete the number sentence.

5. ___  + ___ = ___ in all

6. ___ + ___ = ___ in all

7. ___ + ___ = ___ in all

(pages 35–46)

CHECKPOINT 2   Add.

1. $5 + 0 = \boxed{}$ $0 + 6 = \boxed{}$ $3 + 4 = \boxed{}$

Complete the number sentence.

2. $\boxed{} + \boxed{} = \boxed{}$ in all

Extra practice on page 361

Problem Solving

CHAPTER 2 TEST

Add.

1. $\begin{array}{r} 5 \\ +1 \\ \hline \end{array}$ $\begin{array}{r} 3 \\ +3 \\ \hline \end{array}$ $\begin{array}{r} 4 \\ +2 \\ \hline \end{array}$ $\begin{array}{r} 2 \\ +3 \\ \hline \end{array}$ $\begin{array}{r} 6 \\ +1 \\ \hline \end{array}$ $\begin{array}{r} 3 \\ +1 \\ \hline \end{array}$

2. $3 + 4 =$ ____ $1 + 2 =$ ____ $5 + 2 =$ ____

Color the number of each object you see.

      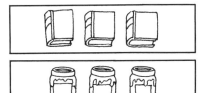

3.

4.

Add.

5. $\begin{array}{r} 4 \\ +0 \\ \hline \end{array}$ $\begin{array}{r} 7 \\ +0 \\ \hline \end{array}$ $\begin{array}{r} 0 \\ +3 \\ \hline \end{array}$ $\begin{array}{r} 5 \\ +0 \\ \hline \end{array}$ $\begin{array}{r} 1 \\ +0 \\ \hline \end{array}$ $\begin{array}{r} 0 \\ +6 \\ \hline \end{array}$

Write the number.

6. ____  + ____   = ____ in all

Extra practice on page 362

MATHEMATICS and READING

Two went to the circus.

They saw three .

Each held two .

There were five .

Each had a .

Two  were dancing.

Write the number.

1. How many in all? _____

2. How many in all? _____

3. How many  and in all? _____

Enrichment

1. Color sums **less** than 5 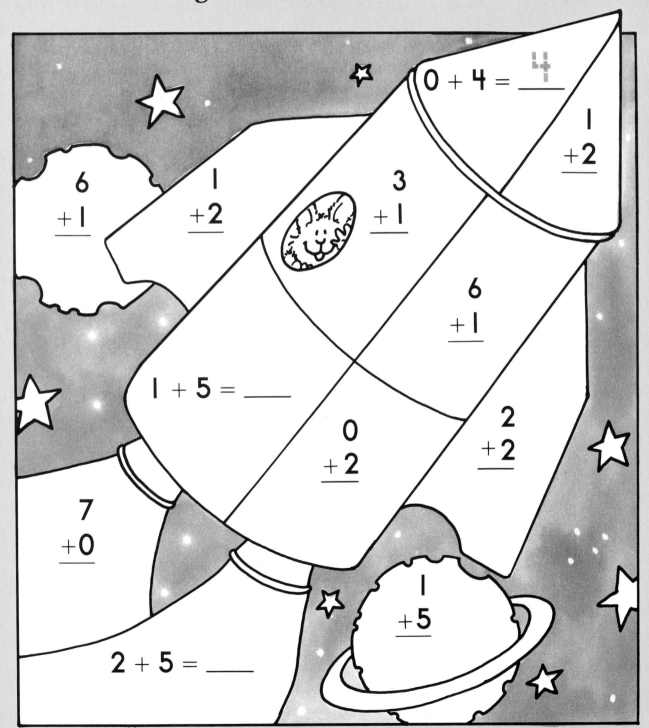.

Color sums **greater** than 5 .

$0 + 4 = \underline{4}$

$\begin{array}{r} 1 \\ +2 \\ \hline \end{array}$

$\begin{array}{r} 6 \\ +1 \\ \hline \end{array}$

$\begin{array}{r} 1 \\ +2 \\ \hline \end{array}$

$\begin{array}{r} 3 \\ +1 \\ \hline \end{array}$

$\begin{array}{r} 6 \\ +1 \\ \hline \end{array}$

$1 + 5 = \underline{}$

$\begin{array}{r} 0 \\ +2 \\ \hline \end{array}$

$\begin{array}{r} 2 \\ +2 \\ \hline \end{array}$

$\begin{array}{r} 7 \\ +0 \\ \hline \end{array}$

$\begin{array}{r} 1 \\ +5 \\ \hline \end{array}$

$2 + 5 = \underline{}$

Add.		Which number is between the sums?
2. 2 + 3 = _5_	4 + 3 = _7_	_6_
3. 2 + 1 = ___	0 + 1 = ___	___
4. 2 + 2 = ___	4 + 2 = ___	___
5. 1 + 4 = ___	3 + 0 = ___	___
6. 7 + 0 = ___	3 + 2 = ___	___
7. 4 + 2 = ___	1 + 3 = ___	___
8. 1 + 2 = ___	0 + 5 = ___	___

Enrichment: Logical Thinking

CUMULATIVE REVIEW

Fill in the ◯ for the correct answer.

How much?

1.	2.
8¢ 9¢ 10¢	6¢ 4¢ 5¢
Ⓐ Ⓑ Ⓒ	Ⓐ Ⓑ Ⓒ

What number is missing?

3. 1 _?_ 3 4 5	4. 7 _?_ 9 10
1 2 6	6 5 8
Ⓐ Ⓑ Ⓒ	Ⓐ Ⓑ Ⓒ

Add.

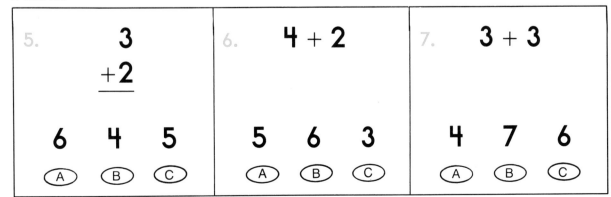

5. 3 +2	6. 4 + 2	7. 3 + 3
6 4 5	5 6 3	4 7 6
Ⓐ Ⓑ Ⓒ	Ⓐ Ⓑ Ⓒ	Ⓐ Ⓑ Ⓒ

Add.

8. $7 + 0$	9. $3 + 0$	10. $4 + 0$
0 7 6	3 0 4	1 4 5
Ⓐ Ⓑ Ⓒ	Ⓐ Ⓑ Ⓒ	Ⓐ Ⓑ Ⓒ

How many 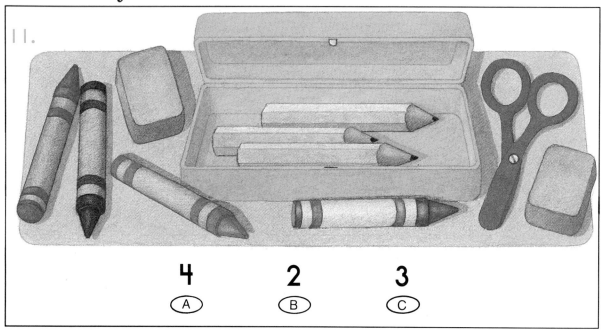 ?

11.

4   2   3
Ⓐ   Ⓑ   Ⓒ

LANGUAGE and VOCABULARY REVIEW

Match. Draw a line from the number to the word.

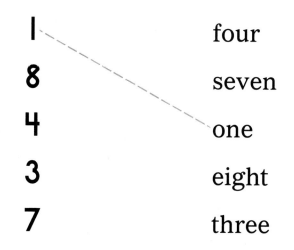

1   four

8   seven

4   one

3   eight

7   three

Language and Vocabulary Review

3

Read with the children:

How many puffins are
on top of the rock?
How many are below?
How many puffins in all?

ADDITION
FACTS THROUGH 10

53

REVIEWING ADDITION

$5 + 2 = \underline{7}$

Add.

1. $2 + 3 = \underline{}$ $2 + 4 = \underline{}$ $2 + 5 = \underline{}$

2. $1 + 6 = \underline{}$ $1 + 5 = \underline{}$ $1 + 4 = \underline{}$

3. $3 + 3 = \underline{}$ $5 + 2 = \underline{}$ $4 + 3 = \underline{}$

4.
$$\begin{array}{r} 3 \\ +3 \\ \hline \end{array} \qquad \begin{array}{r} 0 \\ +7 \\ \hline \end{array} \qquad \begin{array}{r} 2 \\ +3 \\ \hline \end{array}$$

5.
$$\begin{array}{r} 6 \\ +1 \\ \hline \end{array} \qquad \begin{array}{r} 7 \\ +0 \\ \hline \end{array} \qquad \begin{array}{r} 2 \\ +4 \\ \hline \end{array}$$

6.
$$\begin{array}{r} 2 \\ +1 \\ \hline \end{array} \qquad \begin{array}{r} 1 \\ +4 \\ \hline \end{array} \qquad \begin{array}{r} 0 \\ +6 \\ \hline \end{array}$$

7.
$$\begin{array}{r} 3 \\ +4 \\ \hline \end{array} \qquad \begin{array}{r} 1 \\ +3 \\ \hline \end{array} \qquad \begin{array}{r} 5 \\ +2 \\ \hline \end{array}$$

$$\begin{array}{r} 4 \\ +2 \\ \hline 6 \end{array}$$

ADDING THROUGH 8

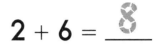

$2 + 6 =$ ___

Add.

1.

$5 + 3 =$ ___

2.

$6 + 1 =$ ___

3.

$1 + 7 =$ ___

4.

$4 + 4 =$ ___

5. $2 + 4 =$ ___ $2 + 5 =$ ___ $2 + 6 =$ ___

6. $3 + 2 =$ ___ $3 + 3 =$ ___ $3 + 4 =$ ___

7. $1 + 7 =$ ___ $1 + 6 =$ ___ $1 + 5 =$ ___

Add.

8. $6 + 0 =$ ___ $7 + 0 =$ ___ $8 + 0 =$ ___

9. $2 + 4 =$ ___ $3 + 4 =$ ___ $4 + 4 =$ ___

10. $3 + 5 =$ ___ $1 + 6 =$ ___ $0 + 8 =$ ___

11. $2 + 6 =$ ___ $1 + 7 =$ ___ $2 + 5 =$ ___

12. $5 + 3 =$ ___ $7 + 0 =$ ___ $6 + 2 =$ ___

13. $0 + 8 =$ ___ $5 + 2 =$ ___ $7 + 1 =$ ___

14. $1 + 5 =$ ___ $3 + 5 =$ ___ $4 + 0 =$ ___

15. $3 + 2 =$ ___ $4 + 2 =$ ___ $1 + 5 =$ ___

Tell the story. Then add.

16.

5 children + **3** children = ___ children

17.

4 children + **3** children = ___ children

Addition Facts through 8

ADDING THROUGH 8

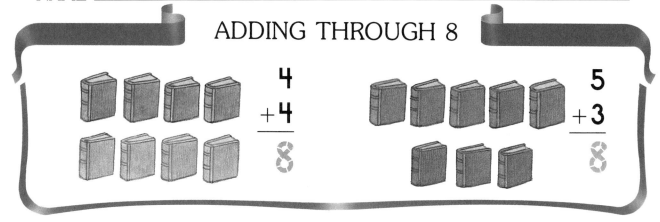

$$\begin{array}{r} 4 \\ +4 \\ \hline 8 \end{array}$$

$$\begin{array}{r} 5 \\ +3 \\ \hline 8 \end{array}$$

Add.

1.

$$\begin{array}{r} 1 \\ +7 \\ \hline \end{array}$$

2.

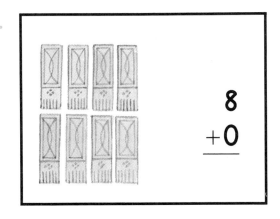

$$\begin{array}{r} 6 \\ +2 \\ \hline \end{array}$$

3.

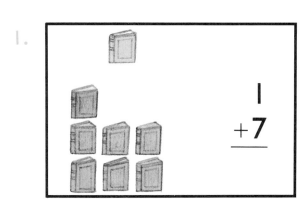

$$\begin{array}{r} 5 \\ +2 \\ \hline \end{array}$$

4.

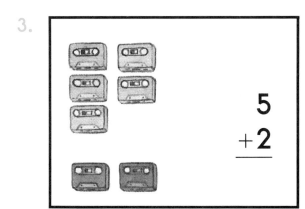

$$\begin{array}{r} 8 \\ +0 \\ \hline \end{array}$$

5.
$$\begin{array}{r} 3 \\ +3 \\ \hline \end{array} \qquad \begin{array}{r} 3 \\ +4 \\ \hline \end{array} \qquad \begin{array}{r} 3 \\ +5 \\ \hline \end{array} \qquad \begin{array}{r} 1 \\ +5 \\ \hline \end{array} \qquad \begin{array}{r} 1 \\ +4 \\ \hline \end{array} \qquad \begin{array}{r} 1 \\ +3 \\ \hline \end{array}$$

6.
$$\begin{array}{r} 5 \\ +1 \\ \hline \end{array} \qquad \begin{array}{r} 5 \\ +2 \\ \hline \end{array} \qquad \begin{array}{r} 5 \\ +3 \\ \hline \end{array} \qquad \begin{array}{r} 4 \\ +4 \\ \hline \end{array} \qquad \begin{array}{r} 3 \\ +4 \\ \hline \end{array} \qquad \begin{array}{r} 2 \\ +4 \\ \hline \end{array}$$

Add.

7. $\begin{array}{r} 8 \\ +0 \\ \hline \end{array}$ $\begin{array}{r} 5 \\ +2 \\ \hline \end{array}$ $\begin{array}{r} 6 \\ +2 \\ \hline \end{array}$ $\begin{array}{r} 3 \\ +5 \\ \hline \end{array}$ $\begin{array}{r} 4 \\ +2 \\ \hline \end{array}$ $\begin{array}{r} 4 \\ +4 \\ \hline \end{array}$

8. $\begin{array}{r} 1 \\ +7 \\ \hline \end{array}$ $\begin{array}{r} 3 \\ +5 \\ \hline \end{array}$ $\begin{array}{r} 5 \\ +1 \\ \hline \end{array}$ $\begin{array}{r} 6 \\ +1 \\ \hline \end{array}$ $\begin{array}{r} 2 \\ +3 \\ \hline \end{array}$ $\begin{array}{r} 5 \\ +1 \\ \hline \end{array}$

9. $\begin{array}{r} 6 \\ +2 \\ \hline \end{array}$ $\begin{array}{r} 4 \\ +1 \\ \hline \end{array}$ $\begin{array}{r} 0 \\ +0 \\ \hline \end{array}$ $\begin{array}{r} 1 \\ +7 \\ \hline \end{array}$ $\begin{array}{r} 2 \\ +5 \\ \hline \end{array}$ $\begin{array}{r} 8 \\ +0 \\ \hline \end{array}$

10. $\begin{array}{r} 4 \\ +4 \\ \hline \end{array}$ $\begin{array}{r} 1 \\ +6 \\ \hline \end{array}$ $\begin{array}{r} 0 \\ +6 \\ \hline \end{array}$ $\begin{array}{r} 5 \\ +3 \\ \hline \end{array}$ $\begin{array}{r} 3 \\ +4 \\ \hline \end{array}$ $\begin{array}{r} 7 \\ +0 \\ \hline \end{array}$

Think of the sum.
Is it greater than 7?
Ring yes or no.

11. 2 + 4   3 + 2   9 + 0

   yes   (no)   yes   no   yes   no

12. 3 + 3   8 + 0   6 + 2

   yes   no   yes   no   yes   no

Addition Facts through 8

ADDING THROUGH 9

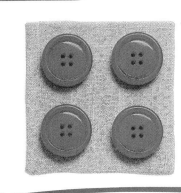 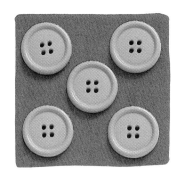

$4 + 5 = \underline{9}$

Add.

1.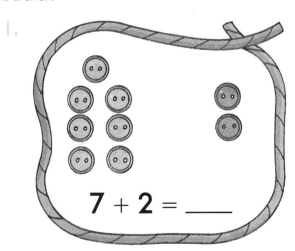

$7 + 2 = \underline{\hspace{1cm}}$

2.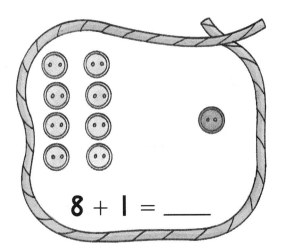

$8 + 1 = \underline{\hspace{1cm}}$

3.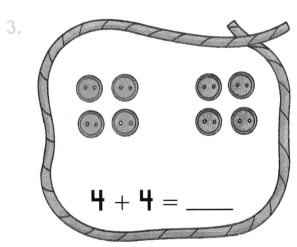

$4 + 4 = \underline{\hspace{1cm}}$

4.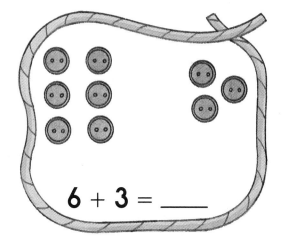

$6 + 3 = \underline{\hspace{1cm}}$

5. $4 + 3 = \underline{\hspace{1cm}}$ $4 + 4 = \underline{\hspace{1cm}}$ $4 + 5 = \underline{\hspace{1cm}}$

6. $3 + 6 = \underline{\hspace{1cm}}$ $3 + 5 = \underline{\hspace{1cm}}$ $3 + 4 = \underline{\hspace{1cm}}$

7. $6 + 1 = \underline{\hspace{1cm}}$ $6 + 2 = \underline{\hspace{1cm}}$ $6 + 3 = \underline{\hspace{1cm}}$

Add.

8. $3 + 4 =$ _____ $4 + 4 =$ _____ $5 + 4 =$ _____

9. $1 + 6 =$ _____ $1 + 7 =$ _____ $1 + 8 =$ _____

10. $3 + 5 =$ _____ $4 + 5 =$ _____ $2 + 7 =$ _____

11. $9 + 0 =$ _____ $2 + 6 =$ _____ $3 + 6 =$ _____

12. $7 + 1 =$ _____ $6 + 2 =$ _____ $5 + 3 =$ _____

13. $8 + 1 =$ _____ $7 + 2 =$ _____ $6 + 3 =$ _____

14. $2 + 5 =$ _____ $4 + 3 =$ _____ $4 + 4 =$ _____

15. $0 + 9 =$ _____ $7 + 0 =$ _____ $0 + 3 =$ _____

☆ Add.

16.

17.

18.

Addition Facts through 9

ADDING THROUGH 9

$$\begin{array}{r} 4 \\ +5 \\ \hline 9 \end{array}$$

Add.

1.
$$\begin{array}{r} 6 \\ +3 \\ \hline \end{array}$$

2.
$$\begin{array}{r} 4 \\ +4 \\ \hline \end{array}$$

3.
$$\begin{array}{r} 5 \\ +4 \\ \hline \end{array}$$

4.
$$\begin{array}{r} 7 \\ +2 \\ \hline \end{array}$$

5.
$$\begin{array}{r} 1 \\ +6 \\ \hline \end{array}\qquad \begin{array}{r} 1 \\ +7 \\ \hline \end{array}\qquad \begin{array}{r} 1 \\ +8 \\ \hline \end{array}\qquad \begin{array}{r} 3 \\ +4 \\ \hline \end{array}\qquad \begin{array}{r} 3 \\ +5 \\ \hline \end{array}\qquad \begin{array}{r} 3 \\ +6 \\ \hline \end{array}$$

6.
$$\begin{array}{r} 3 \\ +3 \\ \hline \end{array}\qquad \begin{array}{r} 4 \\ +3 \\ \hline \end{array}\qquad \begin{array}{r} 5 \\ +3 \\ \hline \end{array}\qquad \begin{array}{r} 4 \\ +5 \\ \hline \end{array}\qquad \begin{array}{r} 3 \\ +5 \\ \hline \end{array}\qquad \begin{array}{r} 2 \\ +5 \\ \hline \end{array}$$

Add.

7.
6	2	6	5	5	0
+1	+7	+2	+2	+4	+9

8.
5	4	4	0	3	1
+3	+4	+5	+5	+6	+8

9.
4	7	6	5	8	3
+4	+2	+3	+4	+1	+4

10.
2	6	8	3	2	9
+6	+3	+0	+5	+7	+0

Think of the sum.
Write the number that comes just after the sum.

11.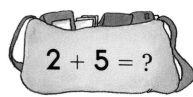

5 + 2 = ?   2 + 3 = ?   2 + 5 = ?

8
___   ___   ___

12.

5 + 0 = ?   4 + 3 = ?   3 + 3 = ?

___   ___   ___

Addition Facts through 9

ADDING IN ANY ORDER

If you know

$$5 + 4 = \underline{9}$$

Then you know

$$4 + 5 = \underline{9}$$

Add.

1. $9 + 0 =$ _____

    $0 + 9 =$ _____

2. $3 + 5 =$ _____

    $5 + 3 =$ _____

3. $2 + 7 =$ _____

    $7 + 2 =$ _____

4. $1 + 8 =$ _____

    $8 + 1 =$ _____

5. $3 + 6 =$ _____

    $6 + 3 =$ _____

6. $2 + 6 =$ _____

    $6 + 2 =$ _____

7. $4 + 3 =$ _____

    $3 + 4 =$ _____

8. $5 + 4 =$ _____

    $4 + 5 =$ _____

Order Property

Add.

9. $\begin{array}{r} 1 \\ +8 \\ \hline \end{array}$ $\begin{array}{r} 8 \\ +1 \\ \hline \end{array}$ 10. $\begin{array}{r} 3 \\ +5 \\ \hline \end{array}$ $\begin{array}{r} 5 \\ +3 \\ \hline \end{array}$ 11. $\begin{array}{r} 1 \\ +7 \\ \hline \end{array}$ $\begin{array}{r} 7 \\ +1 \\ \hline \end{array}$

12. $\begin{array}{r} 6 \\ +3 \\ \hline \end{array}$ $\begin{array}{r} 3 \\ +6 \\ \hline \end{array}$ 13. $\begin{array}{r} 4 \\ +3 \\ \hline \end{array}$ $\begin{array}{r} 3 \\ +4 \\ \hline \end{array}$ 14. $\begin{array}{r} 6 \\ +1 \\ \hline \end{array}$ $\begin{array}{r} 1 \\ +6 \\ \hline \end{array}$

15. $\begin{array}{r} 2 \\ +5 \\ \hline \end{array}$ $\begin{array}{r} 5 \\ +2 \\ \hline \end{array}$ 16. $\begin{array}{r} 4 \\ +5 \\ \hline \end{array}$ $\begin{array}{r} 5 \\ +4 \\ \hline \end{array}$ 17. $\begin{array}{r} 0 \\ +8 \\ \hline \end{array}$ $\begin{array}{r} 8 \\ +0 \\ \hline \end{array}$

18. $\begin{array}{r} 2 \\ +4 \\ \hline \end{array}$ $\begin{array}{r} 4 \\ +2 \\ \hline \end{array}$ 19. $\begin{array}{r} 6 \\ +2 \\ \hline \end{array}$ $\begin{array}{r} 2 \\ +6 \\ \hline \end{array}$ 20. $\begin{array}{r} 2 \\ +7 \\ \hline \end{array}$ $\begin{array}{r} 7 \\ +2 \\ \hline \end{array}$

(pages 53–64)

CHECKPOINT 1

Add.

1. 7 + 1 = ☐   5 + 4 = ☐   4 + 3 = ☐

2. $\begin{array}{r} 2 \\ +6 \\ \hline \end{array}$ $\begin{array}{r} 3 \\ +5 \\ \hline \end{array}$ $\begin{array}{r} 3 \\ +6 \\ \hline \end{array}$ $\begin{array}{r} 9 \\ +0 \\ \hline \end{array}$ $\begin{array}{r} 5 \\ +2 \\ \hline \end{array}$ $\begin{array}{r} 0 \\ +8 \\ \hline \end{array}$

Extra practice on page 363

Order Property

PROBLEM SOLVING

How much in all?

1. _____¢ + _____ 2 ¢ = _____ 5 ¢

2. _____¢ + _____¢ = _____¢

3. _____¢ + _____¢ = _____¢

4. _____¢ + _____¢ = _____¢

5. _____¢ + _____¢ = _____¢

I bought Then I bought How much are both?

6.  _____¢    _____¢   _____¢

7.  _____¢   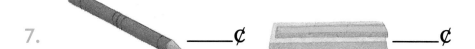 _____¢   _____¢

8.  _____¢    _____¢   _____¢

9. _____¢   _____¢   _____¢

10.  _____¢    _____¢   _____¢

Problem Solving

ADDING THROUGH 10

$3 + 7 = \underline{10}$

Add.

1. 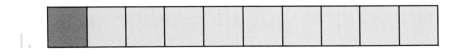 $1 + 9 = \underline{}$

$9 + 1 = \underline{}$

2. $2 + 8 = \underline{}$

$8 + 2 = \underline{}$

3. 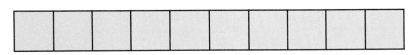 $3 + 7 = \underline{}$

$7 + 3 = \underline{}$

4. $5 + 3 = \underline{}$ $\quad 5 + 4 = \underline{}$ $\quad 5 + 5 = \underline{}$

5. $10 + 0 = \underline{}$ $\quad 9 + 0 = \underline{}$ $\quad 8 + 0 = \underline{}$

Add.

6. 9 + 1 = _____   4 + 6 = _____   5 + 5 = _____

7. 8 + 2 = _____   3 + 6 = _____   2 + 8 = _____

8. 7 + 3 = _____   2 + 7 = _____   1 + 9 = _____

9. 6 + 4 = _____   6 + 3 = _____   7 + 2 = _____

10. 3 + 5 = _____   3 + 7 = _____   4 + 6 = _____

11. 9 + 1 = _____   2 + 8 = _____   1 + 6 = _____

12. 4 + 4 = _____   3 + 6 = _____   9 + 0 = _____

13. 4 + 2 = _____   4 + 5 = _____   6 + 2 = _____

Tell the story.
Write the numbers.
Then add.

14.   _____ children

    + _____ children
    _____
      _____ children

Addition Facts through 10

ADDING FACTS THROUGH 10

$$\begin{array}{r} 4 \\ +6 \\ \hline 10 \end{array}$$

Add.

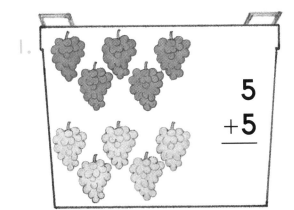

1. $\begin{array}{r} 5 \\ +5 \\ \hline \end{array}$

2. 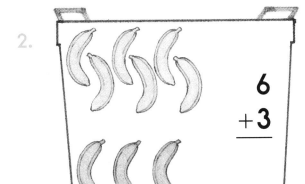 $\begin{array}{r} 6 \\ +3 \\ \hline \end{array}$

3. 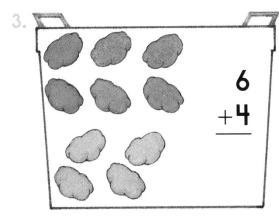 $\begin{array}{r} 6 \\ +4 \\ \hline \end{array}$

4. $\begin{array}{r} 8 \\ +2 \\ \hline \end{array}$

5. $\begin{array}{r} 7 \\ +1 \\ \hline \end{array}$ $\begin{array}{r} 8 \\ +1 \\ \hline \end{array}$ $\begin{array}{r} 9 \\ +1 \\ \hline \end{array}$ $\begin{array}{r} 7 \\ +3 \\ \hline \end{array}$ $\begin{array}{r} 7 \\ +2 \\ \hline \end{array}$ $\begin{array}{r} 7 \\ +1 \\ \hline \end{array}$

6. $\begin{array}{r} 3 \\ +3 \\ \hline \end{array}$ $\begin{array}{r} 3 \\ +4 \\ \hline \end{array}$ $\begin{array}{r} 3 \\ +5 \\ \hline \end{array}$ $\begin{array}{r} 5 \\ +5 \\ \hline \end{array}$ $\begin{array}{r} 4 \\ +5 \\ \hline \end{array}$ $\begin{array}{r} 3 \\ +5 \\ \hline \end{array}$

Complete the tables.

7.

Add 2			
8	3	6	5
10	5		

8.

Add 3			
7	3	5	6

9.

Add 4			
5	6	2	4

10.

Add 5			
4	2	3	5

Think of the sum.
Then write the number that
comes just before the sum.

11.

6 + 3 = ?

8
___

5 + 2 = ?

___

3 + 7 = ?

___

Addition Facts through 10

ADDING THREE NUMBERS

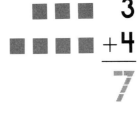 $\begin{array}{r} 3 \\ +4 \\ \hline 7 \end{array}$

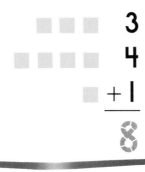 $\begin{array}{r} 3 \\ 4 \\ +1 \\ \hline 8 \end{array}$

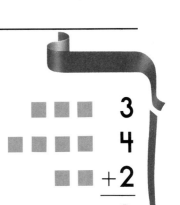 $\begin{array}{r} 3 \\ 4 \\ +2 \\ \hline 9 \end{array}$

Add.

1. $\begin{array}{r} 4 \\ +3 \\ \hline \end{array}$ $\begin{array}{r} 4 \\ 3 \\ +2 \\ \hline \end{array}$ $\begin{array}{r} 4 \\ 3 \\ +3 \\ \hline \end{array}$ 2. $\begin{array}{r} 1 \\ +5 \\ \hline \end{array}$ $\begin{array}{r} 1 \\ 5 \\ +1 \\ \hline \end{array}$ $\begin{array}{r} 1 \\ 5 \\ +2 \\ \hline \end{array}$

3. $\begin{array}{r} 5 \\ +1 \\ \hline \end{array}$ $\begin{array}{r} 5 \\ 1 \\ +2 \\ \hline \end{array}$ $\begin{array}{r} 5 \\ 1 \\ +3 \\ \hline \end{array}$ 4. $\begin{array}{r} 3 \\ +2 \\ \hline \end{array}$ $\begin{array}{r} 3 \\ 2 \\ +4 \\ \hline \end{array}$ $\begin{array}{r} 3 \\ 2 \\ +5 \\ \hline \end{array}$

5. $\begin{array}{r} 5 \\ +2 \\ \hline \end{array}$ $\begin{array}{r} 5 \\ 2 \\ +1 \\ \hline \end{array}$ $\begin{array}{r} 5 \\ 2 \\ +2 \\ \hline \end{array}$ 6. $\begin{array}{r} 2 \\ +2 \\ \hline \end{array}$ $\begin{array}{r} 2 \\ 2 \\ +4 \\ \hline \end{array}$ $\begin{array}{r} 2 \\ 2 \\ +5 \\ \hline \end{array}$

7. $\begin{array}{r} 3 \\ +3 \\ \hline \end{array}$ $\begin{array}{r} 3 \\ 3 \\ +2 \\ \hline \end{array}$ $\begin{array}{r} 3 \\ 3 \\ +3 \\ \hline \end{array}$ 8. $\begin{array}{r} 2 \\ +2 \\ \hline \end{array}$ $\begin{array}{r} 2 \\ 2 \\ +3 \\ \hline \end{array}$ $\begin{array}{r} 2 \\ 2 \\ +4 \\ \hline \end{array}$

Add.

9.
6	6	6	5	5	5
1	1	1	2	2	2
+0	+2	+3	+3	+1	+2

10.
2	6	3	7	3	5
1	1	5	1	3	4
+7	+1	+2	+2	+3	+1

11.
1	2	4	5	3	1
5	2	1	2	1	1
+3	+6	+2	+3	+6	+8

$2 + 1 + 3$

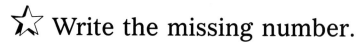 **Write the missing number.**

12.
3	7	5	1	2
2	1	2	3	2
+5	+☐	+☐	+☐	+☐
10	9	10	6	8

Adding Three Numbers

PROBLEM SOLVING

4¢ each
6¢ each
2¢ each
3¢ each
5¢ each

How much in all? Write the numbers. Use ¢.

1.

$$\begin{array}{r} 4¢ \\ +\ 3¢ \\ \hline 7¢ \end{array}$$

2.

$$\begin{array}{r} \underline{} \\ +\ \underline{} \\ \hline \end{array}$$

3.

$$\begin{array}{r} \underline{} \\ +\ \underline{} \\ \hline \end{array}$$

4.

$$\begin{array}{r} \underline{} \\ +\ \underline{} \\ \hline \end{array}$$

How much in all? Write the numbers. Use ¢.

5.  5¢ _____
   + _____
   _____

6.  7¢ _____
   + _____
   _____

7.  _____
   + _____
   _____

8. 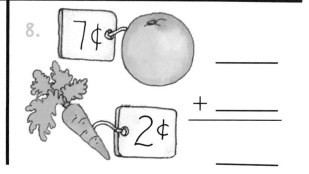 _____
   + _____
   _____

(pages 65–74)

CHECKPOINT 2   Add.

1. **9 + 1 =** ☐   **8 + 2 =** ☐   **7 + 2 =** ☐

2.
2	3	2	5	3	7
5	2	1	1	2	1
+1	+4	+3	+2	+2	+2

3. How much are both?
   Write the numbers. Use ¢.

_____
+ _____

Extra practice on page 363

Problem Solving

CHAPTER 3 TEST

Add.

1.	2	3	0	8	6	4
	+7	+5	+9	+0	+2	+4

Add.

2.	4	3	3	6	7	9
	+6	+7	+6	+4	+2	+1

Add.

3.	4	7	2	5	1	3
	1	1	3	2	4	5
	+3	+2	+2	+3	+4	+1

How much in all?
Write the numbers. Use ¢.

4.

___
+ ___

___

5.

___
+ ___

___

Extra practice on page 364

Chapter 3 Test

MATHEMATICS and SOCIAL STUDIES

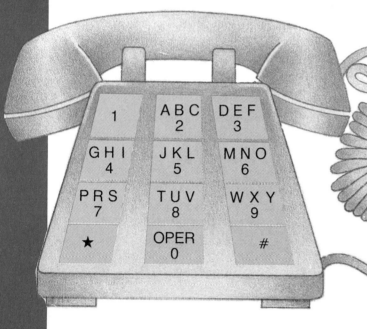

	1	ABC 2	DEF 3
	GHI 4	JKL 5	MNO 6
	PRS 7	TUV 8	WXY 9
	★	OPER 0	#

Write the phone number for the business.

1. P E T   S H O P

___ ___ ___ - ___ ___ ___ ___

2. A L ' S   C A F E

___ ___ ___ - ___ ___ ___ ___

3. T O Y   S H O P

___ ___ ___ - ___ ___ ___ ___

4. C A B   R I D E

___ ___ ___ - ___ ___ ___ ___

5. What is your phone number?

___ ___ ___ - ___ ___ ___ ___

Enrichment

How many animals?
Write the numbers.

A.

B.

C.

1. Table A ____

   Table B +____

   in all ____

2. Table B ____

   Table C +____

   in all ____

3. Table A ____

   Table C +____

   in all ____

4. How many foxes at all the tables? ☐ foxes

5. How many bears at all the tables? ☐ bears

6. How many animals in all? ☐ animals

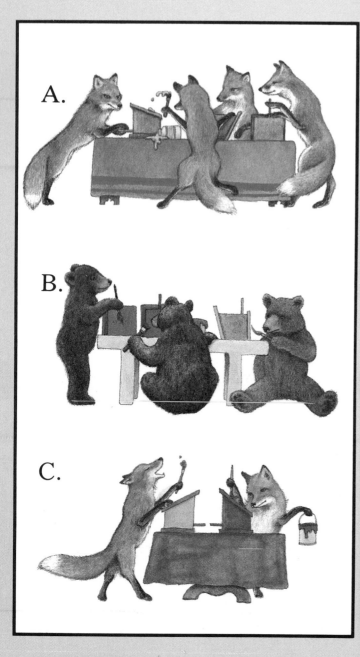

A.

B.

C.

How many animals?
Write the numbers.

7. Table A   ____

    Table B   +____

    in all   ____

8. Table B   ____

    Table C   +____

    in all   ____

9. Table A   ____

    Table C   +____

    in all   ____

10. How many animals
at Table A?   ☐ animals

11. How many animals
at Table A and Table B?   ☐ animals

12. How many animals
are making birdhouses?   ☐ animals

Enrichment: Interpreting a Picture

NAME

CUMULATIVE REVIEW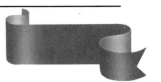

Fill in the ⬭ for the correct answer.

How much?

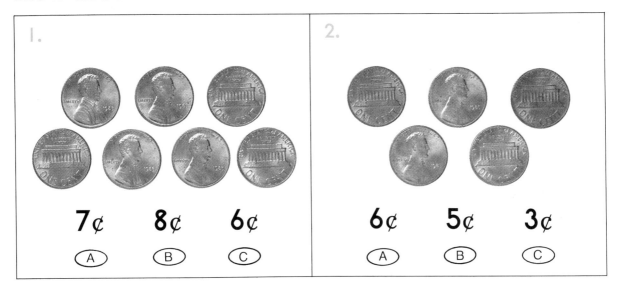

1. 7¢   8¢   6¢
    Ⓐ   Ⓑ   Ⓒ

2. 6¢   5¢   3¢
    Ⓐ   Ⓑ   Ⓒ

What number is missing?

3. 3, 4, __?__

    6   7   5
    Ⓐ Ⓑ Ⓒ

4. 7, _?_, 9

    6   8   7
    Ⓐ Ⓑ Ⓒ

Add.

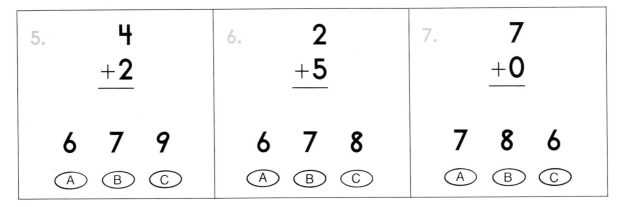

5.   4
    +2

    6   7   9
    Ⓐ Ⓑ Ⓒ

6.   2
    +5

    6   7   8
    Ⓐ Ⓑ Ⓒ

7.   7
    +0

    7   8   6
    Ⓐ Ⓑ Ⓒ

Fill in the ⬭ for the correct answer.

8.

Ⓐ 2 + 2

Ⓑ 3 + 2

Ⓒ 2 + 3

LANGUAGE and VOCABULARY REVIEW

7 is greater than **3**.   **4** is less than **9**.

Write greater or less.

1. **9** is ___greater___ than **7**.

2. **3** is _____ than **4**.

3. **7** is _____ than **10**.

4. **8** is _____ than **6**.

5. **5** is _____ than **3**.

Language and Vocabulary Review

Read with the children:

How many bags of fruit are there?
How many bags of oranges?
How many bags of grapefruit?
If 4 bags are sold, how many are left?

SUBTRACTION FACTS THROUGH 7

4

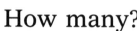

BEGINNING SUBTRACTION

How many?	How many go?	How many are left?

$$3 \ - \ 1 \ = \ 2$$

Write the number. Subtract.

How many?	How many go?	How many are left?

1.

___ − ___ = ___

2.

___ − ___ = ___

3.

___ − ___ = ___

Beginning Subtraction

SUBTRACTING 1, 2, OR 3

$4 - 1 =$ _3_

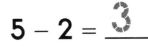

$5 - 2 =$ _3_

How many?

1.

_____ − _____ = _____

2.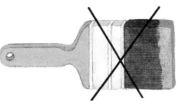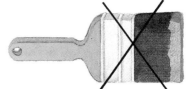

_____ − _____ = _____

3.

_____ − _____ = _____

Subtract.

4.

$$6 - 1 = \rule{1.5cm}{0.15mm}$$

5.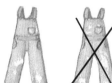

$$4 - 2 = \rule{1.5cm}{0.15mm}$$

6.

$$6 - 3 = \rule{1.5cm}{0.15mm}$$

7.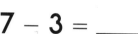

$$7 - 3 = \rule{1.5cm}{0.15mm}$$

Tell the story. Then subtract.

8.

$$6 - 2 = \rule{1.5cm}{0.15mm}$$

9.

$$3 - 2 = \rule{1.5cm}{0.15mm}$$

10.

$$5 - 3 = \rule{1.5cm}{0.15mm}$$

11.

$$7 - 2 = \rule{1.5cm}{0.15mm}$$

Subtracting 1, 2, or 3

SUBTRACTING 1 TO 6

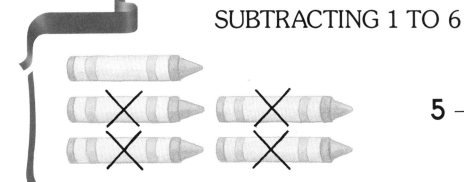

$$5 - 4 = 1$$
⇧
difference

Write the numbers. Then ring the difference.

1.
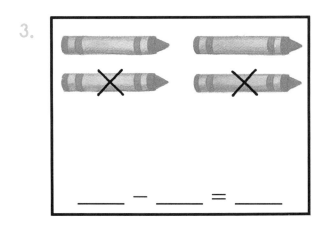

6 – 4 = ②

2.
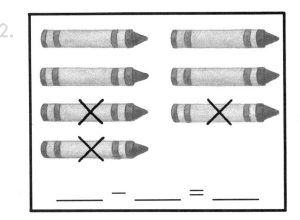

_____ – _____ = _____

3.
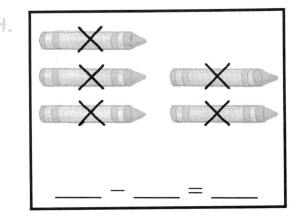

_____ – _____ = _____

4.

_____ – _____ = _____

5.
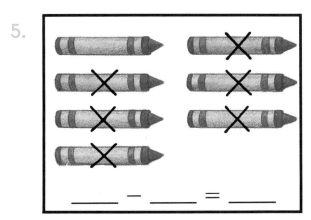

_____ – _____ = _____

6.
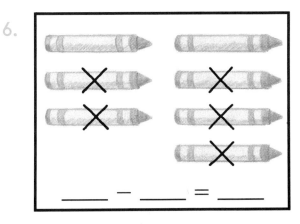

_____ – _____ = _____

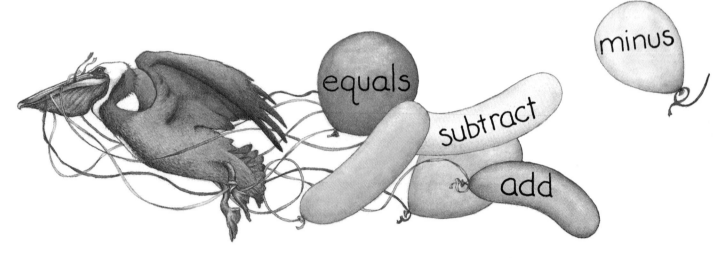

equals

minus

subtract

add

Write the difference.

7. 4 − 1 = _____   5 − 2 = _____   5 − 4 = _____

8. 6 − 5 = _____   2 − 2 = _____   7 − 5 = _____

9. 5 − 1 = _____   6 − 4 = _____   4 − 3 = _____

10. 7 − 6 = _____   7 − 3 = _____   6 − 1 = _____

11. 5 − 3 = _____   2 − 1 = _____   4 − 4 = _____

12. 4 − 2 = _____   6 − 6 = _____   7 − 2 = _____

13. 5 − 5 = _____   6 − 2 = _____   6 − 3 = _____

14. 7 − 1 = _____   7 − 4 = _____   3 − 2 = _____

15. 6 − 5 = _____   3 − 3 = _____   6 − 4 = _____

☆ Write the missing number.

16. 4 − [1] = 3   4 − [ ] = 1   5 − [ ] = 1

17. 5 − [ ] = 4   6 − [ ] = 1   6 − [ ] = 5

Subtracting 1 to 6

RELATED FACTS

If you know **5 − 2** = _3_

Then you know **5 − 3** = _2_

Subtract.

1.

$$5 - 1 = \underline{\hphantom{00}}$$

$$5 - 4 = \underline{\hphantom{00}}$$

2.

$$6 - 1 = \underline{\hphantom{00}}$$

$$6 - 5 = \underline{\hphantom{00}}$$

3.

$$6 - 2 = \underline{\hphantom{00}}$$

$$6 - 4 = \underline{\hphantom{00}}$$

4.

$$3 - 1 = \underline{\hphantom{00}}$$

$$3 - 2 = \underline{\hphantom{00}}$$

5.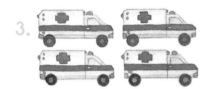

$$4 - 1 = \underline{\hphantom{00}}$$

$$4 - 3 = \underline{\hphantom{00}}$$

6.

$$7 - 5 = \underline{\hphantom{00}}$$

$$7 - 2 = \underline{\hphantom{00}}$$

Subtract.

7. $3 - 1 =$ _____ 8. $6 - 1 =$ _____ 9. $7 - 1 =$ _____

$3 - 2 =$ _____ $6 - 5 =$ _____ $7 - 6 =$ _____

10. $5 - 4 =$ _____ 11. $7 - 1 =$ _____ 12. $6 - 2 =$ _____

$5 - 1 =$ _____ $7 - 6 =$ _____ $6 - 4 =$ _____

13. $7 - 3 =$ _____ 14. $5 - 2 =$ _____ 15. $4 - 1 =$ _____

$7 - 4 =$ _____ $5 - 3 =$ _____ $4 - 3 =$ _____

16. $7 - 1 =$ _____ 17. $7 - 2 =$ _____ 18. $6 - 1 =$ _____

$7 - 6 =$ _____ $7 - 5 =$ _____ $6 - 5 =$ _____

19. $4 - 2 =$ _____ $7 - 4 =$ _____ $6 - 2 =$ _____

20. $5 - 3 =$ _____ $6 - 4 =$ _____ $5 - 1 =$ _____

(pages 81–88)

CHECKPOINT 1

Subtract.

1. $4 - 1 =$ ☐ $5 - 2 =$ ☐ $7 - 5 =$ ☐

2. $6 - 2 =$ ☐ $7 - 4 =$ ☐ $3 - 2 =$ ☐

Extra practice on page 365

Related Subtraction Facts

PROBLEM SOLVING

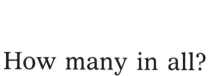

How many in all?

$4\ \boxed{+}\ 1 = \underline{5}$

Write + or − in the ☐.
Add or subtract.

1.

How many are left?

$4\ \boxed{}\ 1 = \underline{}$

2.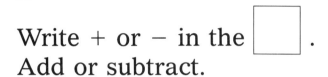

How many in all?

$4\ \boxed{}\ 2 = \underline{}$

3.

How many are left?

$4\ \boxed{}\ 2 = \underline{}$

4.

How many are left?

$4\ \boxed{}\ 3 = \underline{}$

Write + or − in the ☐.
Add or subtract.

5.  How many are left?

$5 \boxed{} 4 = \underline{}$

6.  How many in all?

$3 \boxed{} 2 = \underline{}$

7.  How many in all?

$3 \boxed{} 3 = \underline{}$

8.  How many are left?

$6 \boxed{} 3 = \underline{}$

9.  How many in all?

$2 \boxed{} 2 = \underline{}$

Problem Solving

SUBTRACTION ANOTHER WAY

$$7 - 3 = \underline{}$$

$$\begin{array}{r} 7 \\ -3 \\ \hline \end{array}$$

Subtract.

1.
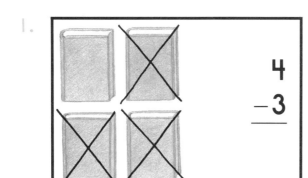
$$\begin{array}{r} 4 \\ -3 \\ \hline \end{array}$$

2.
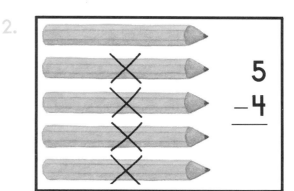
$$\begin{array}{r} 5 \\ -4 \\ \hline \end{array}$$

3.
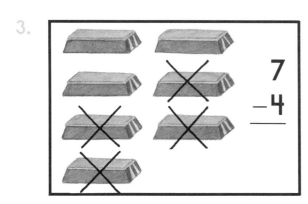
$$\begin{array}{r} 7 \\ -4 \\ \hline \end{array}$$

4.
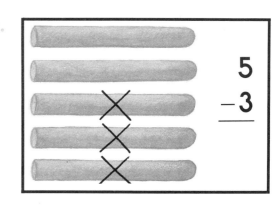
$$\begin{array}{r} 5 \\ -3 \\ \hline \end{array}$$

5.
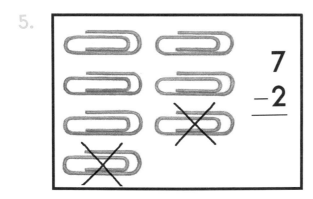
$$\begin{array}{r} 7 \\ -2 \\ \hline \end{array}$$

6.
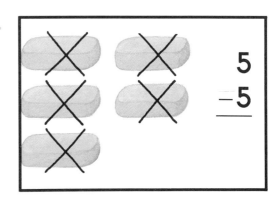
$$\begin{array}{r} 5 \\ -5 \\ \hline \end{array}$$

Subtract.

7.
$$
\begin{array}{r} 5 \\ -2 \\ \hline \end{array}
\quad
\begin{array}{r} 6 \\ -1 \\ \hline \end{array}
\quad
\begin{array}{r} 2 \\ -1 \\ \hline \end{array}
\quad
\begin{array}{r} 4 \\ -3 \\ \hline \end{array}
\quad
\begin{array}{r} 3 \\ -1 \\ \hline \end{array}
\quad
\begin{array}{r} 5 \\ -4 \\ \hline \end{array}
$$

8.
$$
\begin{array}{r} 7 \\ -2 \\ \hline \end{array}
\quad
\begin{array}{r} 6 \\ -4 \\ \hline \end{array}
\quad
\begin{array}{r} 3 \\ -1 \\ \hline \end{array}
\quad
\begin{array}{r} 6 \\ -6 \\ \hline \end{array}
\quad
\begin{array}{r} 5 \\ -1 \\ \hline \end{array}
\quad
\begin{array}{r} 7 \\ -4 \\ \hline \end{array}
$$

9.
$$
\begin{array}{r} 4 \\ -1 \\ \hline \end{array}
\quad
\begin{array}{r} 3 \\ -2 \\ \hline \end{array}
\quad
\begin{array}{r} 4 \\ -4 \\ \hline \end{array}
\quad
\begin{array}{r} 7 \\ -3 \\ \hline \end{array}
\quad
\begin{array}{r} 4 \\ -2 \\ \hline \end{array}
\quad
\begin{array}{r} 1 \\ -1 \\ \hline \end{array}
$$

10.
$$
\begin{array}{r} 7 \\ -5 \\ \hline \end{array}
\quad
\begin{array}{r} 7 \\ -6 \\ \hline \end{array}
\quad
\begin{array}{r} 5 \\ -3 \\ \hline \end{array}
\quad
\begin{array}{r} 7 \\ -7 \\ \hline \end{array}
\quad
\begin{array}{r} 6 \\ -2 \\ \hline \end{array}
\quad
\begin{array}{r} 5 \\ -5 \\ \hline \end{array}
$$

Think of the difference.
If greater than **3**, color 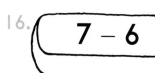 red .

11.
7 – 3

12.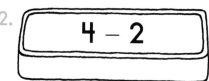
4 – 2

13.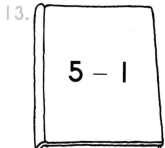
5 – 1

14.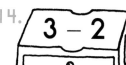
3 – 2

15.
6 – 2

16.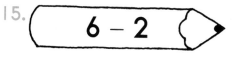
7 – 6

Subtraction, Vertical Form

NAME _____

SUBTRACTING FROM 7

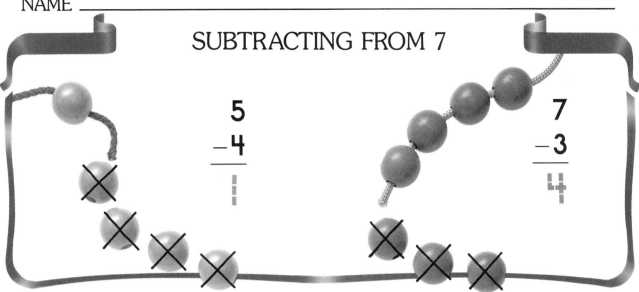

$$\begin{array}{r} 5 \\ -4 \\ \hline 1 \end{array}$$

$$\begin{array}{r} 7 \\ -3 \\ \hline 4 \end{array}$$

Subtract.

1.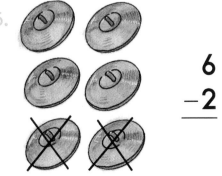
$$\begin{array}{r} 5 \\ -2 \\ \hline \end{array}$$

2.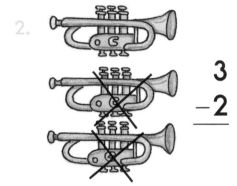
$$\begin{array}{r} 3 \\ -2 \\ \hline \end{array}$$

3.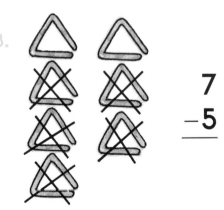
$$\begin{array}{r} 7 \\ -5 \\ \hline \end{array}$$

4.
$$\begin{array}{r} 4 \\ -2 \\ \hline \end{array}$$

5.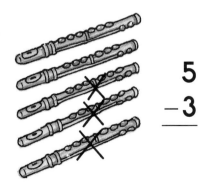
$$\begin{array}{r} 6 \\ -2 \\ \hline \end{array}$$

6.
$$\begin{array}{r} 5 \\ -3 \\ \hline \end{array}$$

Subtraction Facts through 7

Subtract.

7.

4			
−1	−3	−2	−4
3	1		

8.

5			
−1	−3	−2	−4

9.

6			
−5	−3	−4	−6

10.

7			
−1	−5	−6	−4

Tell the story. Then add or subtract.

11.

4 + 2 = _____

12.

7 − 3 = _____

Subtraction Facts through 7

SUBTRACTING WITH ZERO

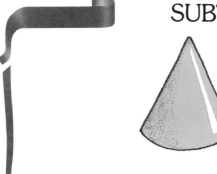 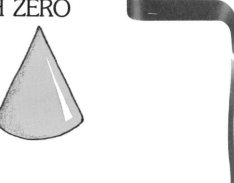

$3 - 0 = \underline{}$

Subtract.

1.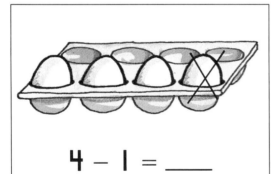

$4 - 3 = \underline{}$

2.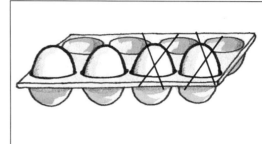

$4 - 2 = \underline{}$

3.

$4 - 1 = \underline{}$

4.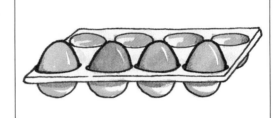

$4 - 0 = \underline{}$

5.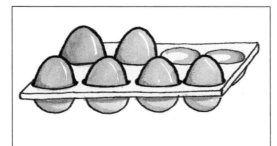

$6 - 0 = \underline{}$

6.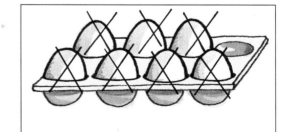

$7 - 7 = \underline{}$

Subtract.

7. $5 - 0 =$ _____ $2 - 1 =$ _____

8. $7 - 6 =$ _____ $4 - 0 =$ _____

9. $1 - 0 =$ _____ $3 - 3 =$ _____

10. $6 - 3 =$ _____ $4 - 3 =$ _____

11. $3 - 0 =$ _____ $4 - 1 =$ _____

12.
$$\begin{array}{r} 6 \\ -0 \\ \hline \end{array} \qquad \begin{array}{r} 4 \\ -2 \\ \hline \end{array} \qquad \begin{array}{r} 2 \\ -2 \\ \hline \end{array} \qquad \begin{array}{r} 7 \\ -0 \\ \hline \end{array} \qquad \begin{array}{r} 7 \\ -5 \\ \hline \end{array} \qquad \begin{array}{r} 6 \\ -6 \\ \hline \end{array}$$

13.
$$\begin{array}{r} 4 \\ -3 \\ \hline \end{array} \qquad \begin{array}{r} 1 \\ -0 \\ \hline \end{array} \qquad \begin{array}{r} 6 \\ -4 \\ \hline \end{array} \qquad \begin{array}{r} 5 \\ -3 \\ \hline \end{array} \qquad \begin{array}{r} 7 \\ -7 \\ \hline \end{array} \qquad \begin{array}{r} 5 \\ -0 \\ \hline \end{array}$$

14.
$$\begin{array}{r} 7 \\ -2 \\ \hline \end{array} \qquad \begin{array}{r} 1 \\ -1 \\ \hline \end{array} \qquad \begin{array}{r} 5 \\ -4 \\ \hline \end{array} \qquad \begin{array}{r} 6 \\ -5 \\ \hline \end{array} \qquad \begin{array}{r} 2 \\ -0 \\ \hline \end{array} \qquad \begin{array}{r} 4 \\ -1 \\ \hline \end{array}$$

☆ **Write the missing number.**

15.
$$\begin{array}{r} 5 \\ -\boxed{3} \\ \hline 2 \end{array} \qquad \begin{array}{r} 3 \\ -\boxed{} \\ \hline 3 \end{array} \qquad \begin{array}{r} 7 \\ -\boxed{} \\ \hline 4 \end{array} \qquad \begin{array}{r} 4 \\ -\boxed{} \\ \hline 0 \end{array} \qquad \begin{array}{r} 2 \\ -\boxed{} \\ \hline 2 \end{array} \qquad \begin{array}{r} 6 \\ -\boxed{} \\ \hline 2 \end{array}$$

Subtracting with Zero

FACT FAMILIES

If you know $2 + 4 = \underline{6}$

Then you know $6 - 4 = \underline{2}$

■ ■   ■ ■   ■ ■ $4 + 2 = \underline{6}$

$6 - 2 = \underline{4}$

Add or subtract.

1.

$5 + 2 = \underline{}$

$7 - 2 = \underline{}$

$2 + 5 = \underline{}$

$7 - 5 = \underline{}$

2.

$2 + 3 = \underline{}$

$5 - 3 = \underline{}$

$3 + 2 = \underline{}$

$5 - 2 = \underline{}$

3.

$3 + 4 = \underline{}$

$7 - 4 = \underline{}$

$4 + 3 = \underline{}$

$7 - 3 = \underline{}$

Add or subtract.

4.

1, 5, 6
1 + 5 = ___
6 − 5 = ___
5 + 1 = ___
6 − 1 = ___

5.

3, 4, 7
3 + 4 = ___
7 − 4 = ___
4 + 3 = ___
7 − 3 = ___

6.

2, 3, 5

$$\begin{array}{cc} 2 & 5 \\ +3 & -3 \\ \hline \end{array}$$

$$\begin{array}{cc} 3 & 5 \\ +2 & -2 \\ \hline \end{array}$$

7.

1, 3, 4

$$\begin{array}{cc} 1 & 4 \\ +3 & -3 \\ \hline \end{array}$$

$$\begin{array}{cc} 3 & 4 \\ +1 & -1 \\ \hline \end{array}$$

Think of the difference.
If less than 4, color blue .

8.
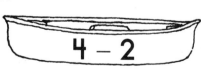
4 − 2

9.
5 − 3

10.
7 − 2

11.
7 − 1

12.
6 − 3

13.

5 − 2

Fact Families

PROBLEM SOLVING

5

2 join.

How many in all?

5
+2
———

5
−2
———

Ring the correct example.

1.

7

2  go away.

How many are left?

7
+2
———

7
−2
———

2.

7

6 go away.

How many are left?

7
−6
———

7
+6
———

Ring the correct example.

3. 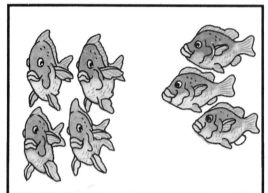   4    join.

$$\begin{array}{r} 4 \\ +3 \\ \hline \end{array}$$

3

How many in all?

$$\begin{array}{r} 4 \\ -3 \\ \hline \end{array}$$

4.    5    goes away.

$$\begin{array}{r} 5 \\ +1 \\ \hline \end{array}$$

1

How many are left?

$$\begin{array}{r} 5 \\ -1 \\ \hline \end{array}$$

(pages 89–100)

CHECKPOINT 2

Subtract.

1.

$$\begin{array}{r} 6 \\ -0 \\ \hline \end{array} \quad \begin{array}{r} 6 \\ -1 \\ \hline \end{array} \quad \begin{array}{r} 3 \\ -3 \\ \hline \end{array} \quad \begin{array}{r} 7 \\ -5 \\ \hline \end{array} \quad \begin{array}{r} 5 \\ -5 \\ \hline \end{array}$$

Ring the correct example.

2.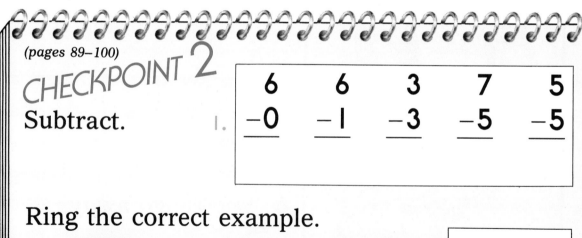

$$\begin{array}{r} 5 \\ +2 \\ \hline \end{array} \quad \begin{array}{r} 5 \\ -2 \\ \hline \end{array}$$

Extra practice on page 365

Problem Solving

CHAPTER 4 TEST

Subtract.

1. $4 - 2 =$ ___ $5 - 3 =$ ___ $6 - 4 =$ ___

2. $7 - 4 =$ ___ $6 - 2 =$ ___ $7 - 5 =$ ___

3.
$$\begin{array}{r} 4 \\ -3 \\ \hline \end{array} \qquad \begin{array}{r} 7 \\ -2 \\ \hline \end{array} \qquad \begin{array}{r} 3 \\ -2 \\ \hline \end{array} \qquad \begin{array}{r} 6 \\ -5 \\ \hline \end{array} \qquad \begin{array}{r} 7 \\ -4 \\ \hline \end{array} \qquad \begin{array}{r} 5 \\ -3 \\ \hline \end{array}$$

Subtract.

4. $5 - 0 =$ ___ $6 - 6 =$ ___ $7 - 0 =$ ___

5. $7 - 3 =$ ___ $6 - 0 =$ ___ $4 - 4 =$ ___

Write + or − in the ☐.
Then add or subtract.

6.

6 ☐ $2 =$ ___

Extra practice on page 366

MATHEMATICS and SCIENCE

Machines can
help us count.
Trace the word.

1.

calculator

2.

computer

3.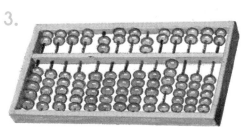

abacus

4.

clock

5.

cash register

Mathematics and Science

Enrichment

Draw a picture. Then write the number.

1.

$5 - \underline{} = 4$

$6 - \underline{} = 4$

2.

$4 - \underline{} = 4$

$7 - \underline{} = 3$

3.

$7 - \underline{} = 2$

$6 - \underline{} = 3$

Draw a picture. Then write the number.

4.
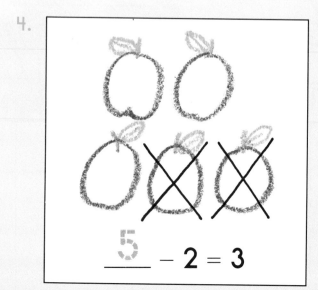

5

_____ $- 2 = 3$

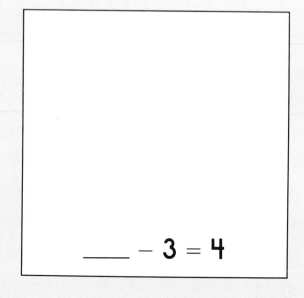

_____ $- 3 = 4$

5.

_____ $- 4 = 3$

_____ $- 2 = 4$

6.

_____ $- 1 = 5$

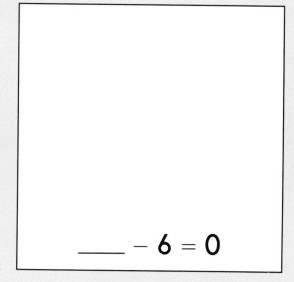

_____ $- 6 = 0$

Enrichment: Drawing a Picture

 CUMULATIVE REVIEW

Fill in the ⬭ for the correct answer.

Add.

1.	2.	3.
5 +0	0 +7	6 + 0
5　6　8 Ⓐ　Ⓑ　Ⓒ	6　8　7 Ⓐ　Ⓑ　Ⓒ	5　6　7 Ⓐ　Ⓑ　Ⓒ

Add.

4.	5.	6.
2 +7	4 +6	3 + 6
8　9　7 Ⓐ　Ⓑ　Ⓒ	10　9　7 Ⓐ　Ⓑ　Ⓒ	9　8　10 Ⓐ　Ⓑ　Ⓒ

Add.

7.	8.	9.
2 4 +3	5 1 +2	3 4 +3
9　8　10 Ⓐ　Ⓑ　Ⓒ	8　9　7 Ⓐ　Ⓑ　Ⓒ	10　9　8 Ⓐ　Ⓑ　Ⓒ

LANGUAGE and VOCABULARY REVIEW

Addition Words

join
add
sum
plus

Subtraction Words

left
minus
subtract
difference
take away

Color the addition words 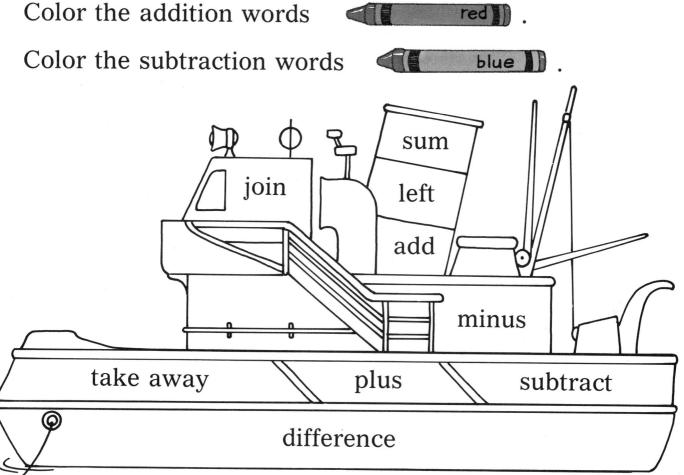 red .

Color the subtraction words blue .

sum

join

left

add

minus

take away   plus   subtract

difference

Language and Vocabulary Review

5

Read with the children:

The farmer has 10 cows.
Some are in the field.
Some are in the barn.
How many in the field?
How many in the barn?

SUBTRACTION
FACTS THROUGH 10

REVIEWING SUBTRACTION

$7 - 3 = \underline{4}$

Subtract.

1. $7 - 1 = \underline{}$ $6 - 1 = \underline{}$ $6 - 6 = \underline{}$

2. $5 - 4 = \underline{}$ $5 - 0 = \underline{}$ $6 - 5 = \underline{}$

3. $6 - 3 = \underline{}$ $6 - 4 = \underline{}$ $4 - 1 = \underline{}$

$$\begin{array}{r} 6 \\ -4 \\ \hline 2 \end{array}$$

4.
$$\begin{array}{r} 7 \\ -1 \\ \hline \end{array}\qquad \begin{array}{r} 7 \\ -4 \\ \hline \end{array}\qquad \begin{array}{r} 4 \\ -3 \\ \hline \end{array}\qquad \begin{array}{r} 6 \\ -3 \\ \hline \end{array}\qquad \begin{array}{r} 3 \\ -2 \\ \hline \end{array}\qquad \begin{array}{r} 4 \\ -1 \\ \hline \end{array}$$

5.
$$\begin{array}{r} 6 \\ -0 \\ \hline \end{array}\qquad \begin{array}{r} 5 \\ -4 \\ \hline \end{array}\qquad \begin{array}{r} 7 \\ -7 \\ \hline \end{array}\qquad \begin{array}{r} 7 \\ -3 \\ \hline \end{array}\qquad \begin{array}{r} 4 \\ -0 \\ \hline \end{array}\qquad \begin{array}{r} 6 \\ -3 \\ \hline \end{array}$$

Reviewing Subtraction

SUBTRACTING FROM 8

$8 - 3 = \underline{5}$

Subtract.

1.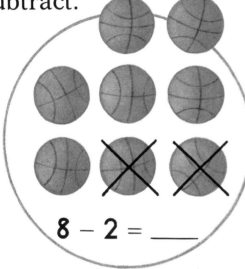

$8 - 2 = \underline{}$

2.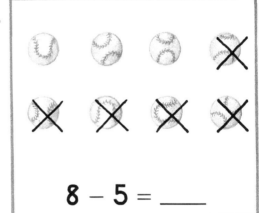

$8 - 5 = \underline{}$

3.

$7 - 6 = \underline{}$

4.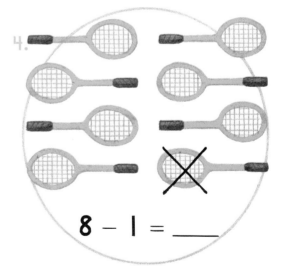

$8 - 1 = \underline{}$

5. $8 - 5 = \underline{}$ $8 - 4 = \underline{}$ $8 - 3 = \underline{}$

6. $8 - 2 = \underline{}$ $7 - 2 = \underline{}$ $6 - 2 = \underline{}$

7. $8 - 6 = \underline{}$ $8 - 7 = \underline{}$ $8 - 8 = \underline{}$

Subtract.

8. $6 - 2 =$ ___ $7 - 2 =$ ___ $8 - 2 =$ ___

9. $6 - 3 =$ ___ $7 - 3 =$ ___ $8 - 3 =$ ___

10. $6 - 4 =$ ___ $7 - 4 =$ ___ $8 - 4 =$ ___

11. $8 - 5 =$ ___ $7 - 6 =$ ___ $8 - 8 =$ ___

12. $8 - 7 =$ ___ $6 - 1 =$ ___ $8 - 6 =$ ___

13. $5 - 4 =$ ___ $8 - 1 =$ ___ $7 - 7 =$ ___

14. $8 - 2 =$ ___ $6 - 0 =$ ___ $5 - 3 =$ ___

15. $8 - 0 =$ ___ $8 - 5 =$ ___ $7 - 4 =$ ___

16. $6 - 2 =$ ___ $8 - 3 =$ ___ $5 - 1 =$ ___

Tell the story. Then add or subtract.

17.

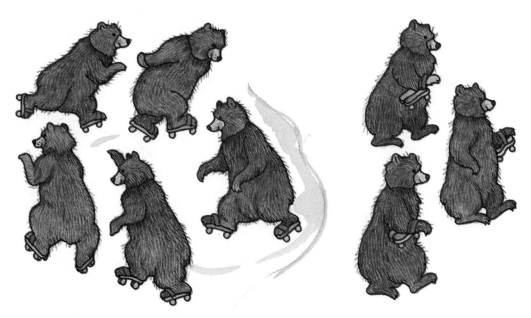

8 bears − **3** bears = ___ bears

Subtraction Facts through 8

SUBTRACTING FROM 8

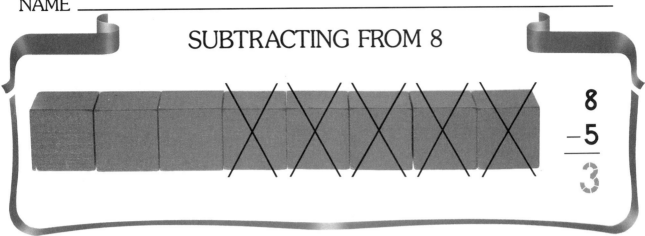

$$\begin{array}{r} 8 \\ -5 \\ \hline 3 \end{array}$$

Subtract.

1.
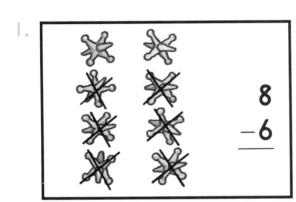
$$\begin{array}{r} 8 \\ -6 \\ \hline \end{array}$$

2.
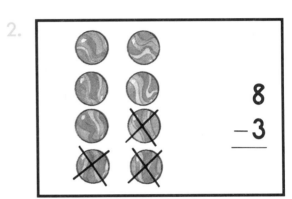
$$\begin{array}{r} 8 \\ -3 \\ \hline \end{array}$$

3.
$$\begin{array}{r} 7 \\ -5 \\ \hline \end{array}$$

4.
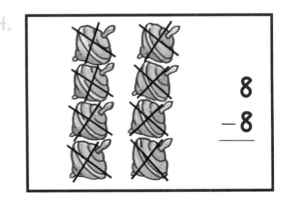
$$\begin{array}{r} 8 \\ -8 \\ \hline \end{array}$$

5.
$$\begin{array}{r} 8 \\ -0 \\ \hline \end{array} \qquad \begin{array}{r} 8 \\ -1 \\ \hline \end{array} \qquad \begin{array}{r} 8 \\ -2 \\ \hline \end{array} \qquad \begin{array}{r} 8 \\ -6 \\ \hline \end{array} \qquad \begin{array}{r} 7 \\ -6 \\ \hline \end{array} \qquad \begin{array}{r} 6 \\ -6 \\ \hline \end{array}$$

6.
$$\begin{array}{r} 8 \\ -4 \\ \hline \end{array} \qquad \begin{array}{r} 8 \\ -5 \\ \hline \end{array} \qquad \begin{array}{r} 8 \\ -6 \\ \hline \end{array} \qquad \begin{array}{r} 5 \\ -5 \\ \hline \end{array} \qquad \begin{array}{r} 5 \\ -4 \\ \hline \end{array} \qquad \begin{array}{r} 5 \\ -3 \\ \hline \end{array}$$

Subtract.

7.
$$\begin{array}{r} 8 \\ -2 \\ \hline \end{array}$$
$$\begin{array}{r} 7 \\ -6 \\ \hline \end{array}$$
$$\begin{array}{r} 6 \\ -1 \\ \hline \end{array}$$
$$\begin{array}{r} 8 \\ -3 \\ \hline \end{array}$$
$$\begin{array}{r} 6 \\ -4 \\ \hline \end{array}$$
$$\begin{array}{r} 8 \\ -6 \\ \hline \end{array}$$

8.
$$\begin{array}{r} 7 \\ -7 \\ \hline \end{array}$$
$$\begin{array}{r} 8 \\ -4 \\ \hline \end{array}$$
$$\begin{array}{r} 7 \\ -5 \\ \hline \end{array}$$
$$\begin{array}{r} 6 \\ -6 \\ \hline \end{array}$$
$$\begin{array}{r} 7 \\ -2 \\ \hline \end{array}$$
$$\begin{array}{r} 8 \\ -7 \\ \hline \end{array}$$

9.
$$\begin{array}{r} 8 \\ -3 \\ \hline \end{array}$$
$$\begin{array}{r} 7 \\ -4 \\ \hline \end{array}$$
$$\begin{array}{r} 6 \\ -3 \\ \hline \end{array}$$
$$\begin{array}{r} 8 \\ -5 \\ \hline \end{array}$$
$$\begin{array}{r} 7 \\ -3 \\ \hline \end{array}$$
$$\begin{array}{r} 8 \\ -0 \\ \hline \end{array}$$

10.
$$\begin{array}{r} 8 \\ -8 \\ \hline \end{array}$$
$$\begin{array}{r} 6 \\ -2 \\ \hline \end{array}$$
$$\begin{array}{r} 8 \\ -1 \\ \hline \end{array}$$
$$\begin{array}{r} 7 \\ -0 \\ \hline \end{array}$$
$$\begin{array}{r} 8 \\ -4 \\ \hline \end{array}$$
$$\begin{array}{r} 5 \\ -5 \\ \hline \end{array}$$

Think of the difference.
Is it **greater** than **6**?
Ring yes or no.

11. $8 - 1$ $8 - 4$ $7 - 3$

 (yes)   no   yes   no   yes   no

12. $7 - 5$ $8 - 3$ $7 - 0$

 yes   no   yes   no   yes   no

Subtraction Facts through 8

NAME _____

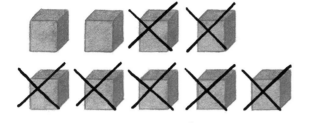 

$9 - 7 = \underline{2}$ $9 - 5 = \underline{4}$

Subtract.

1.

$9 - 1 = \underline{}$

2.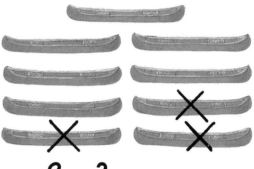

$9 - 3 = \underline{}$

3.

$8 - 4 = \underline{}$

4.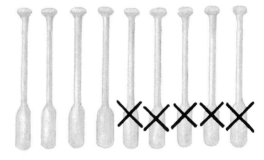

$9 - 5 = \underline{}$

5. $9 - 2 = \underline{}$ $9 - 3 = \underline{}$ $9 - 4 = \underline{}$

6. $8 - 6 = \underline{}$ $7 - 6 = \underline{}$ $6 - 6 = \underline{}$

7. $9 - 9 = \underline{}$ $9 - 8 = \underline{}$ $9 - 7 = \underline{}$

8. Subtract.
Color

5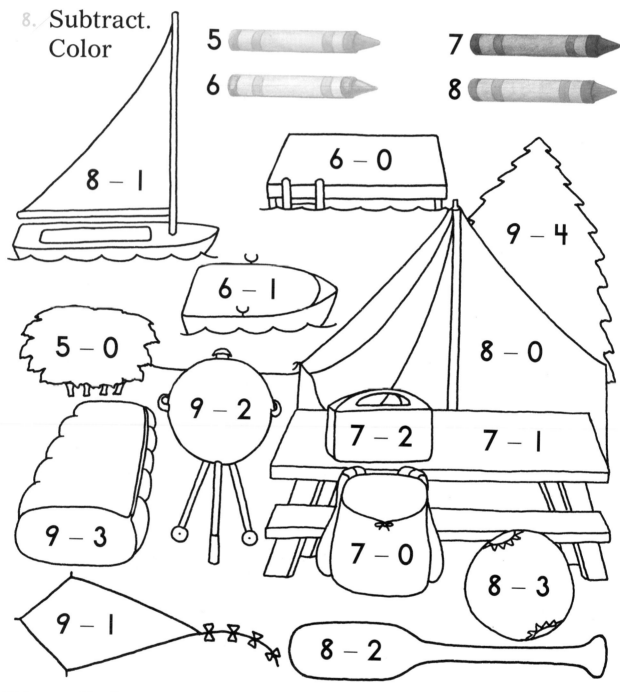
6
7
8

6 − 0

9 − 4

8 − 1

6 − 1

5 − 0

8 − 0

9 − 2

7 − 2   7 − 1

9 − 3

7 − 0

8 − 3

9 − 1

8 − 2

☆ Ring all the names for the number.

9.   [6]   (7 − 1)   (8 − 2)   8 − 1

10.   [7]   8 − 3   8 − 1   7 − 0

11.   [8]   9 − 1   7 − 6   8 − 0

114   one hundred fourteen

Subtraction Facts through 9

SUBTRACTING FROM 9

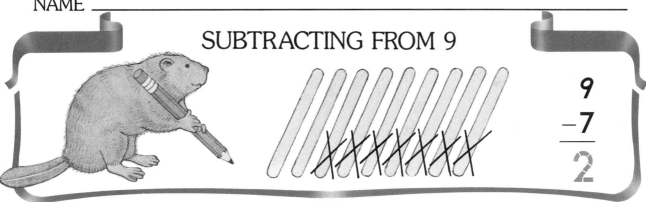

$$\begin{array}{r} 9 \\ -7 \\ \hline 2 \end{array}$$

Subtract.

1.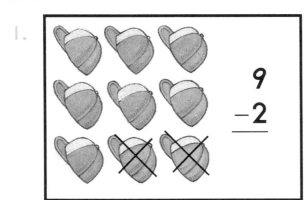

$$\begin{array}{r} 9 \\ -2 \\ \hline \end{array}$$

2.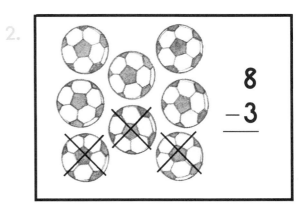

$$\begin{array}{r} 8 \\ -3 \\ \hline \end{array}$$

3.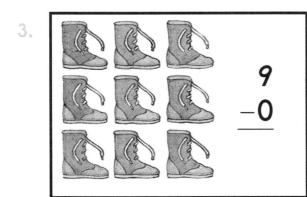

$$\begin{array}{r} 9 \\ -0 \\ \hline \end{array}$$

4.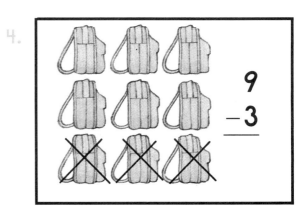

$$\begin{array}{r} 9 \\ -3 \\ \hline \end{array}$$

5.
$$\begin{array}{r} 9 \\ -1 \\ \hline \end{array} \qquad \begin{array}{r} 9 \\ -2 \\ \hline \end{array} \qquad \begin{array}{r} 9 \\ -3 \\ \hline \end{array} \qquad \begin{array}{r} 9 \\ -8 \\ \hline \end{array} \qquad \begin{array}{r} 9 \\ -7 \\ \hline \end{array} \qquad \begin{array}{r} 9 \\ -6 \\ \hline \end{array}$$

6.
$$\begin{array}{r} 9 \\ -4 \\ \hline \end{array} \qquad \begin{array}{r} 8 \\ -4 \\ \hline \end{array} \qquad \begin{array}{r} 7 \\ -4 \\ \hline \end{array} \qquad \begin{array}{r} 9 \\ -2 \\ \hline \end{array} \qquad \begin{array}{r} 9 \\ -3 \\ \hline \end{array} \qquad \begin{array}{r} 9 \\ -4 \\ \hline \end{array}$$

Subtract.

7.
$$\begin{array}{r} 9 \\ -7 \\ \hline \end{array}$$
$$\begin{array}{r} 9 \\ -5 \\ \hline \end{array}$$
$$\begin{array}{r} 8 \\ -8 \\ \hline \end{array}$$
$$\begin{array}{r} 9 \\ -6 \\ \hline \end{array}$$
$$\begin{array}{r} 7 \\ -4 \\ \hline \end{array}$$
$$\begin{array}{r} 9 \\ -3 \\ \hline \end{array}$$

8.
$$\begin{array}{r} 9 \\ -0 \\ \hline \end{array}$$
$$\begin{array}{r} 8 \\ -5 \\ \hline \end{array}$$
$$\begin{array}{r} 9 \\ -2 \\ \hline \end{array}$$
$$\begin{array}{r} 8 \\ -4 \\ \hline \end{array}$$
$$\begin{array}{r} 7 \\ -5 \\ \hline \end{array}$$
$$\begin{array}{r} 9 \\ -9 \\ \hline \end{array}$$

9.
$$\begin{array}{r} 8 \\ -7 \\ \hline \end{array}$$
$$\begin{array}{r} 7 \\ -3 \\ \hline \end{array}$$
$$\begin{array}{r} 9 \\ -8 \\ \hline \end{array}$$
$$\begin{array}{r} 8 \\ -1 \\ \hline \end{array}$$
$$\begin{array}{r} 7 \\ -2 \\ \hline \end{array}$$
$$\begin{array}{r} 9 \\ -1 \\ \hline \end{array}$$

10.
$$\begin{array}{r} 9 \\ -4 \\ \hline \end{array}$$
$$\begin{array}{r} 9 \\ -1 \\ \hline \end{array}$$
$$\begin{array}{r} 8 \\ -8 \\ \hline \end{array}$$
$$\begin{array}{r} 9 \\ -2 \\ \hline \end{array}$$
$$\begin{array}{r} 7 \\ -7 \\ \hline \end{array}$$
$$\begin{array}{r} 9 \\ -0 \\ \hline \end{array}$$

(pages 107–116)

CHECKPOINT 1   Subtract.

1. $9 - 6 = \boxed{}$ $8 - 3 = \boxed{}$ $8 - 6 = \boxed{}$

2.
$$\begin{array}{r} 9 \\ -3 \\ \hline \end{array}$$
$$\begin{array}{r} 7 \\ -5 \\ \hline \end{array}$$
$$\begin{array}{r} 8 \\ -7 \\ \hline \end{array}$$
$$\begin{array}{r} 9 \\ -2 \\ \hline \end{array}$$
$$\begin{array}{r} 6 \\ -4 \\ \hline \end{array}$$
$$\begin{array}{r} 8 \\ -3 \\ \hline \end{array}$$

Extra practice on page 367

116 one hundred sixteen

Subtraction Facts through 9

PROBLEM SOLVING

6 + 2

6 − 2

3 + 3

Ring the correct example.

1.

3 + 2

5 + 2

5 − 3

2.

7 − 2

7 − 5

5 + 2

3.

8 − 3

5 + 3

7 − 4

Ring the correct example.

4.

$$5 + 2$$

$$3 + 5$$

$$5 - 3$$

5.

$$4 + 3$$

$$7 + 0$$

$$4 - 3$$

6.

$$8 - 5$$

$$5 + 3$$

$$8 - 4$$

7.

$$6 + 2$$

$$7 + 1$$

$$6 - 2$$

8.

$$8 - 8$$

$$8 - 0$$

$$8 + 1$$

Problem Solving

SUBTRACTING FROM 10

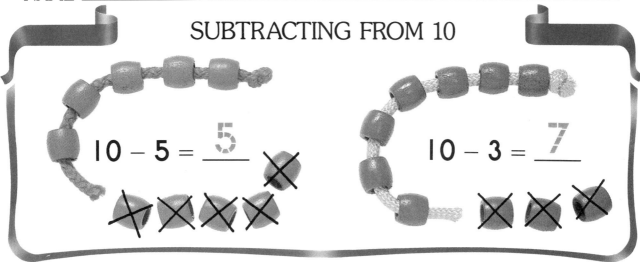

$$10 - 5 = \underline{5}$$

$$10 - 3 = \underline{7}$$

Subtract.

1.
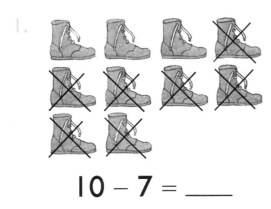

$$10 - 7 = \underline{}$$

2.
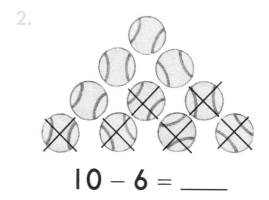

$$10 - 6 = \underline{}$$

3.
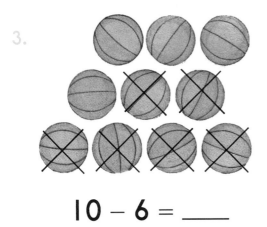

$$10 - 6 = \underline{}$$

4.

$$10 - 4 = \underline{}$$

5. $10 - 7 = \underline{}$ $\quad$ $10 - 6 = \underline{}$ $\quad$ $10 - 5 = \underline{}$

6. $10 - 9 = \underline{}$ $\quad$ $10 - 8 = \underline{}$ $\quad$ $10 - 7 = \underline{}$

7. $10 - 1 = \underline{}$ $\quad$ $9 - 1 = \underline{}$ $\quad$ $8 - 1 = \underline{}$

Subtract.

8. 8 – 2 = ____   9 – 2 = ____   10 – 2 = ____

9. 8 – 3 = ____   9 – 3 = ____   10 – 3 = ____

10. 8 – 4 = ____   9 – 4 = ____   10 – 4 = ____

11. 8 – 5 = ____   9 – 5 = ____   10 – 5 = ____

12. 10 – 4 = ____   10 – 6 = ____   10 – 7 = ____

13. 9 – 8 = ____   8 – 7 = ____   10 – 2 = ____

14. 10 – 3 = ____   9 – 5 = ____   10 – 1 = ____

15. 9 – 4 = ____   10 – 5 = ____   9 – 3 = ____

16. 10 – 6 = ____   9 – 3 = ____   10 – 7 = ____

Think of the difference.
Then write the number
just after the difference.

17.
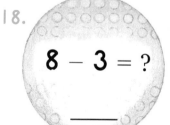
10 – 2 = ?
____

18.
8 – 3 = ?
____

19.
7 – 2 = ?
____

20.
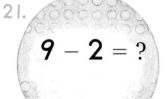
8 – 1 = ?
____

21.
9 – 2 = ?
____

22.
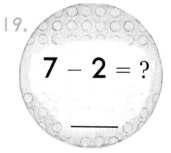
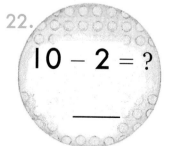
10 – 2 = ?
____

Subtraction Facts through 10

SUBTRACTING FROM 10

$$\begin{array}{r} 10 \\ -\ 3 \\ \hline 7 \end{array}$$

Subtract.

1.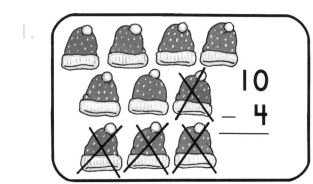

$$\begin{array}{r} 10 \\ -\ 4 \\ \hline \end{array}$$

2.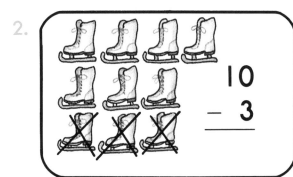

$$\begin{array}{r} 10 \\ -\ 3 \\ \hline \end{array}$$

3.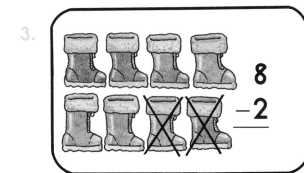

$$\begin{array}{r} 8 \\ -2 \\ \hline \end{array}$$

4.

$$\begin{array}{r} 10 \\ -\ 6 \\ \hline \end{array}$$

5.
$$\begin{array}{r} 10 \\ -\ 5 \\ \hline \end{array} \quad \begin{array}{r} 10 \\ -\ 4 \\ \hline \end{array} \quad \begin{array}{r} 10 \\ -\ 3 \\ \hline \end{array} \quad \begin{array}{r} 8 \\ -4 \\ \hline \end{array} \quad \begin{array}{r} 7 \\ -4 \\ \hline \end{array} \quad \begin{array}{r} 6 \\ -4 \\ \hline \end{array}$$

6.
$$\begin{array}{r} 10 \\ -\ 1 \\ \hline \end{array} \quad \begin{array}{r} 10 \\ -\ 2 \\ \hline \end{array} \quad \begin{array}{r} 10 \\ -\ 3 \\ \hline \end{array} \quad \begin{array}{r} 10 \\ -10 \\ \hline \end{array} \quad \begin{array}{r} 10 \\ -\ 9 \\ \hline \end{array} \quad \begin{array}{r} 10 \\ -\ 8 \\ \hline \end{array}$$

Subtract.

7.
10	9	10	8	10	8
− 2	−4	− 1	−5	− 8	−3

8.
10	7	9	10	8	9
− 9	−5	−3	− 5	−8	−2

9.
10	9	10	8	10	9
− 4	−1	− 7	−6	− 3	−0

Tell a story.
Write the numbers. Write + or − in the ☐ .
Then add or subtract.

10.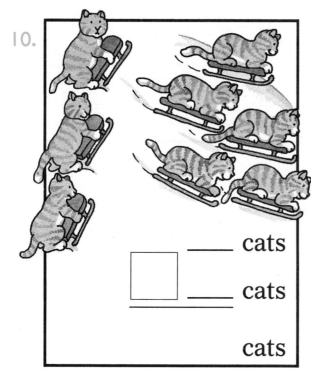

_____ cats
☐ _____ cats
_____ cats

11.

_____ dogs
☐ _____ dogs
_____ dogs

Subtraction Facts through 10

PROBLEM SOLVING

Bob has **7**¢.

He spends **6**¢.

How much does he have left?

$$\begin{array}{r} 7¢ \\ -\,6¢ \\ \hline 1¢ \end{array}$$

Write + or − in the ☐. Then add or subtract.

1. Kim has **5**¢.

She earns **3**¢.

How much does she have now?

$$\begin{array}{r} ☐\ 5¢ \\ 3¢ \\ \hline ¢ \end{array}$$

2. Maria has **8**¢.

She buys an apple for **6**¢.

How much does she have left?

$$\begin{array}{r} ☐\ 8¢ \\ 6¢ \\ \hline ¢ \end{array}$$

3. Jane has **4**¢.

She saved **3**¢ more.

How much does she have in all?

$$\begin{array}{r} ☐\ 4¢ \\ 3¢ \\ \hline ¢ \end{array}$$

Write + or − in the ☐ . Then add or subtract.

4. Jessica had **5¢**.
   She earned **2¢**.
   How much does she have now?

☐ 5¢
  2¢
——
  ¢

5. Michael had **4¢**.
   He gave **2¢** to Jessica.
   How much does he have now?

☐ 4¢
  2¢
——
  ¢

6. Kathy has **7¢**.
   She lost **2¢**.
   How much does she have left?

☐ 7¢
  2¢
——
  ¢

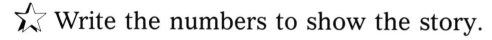

☆ Write the numbers to show the story.

7. Roberto bought a car for **3¢**.
   Then he bought a truck for **6¢**.
   How much did he spend?

☐ ___ ¢
  ___ ¢
——
  ¢

124   one hundred twenty-four

Problem Solving

FAMILY OF FACTS

If you know $2 + 8 = \underline{10}$

Then you know $10 - 8 = \underline{2}$

$8 + 2 = \underline{10}$

2   **8**   **10** $10 - 2 = \underline{8}$

Write the three numbers.   Add or subtract.

1.

$4 + 5 = \underline{}$ $5 + 4 = \underline{}$

$9 - 5 = \underline{}$ $9 - 4 = \underline{}$

_____ , _____ , _____

2.

$3 + 6 = \underline{}$ $6 + 3 = \underline{}$

$9 - 6 = \underline{}$ $9 - 3 = \underline{}$

_____ , _____ , _____

3.

$1 + 9 = \underline{}$ $9 + 1 = \underline{}$

$10 - 9 = \underline{}$ $10 - 1 = \underline{}$

_____ , _____ , _____

4.

2, 7, 9
2 + 7 = ___
9 − 7 = ___
7 + 2 = ___
9 − 2 = ___

5.

3, 5, 8
3 + 5 = ___
8 − 5 = ___
5 + 3 = ___
8 − 3 = ___

6.

5, 2, 7	
5 +2	7 −2
2 +5	7 −5

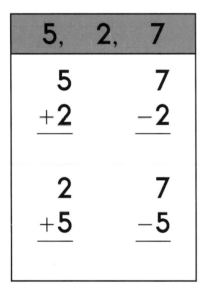

7.

3, 4, 7	
3 +4	7 −4
4 +3	7 −3

(pages 117–126)

CHECKPOINT 2   Subtract.

1. 10 − 6 = ☐   9 − 5 = ☐   10 − 2 = ☐

Write + or − in the ☐.
Then add or subtract.

2. Tim had **5¢**. He saved **2¢** more.
   How much does he have now?

☐
5¢
2¢
———
☐ ¢

Extra practice on page 367

Family of Facts

CHAPTER 5 TEST

Subtract.

1.   8   9   8   8   9   8
    −3   −6   −3   −2   −4   −2

2. $8 - 4 =$ ___ $9 - 8 =$ ___ $9 - 2 =$ ___

Ring the correct example.

3.

$3 + 5$
$5 - 3$
$5 - 2$

4.

$8 + 2$
$10 - 8$
$8 - 2$

Subtract.

5.   10   9   10   10   9   10
    − 6   −9   − 1   − 3   −7   − 5

6. $10 - 7 =$ ___ $10 - 2 =$ ___ $10 - 8 =$ ___

Extra practice on page 368

MATHEMATICS and LANGUAGE

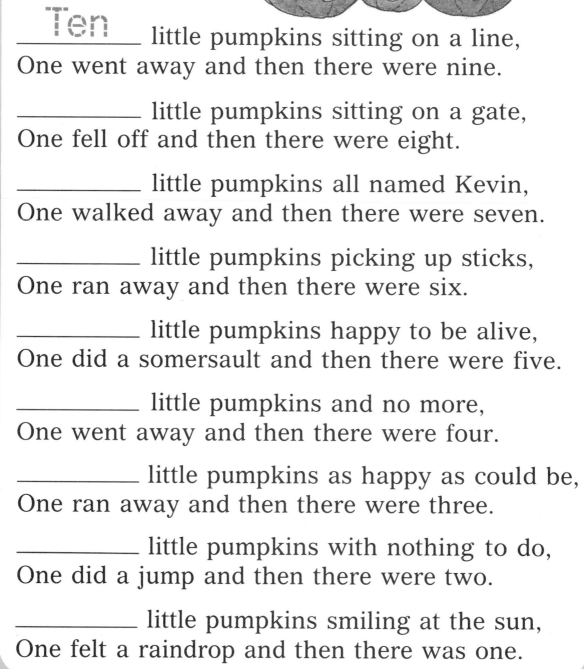

Write the word.

_____Ten_____ little pumpkins sitting on a line,
One went away and then there were nine.

_____ little pumpkins sitting on a gate,
One fell off and then there were eight.

_____ little pumpkins all named Kevin,
One walked away and then there were seven.

_____ little pumpkins picking up sticks,
One ran away and then there were six.

_____ little pumpkins happy to be alive,
One did a somersault and then there were five.

_____ little pumpkins and no more,
One went away and then there were four.

_____ little pumpkins as happy as could be,
One ran away and then there were three.

_____ little pumpkins with nothing to do,
One did a jump and then there were two.

_____ little pumpkins smiling at the sun,
One felt a raindrop and then there was one.

Mathematics and Language

Enrichment

Draw a picture to help.
Write the numbers.
Then add or subtract.

1.

There are **6** bugs on the ____ .
There are **2** bugs on the ground.
How many in all?

$$\begin{array}{r} 6 \\ +\ 2 \\ \hline 8 \end{array}$$

2.

There are **6** birds in the ____ .
3 birds fly away.
How many are left?

$$\begin{array}{r} \underline{} \\ -\ \underline{} \\ \hline \underline{} \end{array}$$

Draw a picture to help.
Write the numbers.
Then add or subtract.

3.

There are **2** plates on the ___ .
5 plates are on the ___ .
How many plates are there?

___
\+ ___
___

4.

There are **6** bees on the ___ .
Then **4** bees fly away.
How many bees are left?

___
− ___
___

Enrichment: Drawing a Picture

NAME _____

 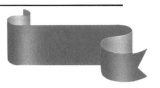

CUMULATIVE REVIEW

Fill in the ⬭ for the correct answer.

Choose the missing numbers.

1. 0, 1, 2, 3, 4, __?__, __?__, __?__, __?__, 9, 10

6,5,7,8	5,7,6,8	5,6,7,8
Ⓐ	Ⓑ	Ⓒ

Add.

2. 5 + 2	3. 7 + 3	4. 8 + 1
3 4 7	10 8 4	7 8 9
Ⓐ Ⓑ Ⓒ	Ⓐ Ⓑ Ⓒ	Ⓐ Ⓑ Ⓒ

Subtract.

5. $\begin{array}{r} 6 \\ -1 \\ \hline \end{array}$	6. $\begin{array}{r} 7 \\ -2 \\ \hline \end{array}$	7. $\begin{array}{r} 5 \\ -5 \\ \hline \end{array}$
7 5 4	5 9 4	10 5 0
Ⓐ Ⓑ Ⓒ	Ⓐ Ⓑ Ⓒ	Ⓐ Ⓑ Ⓒ
8. $\begin{array}{r} 5 \\ -3 \\ \hline \end{array}$	9. $\begin{array}{r} 6 \\ -5 \\ \hline \end{array}$	10. $\begin{array}{r} 1 \\ -0 \\ \hline \end{array}$
4 2 1	2 3 1	0 1 2
Ⓐ Ⓑ Ⓒ	Ⓐ Ⓑ Ⓒ	Ⓐ Ⓑ Ⓒ

Choose the correct number sentence.

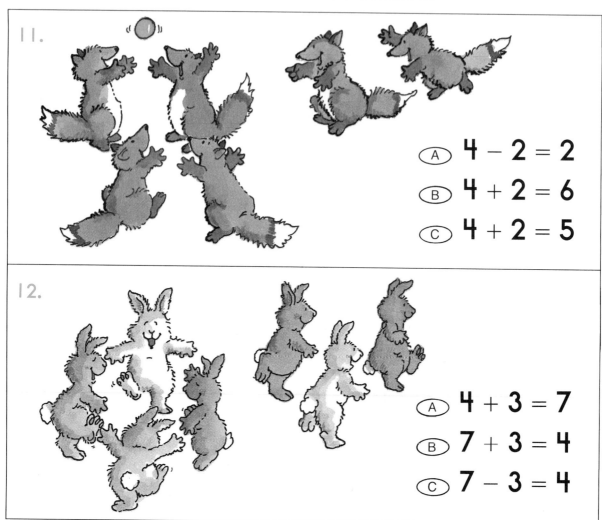

11.

    Ⓐ $4 - 2 = 2$

    Ⓑ $4 + 2 = 6$

    Ⓒ $4 + 2 = 5$

12.

    Ⓐ $4 + 3 = 7$

    Ⓑ $7 + 3 = 4$

    Ⓒ $7 - 3 = 4$

LANGUAGE and VOCABULARY REVIEW

Write the sign next to the word.
Use the signs in the box.

| + | − | ¢ | = |

1. equals ____

2. subtract ____

3. cents ____

4. add ____

Ring the computer parts.

1.

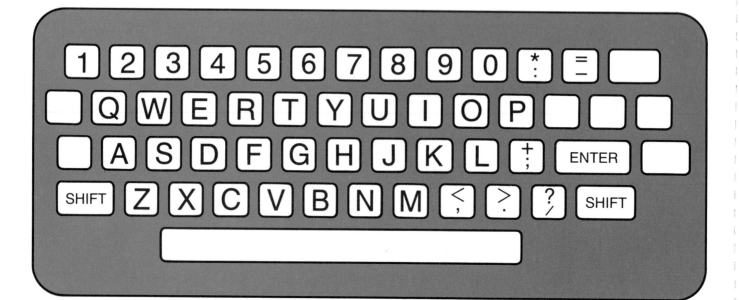

Write the letter.

2. Which ☐ is below Q ?

3. Which ☐ is to the left of K ?

4. Which ☐ is to the right of U ?

5. Which ☐ is below S and

to the right of X ?

6. Which ☐ is above S and

to the left of E ?

A

☐

☐

☐

☐

7. Write the number.

| 1 | ☐ | 3 | ☐ | ☐ | ☐ | ☐ | ☐ | ☐ | 0 |

Computer Keyboard

6

Read with the children:

Suppose you have 14 balloons. If you gave 10 balloons to a friend, how many balloons would you still have?

PLACE VALUE THROUGH 99

135

TENS AND ONES TO 15

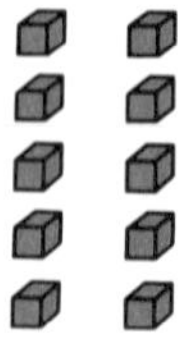

10 ones   is   1 ten

Write the number of tens and ones.
Then write the number.

1. 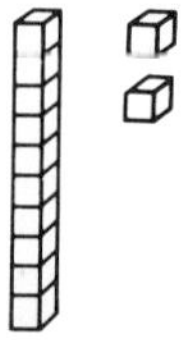
_1_ ten   _2_ ones

_12_

2. 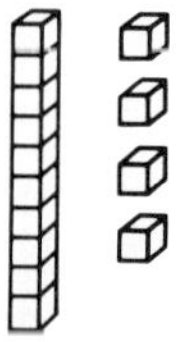
___ ten   ___ ones

___

3. 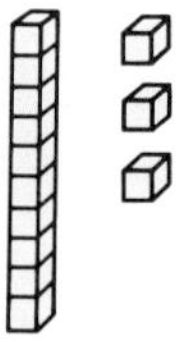
___ ten   ___ ones

___

4. 
___ ten   ___ ones

___

5. 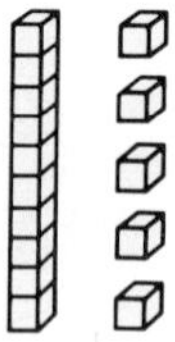
___ ten   ___ ones

___

6. 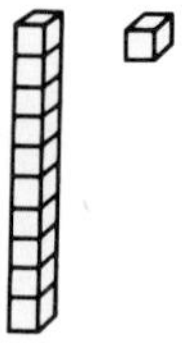
___ ten   ___ one

___

Identifying Tens and Ones to 15

TENS AND ONES TO 19

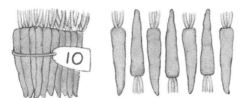

1 ten   **7** ones   is   **17**

Write the number of tens and ones.
Then write the number.

1.
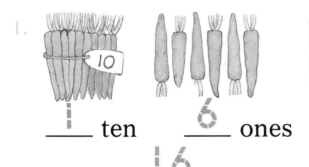

____ ten   __6__ ones

__16__

2.
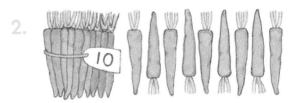

____ ten   ____ ones

_____

3.
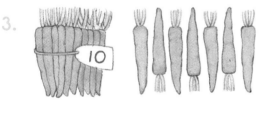

____ ten   ____ ones

_____

4.
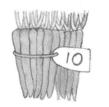

____ ten   ____ ones

_____

5.

____ ten   ____ ones

_____

6.

____ ten   ____ ones

_____

Ring the number.

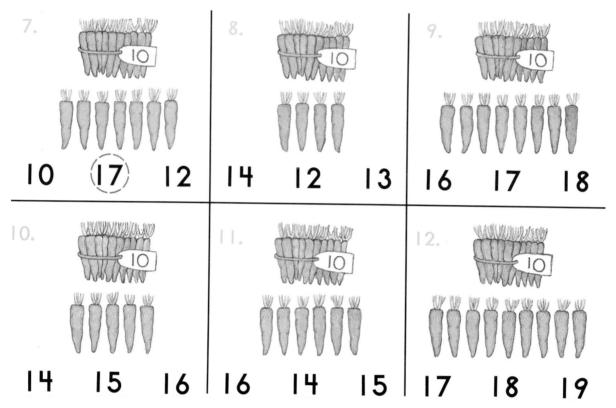

7. 10 (17) 12

8. 14 12 13

9. 16 17 18

10. 14 15 16

11. 16 14 15

12. 17 18 19

Write the number.

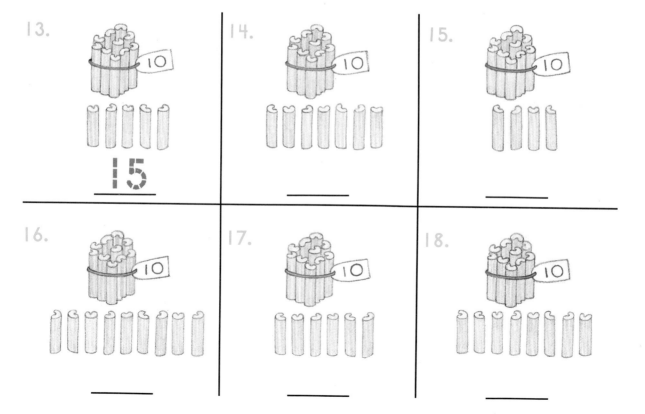

13. 15

14. _____

15. _____

16. _____

17. _____

18. _____

Identifying Tens and Ones to 19

TENS TO 90

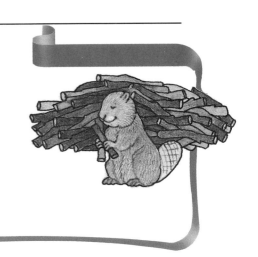

7 tens is **7** tens **0** ones   **70**

Write the number of tens and ones.
Then write the number.

1.

____3____ tens ____0____ ones

____30____

2.
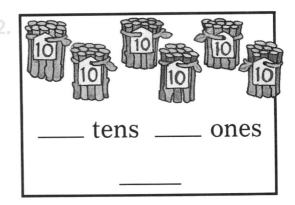

____ tens ____ ones

____

3.

____ tens ____ ones

____

4.

____ tens ____ ones

____

5.
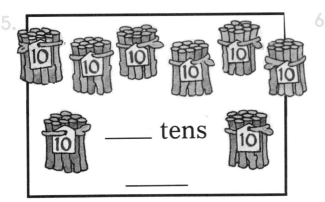

____ tens

____

6.
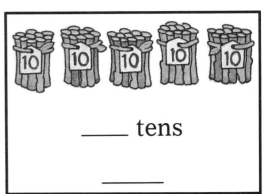

____ tens

____

Write the number.

7.
_____

8.
_____

9.
_____

10.
_____

Count by tens.
Write the missing numbers.

11.

10	20	30	40	50				90

12.

10					60			

13.

		30				70		

14.

	20		40					

15.

10								

Identifying Tens to 90

NUMBERS TO 50

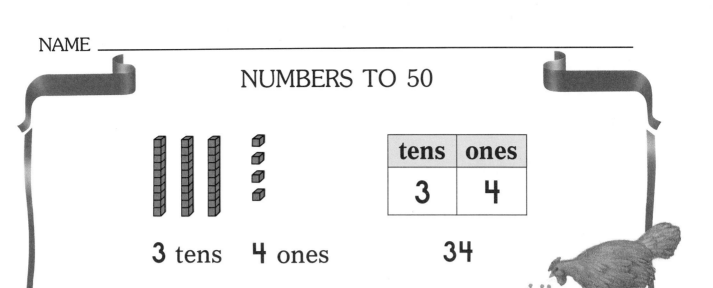

3 tens   4 ones

tens	ones
3	4

34

Write the number of tens and ones.

1.

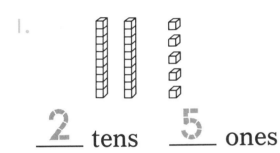

__2__ tens   __5__ ones

tens	ones
2	5

2.

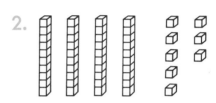

___ tens   ___ ones

tens	ones

3.

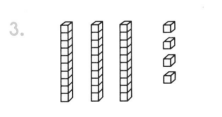

___ tens   ___ ones

tens	ones

4.

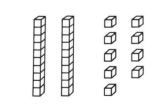

___ tens   ___ ones

tens	ones

Write the number of tens and ones.
Then write the number.

5.
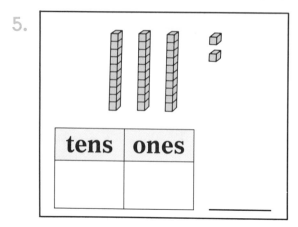

tens	ones

_____

6.
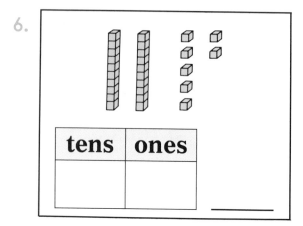

tens	ones

_____

7.
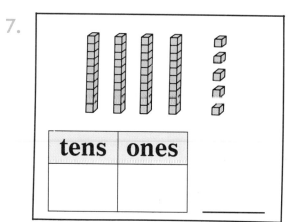

tens	ones

_____

8.
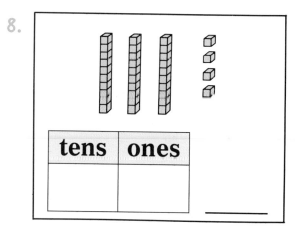

tens	ones

_____

How many in all?

9.

_____ chicks

10.
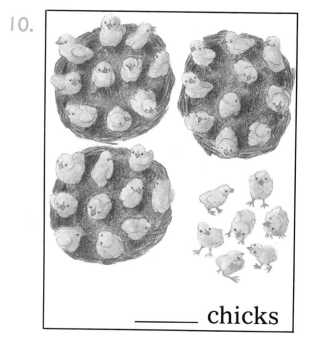

_____ chicks

Identifying Tens and Ones to 50

NUMBERS TO 80

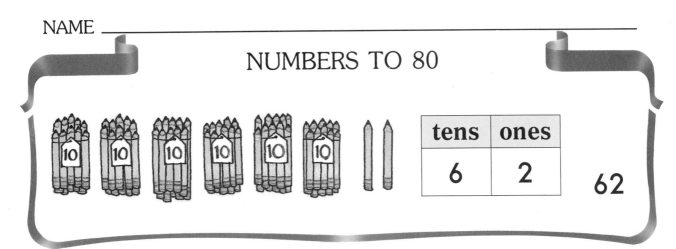

tens	ones
6	2

62

Write the number of tens and ones.
Then write the number.

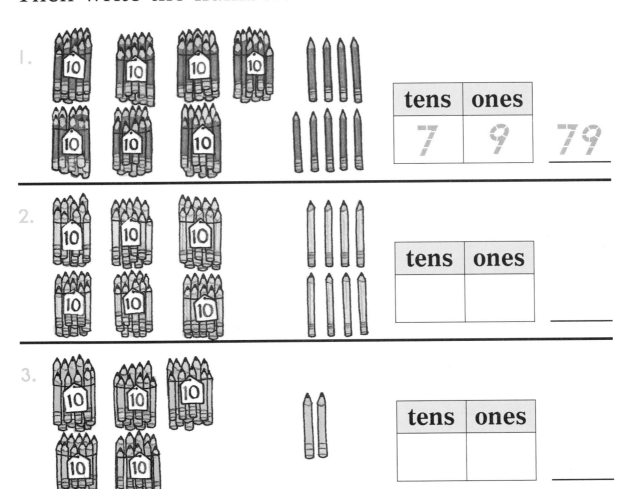

1.

tens	ones
7	9

79

2.

tens	ones

____

3.

tens	ones

____

4.

tens	ones

____

Write the number of tens and ones.

5.

65	53	34	27
__5__ ones	___ ones	___ ones	___ ones
__6__ tens	___ tens	___ tens	___ tens

6.

48	50	75	42
___ ones	___ ones	___ ones	___ ones
___ tens	___ tens	___ tens	___ tens

7.

45	56	63	77
___ ones	___ ones	___ ones	___ ones
___ tens	___ tens	___ tens	___ tens

If you know $2 + 3 = 5$,
then you know $2 + 4 = 6$.
Add.

8.

$4 + 1 =$ _____ $3 + 3 =$ _____ $5 + 2 =$ _____

$4 + 2 =$ _____ $3 + 4 =$ _____ $5 + 3 =$ _____

9.

$4 + 2 =$ _____ $7 + 1 =$ _____ $3 + 6 =$ _____

$4 + 3 =$ _____ $7 + 2 =$ _____ $3 + 7 =$ _____

Identifying Tens and Ones to 80

NUMBERS TO 99

tens	ones
9	4

94

Write the number of tens and ones.
Then write the number.

1.

tens	ones
8	3

83

2.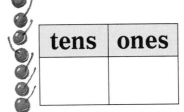

tens	ones

____

3.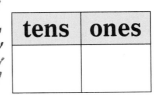

tens	ones

____

4.

tens	ones

____

Identifying Tens and Ones to 99

Write the number of tens and ones.

5.

38	**64**	**75**	**19**
_3_ tens	____ ones	____ ones	____ ten
_8_ ones	____ tens	____ tens	____ ones

6.

29	**47**	**57**	**62**
____ tens	____ ones	____ tens	____ tens
____ ones	____ tens	____ ones	____ ones

7.

73	**97**	**86**	**59**
____ ones	____ tens	____ tens	____ ones
____ tens	____ ones	____ ones	____ tens

☆ Color all the numbers in the **60**'s.

8.

Identifying Tens and Ones to 99

ORDER TO 100

1. Write the missing numbers.

1	2	3			6				10
11		13				17			20
21			24				28		
			34			37			
41							48		50
					56				
								69	
	72								
		93							100

Write the missing numbers.

2.

61		63

63		65

66		68

3.

90		92

89		91

97		99

4.

32		34

35		37

38		40

5.

61	62			66		69	

6.

21	22		24			27		29	

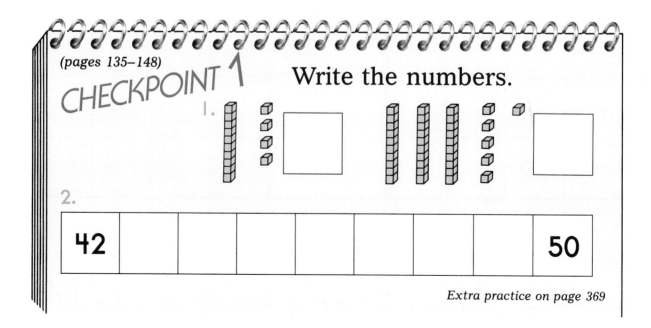

(pages 135–148)

CHECKPOINT 1   Write the numbers.

1.

2.

42								50

Extra practice on page 369

148 one hundred forty-eight

Ordering Numbers through 99

PROBLEM SOLVING

The **graph** shows how many pets.

PETS

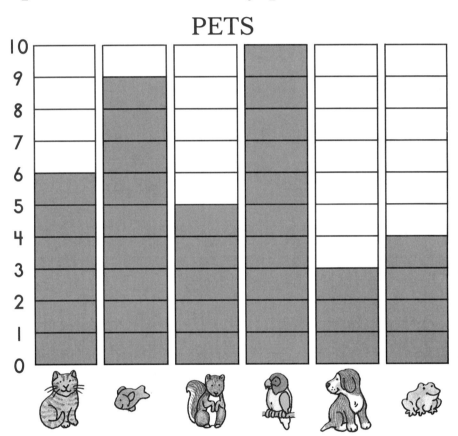

Write how many.

 1. ____6____

2. ____

 3. ____

4. ____

 5. ____

6. ____

7. Color boxes to show how many.

FOREST ANIMALS

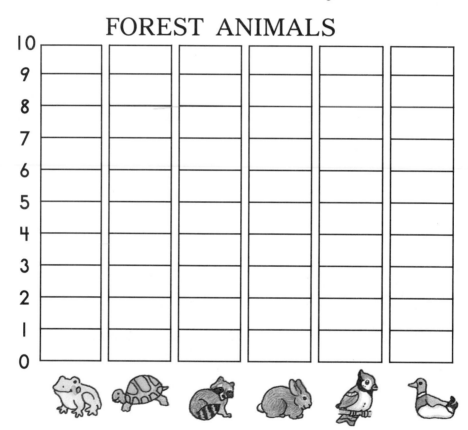

Write how many. Then add.

8. _____ + _____ = _____ in all.

9. _____ + _____ = _____ in all.

10. _____ + _____ = _____ in all.

Problem Solving

GREATER THAN

62   **46**

62 is **greater than 46**

Write the number.
Then ring the number that is greater.

1.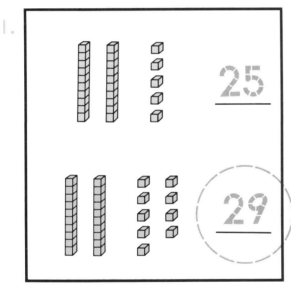

25

29

2.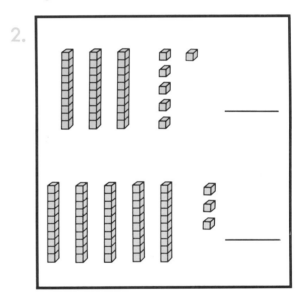

_____

_____

3.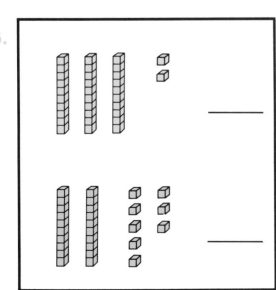

_____

_____

4.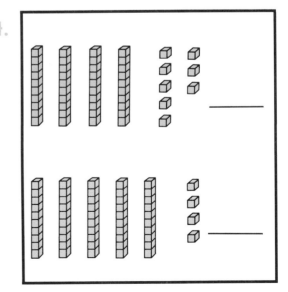

_____

_____

Ring the number that is greater.

5.
(28 / **37**) (62 / 56) (71 / 83) (96 / 86)

6.

37 / 53   13 / 19   25 / 26   34 / 73

7.
| 56 | 87 | 37 | 46 |
| 92 | 78 | 30 | 52 |

Write the number between the two sums.

8. **5 + 1** and **5 + 3** ____

9. **2 + 5** and **2 + 7** ____

10. **4 + 2** and **4 + 4** ____

11. **5 + 3** and **5 + 5** ____

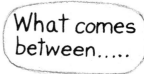

What comes between.....

Greater Than

LESS THAN

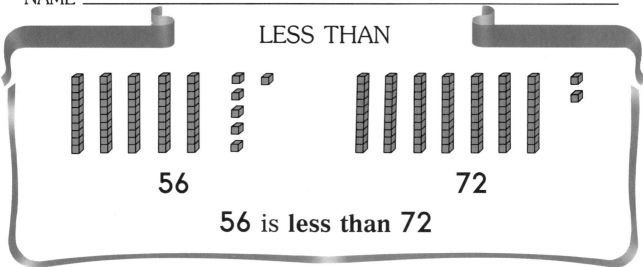

56   **72**

56 is **less than 72**

Write the number.
Then ring the number that is less.

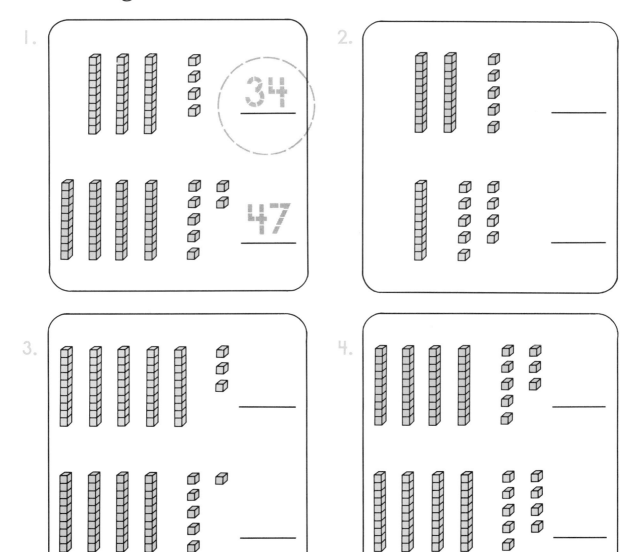

1.   (34)
      47

2.   _____
      _____

3.   _____
      _____

4.   _____
      _____

Ring the number that is less.

5.
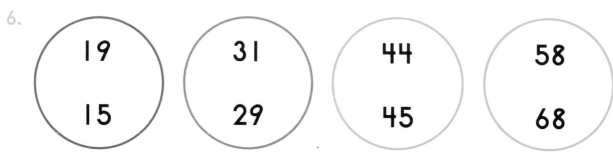

6.
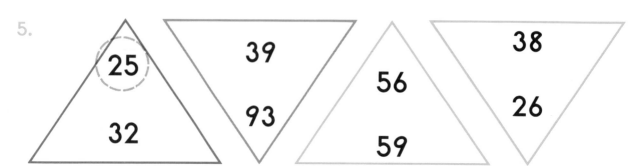

7.
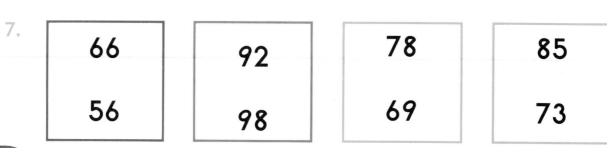

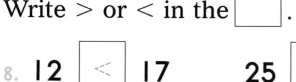

5 is greater than **3**
5 > 3

3 is less than **5**
3 < 5

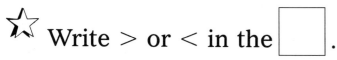 Write > or < in the ☐.

8. 12 | < | 17   25 | ☐ | 37   42 | ☐ | 26

9. 37 | ☐ | 32   47 | ☐ | 65   98 | ☐ | 89

Less Than

ORDINALS

first · second · third · fourth · fifth · sixth · seventh · eighth · ninth · tenth

Ring the animal.

1.

first

2.

fourth

3.

seventh

4.

eighth

5.

tenth

Color the objects.

6.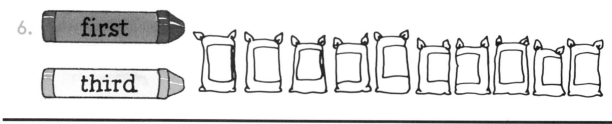

7.

8.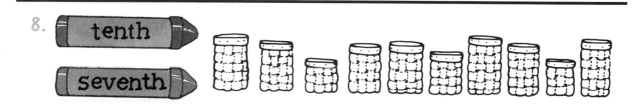

9.

Write the number.

10. Lila filled boxes with berries.
Each box holds **10** berries.
She filled **4** boxes.
How many berries were
put into boxes?

□ berries

11. How many berries would it take
to fill **8** boxes?

□ berries

Identifying Ordinals

PROBLEM SOLVING

Ring what comes next.

1.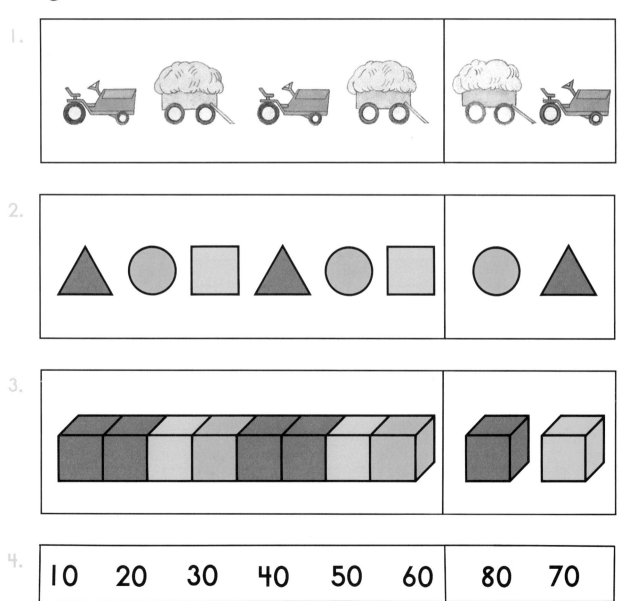

2.

3.

4. | 10 | 20 | 30 | 40 | 50 | 60 | 80 | 70 |

Draw what comes next.

5.

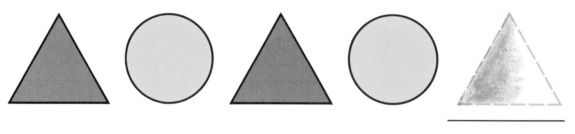

6.

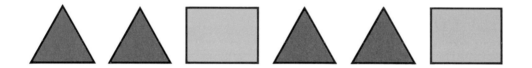

7.

8.

☆ **9.**

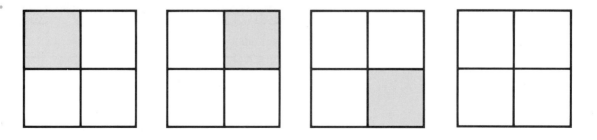

Problem Solving

COUNTING BY TWOS

| 2 | 4 | 6 | 8 | 10 | 12 |

Count by twos. Ring the numbers.

1.

1	(2)	3	(4)	5	(6)	7	8	9	10
11	12	13	14	15	16	17	18	19	20
21	22	23	24	25	26	27	28	29	30
31	32	33	34	35	36	37	38	39	40

Count by twos.
Write the numbers.

2.

2, 4, _6_, _____, _____, _____, _____, _____, _____

3.

34, 36, _____, _____, _____, _____, _____, _____, _____

4.

56, 58, _____, _____, _____, _____, _____, _____, _____

5. Count by twos to connect the dots in order.

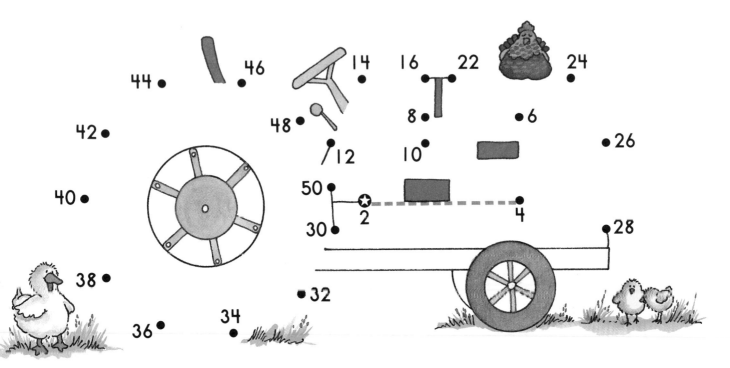

(pages 149–160)

CHECKPOINT 2

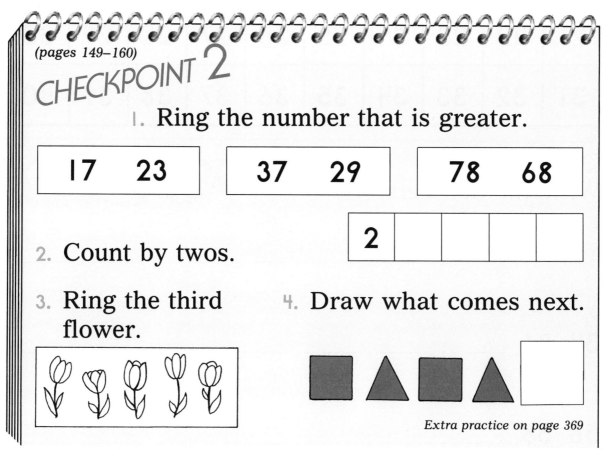

1. Ring the number that is greater.

17	23
37	29
78	68

2. Count by twos.

| 2 | | | | |

3. Ring the third flower.

4. Draw what comes next.

Extra practice on page 369

160 one hundred sixty

Counting by Twos

CHAPTER 6 TEST

Write the number.

1. _____

2. 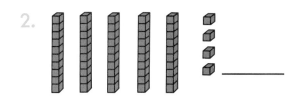 _____

Write the missing numbers.

3. 51, 52, _____, 54, _____, _____, 57, _____, 59

4. 12, 14, _____, _____, _____, _____, _____

Ring the number that is less.

5. 23   12   31   36   46   36

Ring the third animal.

6.

Look at the graph. Write how many.

7. How many  ? _____

8. How many ? _____

Extra practice on page 370

MATHEMATICS and LANGUAGE

ten	10	one	1
twenty	20	two	2
thirty	30	three	3
forty	40	four	4
fifty	50	five	5
sixty	60	six	6
seventy	70	seven	7
eighty	80	eight	8
ninety	90	nine	9

Write the number for the word.

1. sixty-nine _69_   fifty-three _____

2. forty-eight _____   thirty-six _____

3. seventy-two _____   eighty-five _____

4. sixty-seven _____   ninety-one _____

Write the word for the number.

5. 61 _sixty-one_____   43 _____

6. 97 _____   82 _____

7. 56 _____   35 _____

8. 29 _____   78 _____

Enrichment

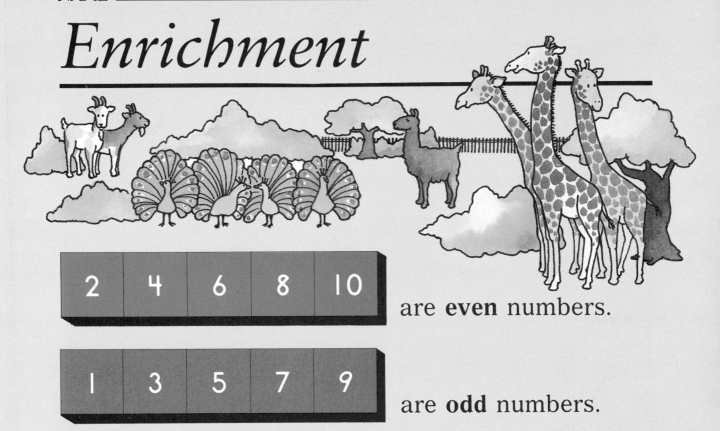

| 2 | 4 | 6 | 8 | 10 |

are **even** numbers.

| 1 | 3 | 5 | 7 | 9 |

are **odd** numbers.

Write the next 4 odd numbers.

1. 1   3   5   7   9 ____ ____ ____ ____

2. 21 23 25 27 ____ ____ ____ ____

3. 37 39 41 43 ____ ____ ____ ____

4. 45 47 49 51 ____ ____ ____ ____

Write the next 4 even numbers.

5. 0   2   4   6   8 ____ ____ ____ ____

6. 20 22 24 26 ____ ____ ____ ____

7. 34 36 38 40 ____ ____ ____ ____

8. 50 52 54 56 ____ ____ ____ ____

Odd and Even Numbers

9. Color the odd numbers .

10. Color the even numbers .

Add or subtract.
Then ring the even answers
and ✔ the odd answers.

11.
$$3 + 2 = \boxed{\checkmark 5}$$ $$4 - 3 = \boxed{}$$ $$5 + 3 = \boxed{}$$ $$2 + 2 = \boxed{}$$ $$5 + 4 = \boxed{}$$ $$3 + 6 = \boxed{}$$

12.
$$5 + 4 = \boxed{}$$ $$8 - 6 = \boxed{}$$ $$9 - 6 = \boxed{}$$ $$4 + 4 = \boxed{}$$ $$6 - 6 = \boxed{}$$ $$7 - 3 = \boxed{}$$

164 one hundred sixty-four

Enrichment: Odd and Even Numbers

 CUMULATIVE REVIEW

Fill in the ◯ for the correct answer.

Add.

1. **7 + 0**	2. **6 + 4**	3. **5 + 3**
0 6 7 Ⓐ Ⓑ Ⓒ	8 10 2 Ⓐ Ⓑ Ⓒ	2 8 5 Ⓐ Ⓑ Ⓒ

4.   8
    +1
	5. 3
	    +7
		6. 6
		    +2

7 8 9 Ⓐ Ⓑ Ⓒ	4 10 7 Ⓐ Ⓑ Ⓒ	6 8 4 Ⓐ Ⓑ Ⓒ

How much in all?

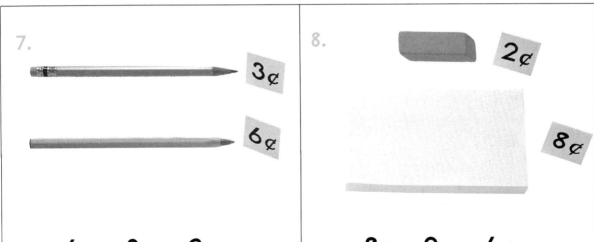

7.

Ⓐ 6¢ + 3¢ = 9¢
Ⓑ 6¢ + 3¢ = 3¢
Ⓒ 3¢ + 3¢ = 6¢

8.

Ⓐ 8¢ + 2¢ = 6¢
Ⓑ 2¢ + 2¢ = 4¢
Ⓒ 8¢ + 2¢ = 10¢

Subtract.

9.	10.	11.
$\begin{array}{r} 9 \\ -1 \\ \hline \end{array}$	$\begin{array}{r} 8 \\ -4 \\ \hline \end{array}$	$\begin{array}{r} 10 \\ -7 \\ \hline \end{array}$
8 10 7 (A) (B) (C)	6 8 4 (A) (B) (C)	3 2 1 (A) (B) (C)
12. 10 – 4	13. 7 – 5	14. 9 – 0
6 8 4 (A) (B) (C)	1 2 5 (A) (B) (C)	0 9 10 (A) (B) (C)

LANGUAGE and VOCABULARY REVIEW

Ring the sentence if it is correct.

1. (5 is less than 7.)

2. 29 is greater than 63.

3. A graph may show how many.

4. You say 1, 2, 3, 4, 5 when you count by twos.

5. 5 tens make 60.

6. 27 is 2 tens and 7 ones.

☆ 7. 2 + 2 is one less than 2 + 3.

Language and Vocabulary Review

Read with the children:

What is the toll?
A quarter is worth **25¢**.
If five red cars and three
blue cars each pay
the toll, how many
quarters is that?

7

MONEY

PENNY AND NICKEL

penny
1 cent
1¢

nickel
5 cents
5¢

Write the amount.

1.

_**5**_ ¢

2.

_____ ¢

3.

_____ ¢

4.

_____ ¢

5.

_____ ¢

6.

_____ ¢

7.

_____ ¢

8.

_____ ¢

9.

_____ ¢

Penny and Nickel

COUNTING BY FIVES

Think   5¢   10¢   15¢   20¢   25¢   _30_ ¢

Count by fives.

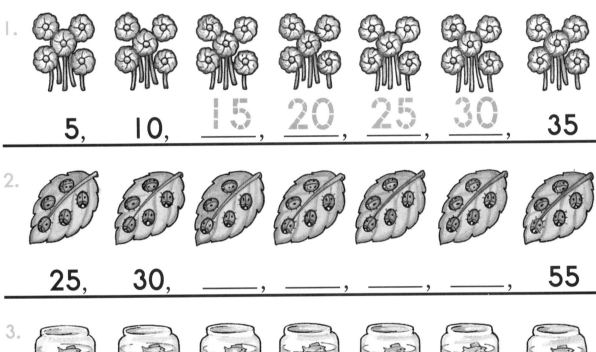

1. 5,   10,   15,   20,   25,   30,   35

2. 25,   30,   ____,   ____,   ____,   ____,   55

3. 40,   45,   ____,   ____,   ____,   ____,   70

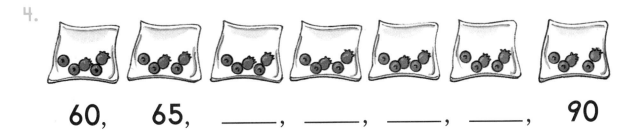

4. 60,   65,   ____,   ____,   ____,   ____,   90

Count by fives.

5.

1	2	3	4	5	6	7	8	9	10
11	12	13	14		16	17	18	19	
21	22	23	24		26	27	28	29	
31	32	33	34		36	37	38	39	
41	42	43	44		46	47	48	49	
51	52	53	54		56	57	58	59	
61	62	63	64		66	67	68	69	
71	72	73	74		76	77	78	79	
81	82	83	84		86	87	88	89	
91	92	93	94		96	97	98	99	100

6. 5, 10, __15__, ____, ____, 30, ____, ____, ____

7. 60, 65, ____, ____, ____, ____, 90, ____, ____

Think of the amount.
If greater than 8¢, color Red

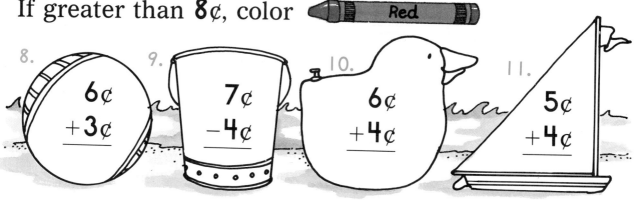

8.
6¢
+3¢
___

9.
7¢
−4¢
___

10.
6¢
+4¢
___

11.
5¢
+4¢
___

Counting by Fives

DIME

Count by tens to find the amount.

dime

10 cents

10¢

(Think) **10¢   20¢   30¢   ___ 40 ¢**

Count by tens. Write the amount.

_____ ¢

2.

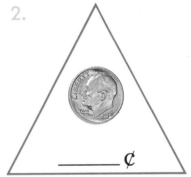

_____ ¢

3.

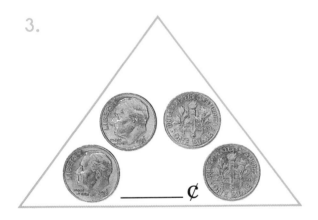

_____ ¢

4.

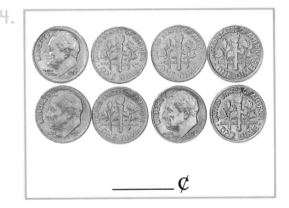

_____ ¢

5.

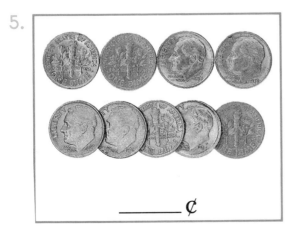

_____ ¢

6.

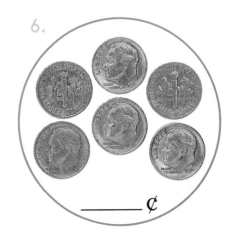

_____ ¢

Write the number.

7. 30¢ = **3** dimes   50¢ = ____ dimes

8. 60¢ = ____ dimes   70¢ = ____ dimes

9. 80¢ = ____ dimes   40¢ = ____ dimes

10. 90¢ = ____ dimes   20¢ = ____ dimes

11. 3 dimes = **30** ¢   6 dimes = ____ ¢

12. 7 dimes = ____ ¢   9 dimes = ____ ¢

13. 2 dimes = ____ ¢   6 dimes = ____ ¢

Ring enough dimes.

Juice 10¢ A Glass

14.

15.

16.

Identifying Value of Dimes

NICKEL AND DIME

Count by tens, then fives to find the amount.

(Think) 10¢   20¢   25¢   30¢

Write the amount.

1.

10 ¢   20 ¢   25 ¢   30 ¢   35 ¢

2.

_____¢   _____¢   _____¢   _____¢   _____¢

3.

_____¢   _____¢   _____¢   _____¢   _____¢   _____¢

4.

_____¢   _____¢   _____¢   _____¢   _____¢   _____¢

Ring the coins to show the amount.

5. **30¢**

6. **40¢**

7. **30¢**

8. **40¢**

9. **20¢**

10. **50¢**

⭐ Write the number.

11. **I**  = _2_

12. **3**  = ____

13. **4** = ____

14. **8** = ____

Identifying Value of Nickels and Dimes

COUNTING MONEY

Count by tens, fives, and ones to find the amount.

(Think) 10¢   20¢   25¢   30¢   35¢   36¢   _37_ ¢

Write the amount.

1.

_10_ ¢   _20_ ¢   _25_ ¢   _30_ ¢   _35_ ¢

2.

_____ ¢   _____ ¢   _____ ¢   _____ ¢   _____ ¢

3.

_____ ¢ _____ ¢ _____ ¢ _____ ¢ _____ ¢ _____ ¢

4.

_____ ¢ _____ ¢ _____ ¢ _____ ¢ _____ ¢ _____ ¢

Write the amount.

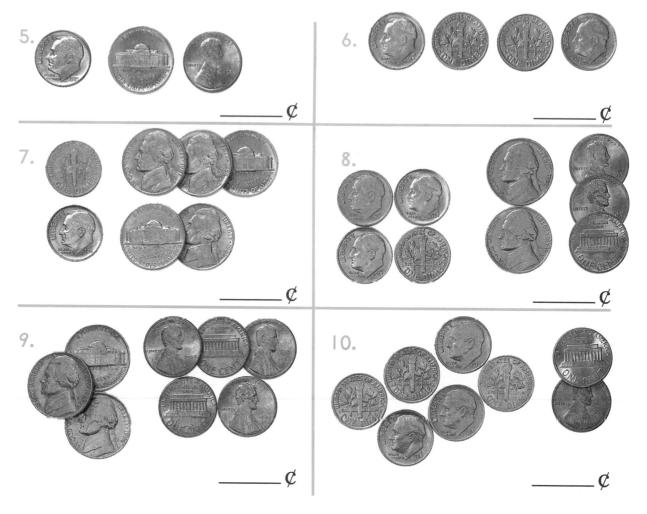

5. _____ ¢

6. _____ ¢

7. _____ ¢

8. _____ ¢

9. _____ ¢

10. _____ ¢

(pages 167–176)

CHECKPOINT 1

Write the amount.

1. _____ ¢

2. _____ ¢

3. **Count by fives.**

5	10				

Extra practice on page 371

Counting Pennies, Nickels, and Dimes

PROBLEM SOLVING

You have **75¢**.

You could buy  or  or 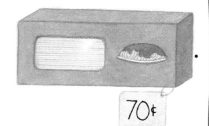.

You could not buy  97¢ .

Ring any of the items you could buy.

1. You have **45¢**.

2. You have **70¢**.

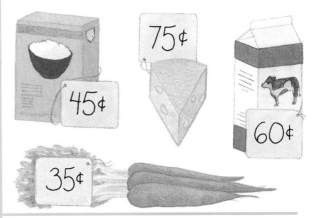

3. You have **95¢**.

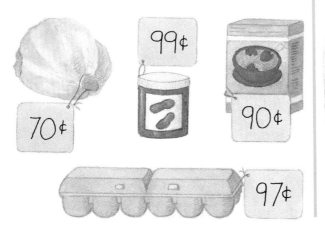

4. You have **85¢**.

Ring any of the items you could buy.

5. You have **25¢**.

15¢   35¢   42¢   23¢

6. You have **40¢**.

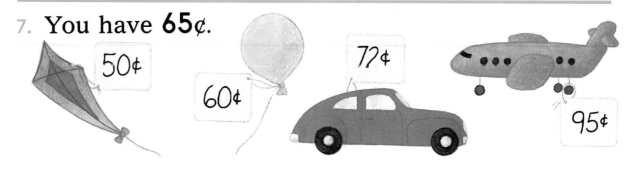

46¢   35¢   27¢   32¢

7. You have **65¢**.

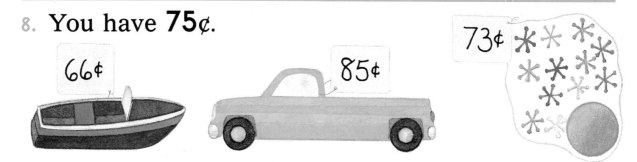

50¢   72¢   60¢   95¢

8. You have **75¢**.

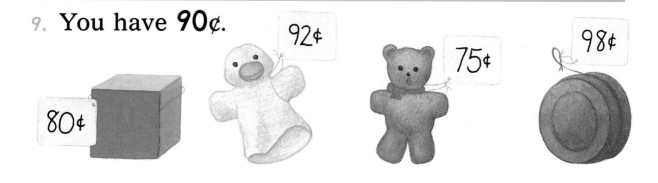

66¢   85¢   73¢

9. You have **90¢**.

92¢   75¢   98¢   80¢

Problem Solving

QUARTER

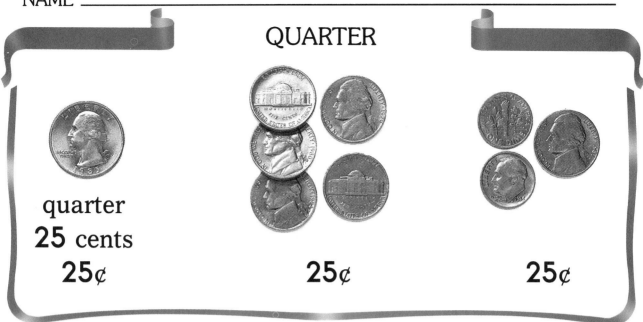

quarter
25 cents
25¢   **25**¢   **25**¢

Ring the coins to show **25**¢.

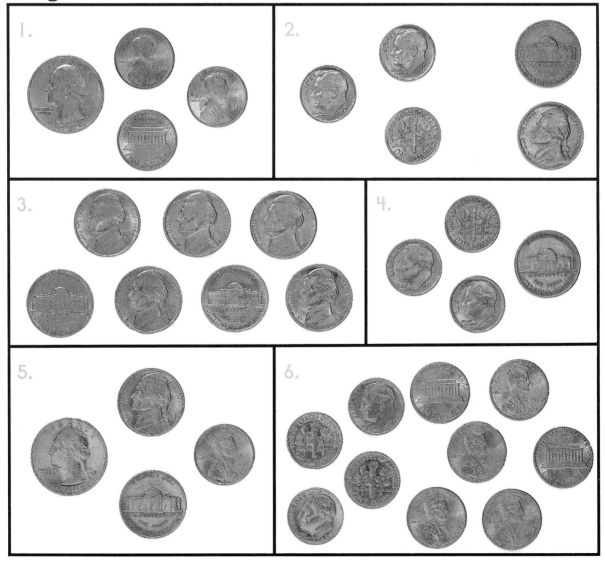

1.

2.

3.

4.

5.

6.

Ring the name to show
who can buy an orange.

 7.

8.

9.

| Steve | Marcia | Jan |

 10.

11.

12.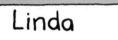

| Linda | Laura | Bob |

Ring yes or no.

13. Anna has

She wants to buy

Does she have
enough money?

yes   no

14. Matt has

He wants to buy

Does he have
enough money?

yes   no

Identifying Value of Quarter

NAME _____

COUNTING MONEY

Start with **25¢**.
Then count by tens and fives to find the amount.

Think   **25**¢   **35**¢   **45**¢   **50**¢   ¢

Count. Write the amount.

1.

   25 ¢   35 ¢   45 ¢

45¢ in all

2.

_____¢ _____¢ _____¢ _____¢ _____¢

3.

_____¢ _____¢ _____¢ _____¢ _____¢

4.

_____¢ _____¢ _____¢ _____¢ _____¢ _____¢

Write the amount.

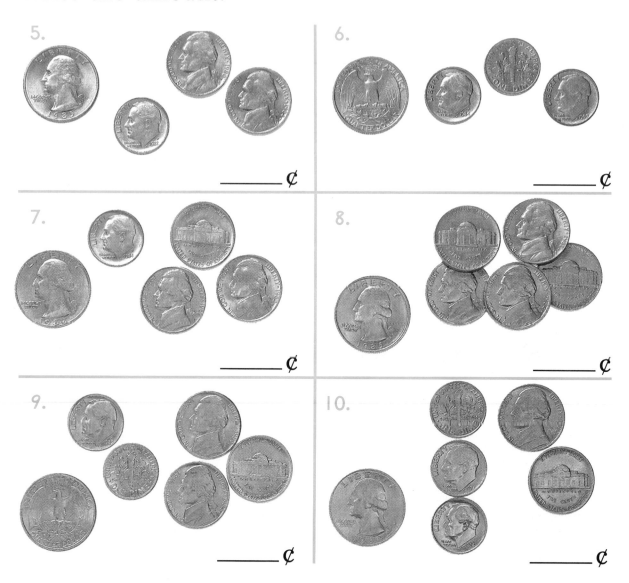

5. _____ ¢

6. _____ ¢

7. _____ ¢

8. _____ ¢

9. _____ ¢

10. _____ ¢

☆ Ring the greater.

11. 2 or 5

12. 8 or 1

13. 1 or 11

14. 3 or 10

15. 3 or 4

16. 2 or 19

Counting Nickels, Dimes, and Quarters

NAME _____

COUNTING MONEY

Start with **25**.
Then count by tens, fives, and ones
to find the amount.

(Think) **25¢**   **35¢**   **40¢**   **41¢**   **42** ¢

Write the amount.

1.

25 ¢   **35** ¢   **45** ¢   **46** ¢

2.

_____ ¢ _____ ¢ _____ ¢ _____ ¢ _____ ¢ _____ ¢

3.

_____ ¢ _____ ¢ _____ ¢ _____ ¢ _____ ¢ _____ ¢

4.

_____ ¢ _____ ¢ _____ ¢ _____ ¢ _____ ¢ _____ ¢

Write the amount.

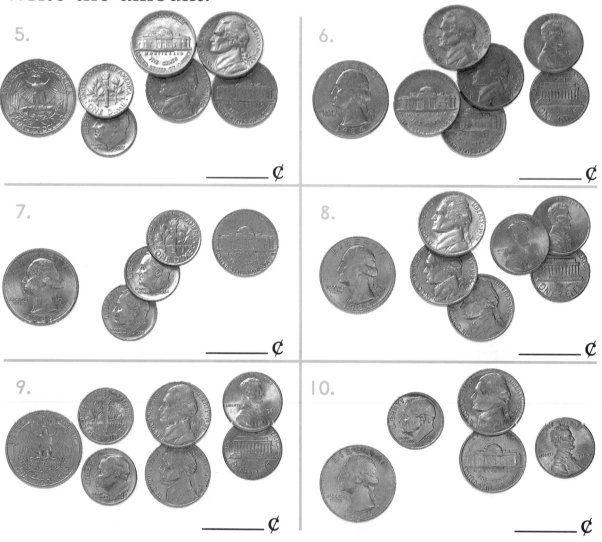

5. _____ ¢

6. _____ ¢

7. _____ ¢

8. _____ ¢

9. _____ ¢

10. _____ ¢

11. Tom has

He buys  35¢

Ring the coins he has left.

12. Sarah has

She buys 45¢

Ring the coins she has left.

Counting Pennies, Nickels, Dimes, and Quarters

COMPARING MONEY

Different sets of coins will buy the toy.

40¢   40¢

Ring the coins to show the amount.

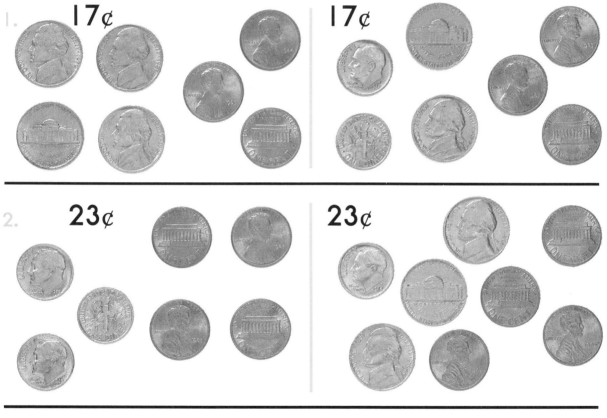

1.   17¢   17¢

2.   23¢   23¢

3.   31¢   31¢

Write the amount.

Can you trade the amount?
Ring yes or no.

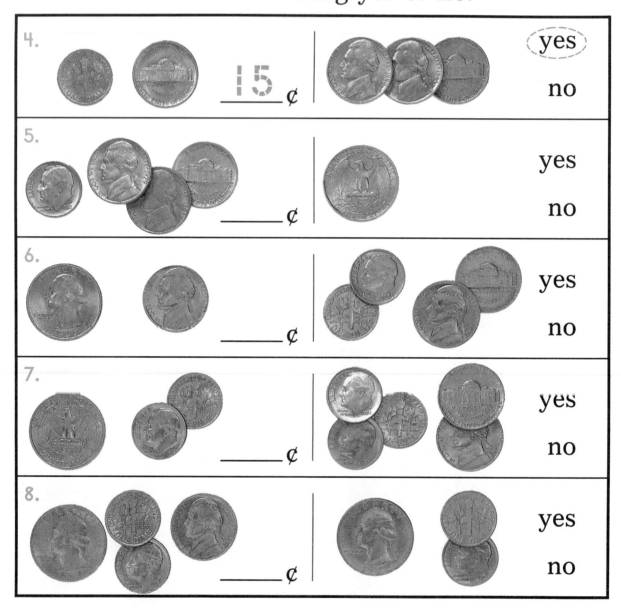

4. _1 5_ ¢   (yes)   no

5. _____ ¢   yes   no

6. _____ ¢   yes   no

7. _____ ¢   yes   no

8. _____ ¢   yes   no

Think of the amount.
If less than 5¢, color **blue** .

9.
$$7¢ - 4¢$$

10.
$$10¢ - 2¢$$

11.
$$6¢ - 3¢$$

12.
$$2¢ + 7¢$$

186   one hundred eighty-six

Equivalent Value of Coins

PROBLEM SOLVING

Find the number pattern.

| 2 | 4 | 6 | 8 | 10 | 12 | 14 | 16 |

Continue the number pattern.

1. Patterns by ones.

   25, 26, 27, __28__, ____, ____, ____

2. Patterns by twos.

   23, 25, 27, ____, ____, ____, ____

3. Patterns by fives.

   45, 50, 55, ____, ____, ____, ____

4. Patterns by tens.

   37, 47, 57, ____, ____, ____, ____

5. Patterns that repeat.

   1, 2, 1, 2, 1, 2, ____, ____, ____, ____, ____, ____

Continue the number pattern.

6. **23, 25, 27,** ____, ____, ____, ____

7. **21, 22, 23,** ____, ____, ____, ____

8. **4, 5, 5, 4, 5, 5, 4, 5,** ____, ____, ____, ____

9. **65, 70, 75,** ____, ____, ____, ____, ____

10. **2, 3, 5, 2, 3, 5, 2,** ____, ____, ____, ____, ____

(pages 177–188)

CHECKPOINT 2

Write the amount.

1. [coins] [¢]

Continue the number pattern.

2. **1 2 3 1 2 3 1** ☐ ☐ ☐

Extra practice on page 371

Problem Solving

CHAPTER 7 TEST

Count by fives.

1. **5, 10,** _____, _____, _____, _____, _____, _____

Ring the coins to show the amount.

2. **50¢**

Write the amount.

3.

   _____ ¢

Write the amount.

4.

    _____ ¢

Continue the number pattern.

5. **35, 37, 39,** _____, _____, _____, _____

6. **39, 49, 59,** _____, _____, _____, _____

Extra practice on page 372

MATHEMATICS and HEALTH

You can save money if you buy .

Ring the one that costs less.

1.

    75¢   69¢

2.

    80¢   85¢

3.

    35¢   32¢

4. 92¢   93¢

5.

    79¢   83¢

6.

    69¢   65¢

Enrichment

Name the coins to make the amount.
Use the number of coins given.

1.	**20¢**	(10¢)	(10¢)		
2.	**20¢**	◯	◯	◯	
3.	**25¢**	◯	◯	◯	◯
4.	**25¢**	◯	◯	◯	
5.	**30¢**	◯	◯	◯	
6.	**30¢**	◯	◯	◯	◯	◯

Name the coins to make
the amount.
Use the number of coins given.

7.	**50¢**	◯	◯		
8.	**50¢**	◯	◯	◯	◯
9.	**60¢**	◯	◯	◯	
10.	**60¢**	◯	◯	◯	◯
11.	**75¢**	◯	◯	◯	
12.	**75¢**	◯	◯	◯	◯ ◯

Enrichment: Logical Reasoning

NAME _____

 CUMULATIVE REVIEW

Fill in the ◯ for the correct answer.

How many tens and ones?

1. 43	2. 82
Ⓐ **3** tens **4** ones	Ⓐ **8** tens **2** ones
Ⓑ **4** tens **3** ones	Ⓑ **2** tens **8** ones
Ⓒ **4** tens **4** ones	Ⓒ **2** tens **2** ones

Choose the missing numbers.

3. 55, __?__, __?__, 58	4. 78, __?__, __?__, 81
Ⓐ 52, 53	Ⓐ 77, 76
Ⓑ 57, 56	Ⓑ 79, 80
Ⓒ 56, 57	Ⓒ 80, 90

Choose the number that is greater.

5. 51 35	6. 64 68	7. 62 72
51 35 15	68 46 64	27 62 72
Ⓐ Ⓑ Ⓒ	Ⓐ Ⓑ Ⓒ	Ⓐ Ⓑ Ⓒ

Choose the number that is less.

8. 85 43	9. 57 67	10. 19 18
85 43 34	57 77 67	81 18 19
Ⓐ Ⓑ Ⓒ	Ⓐ Ⓑ Ⓒ	Ⓐ Ⓑ Ⓒ

PLAYTHINGS AT THE PARK

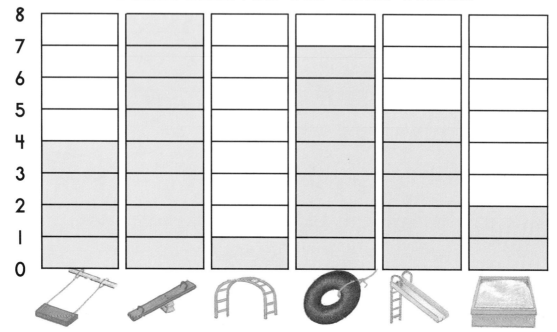

Use the graph to choose the number.

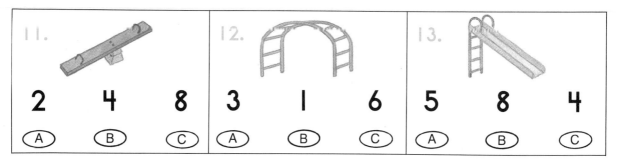

11.	12.	13.
2 (A) **4** (B) **8** (C)	**3** (A) **1** (B) **6** (C)	**5** (A) **8** (B) **4** (C)

LANGUAGE and VOCABULARY REVIEW

Match the word with the amount.
Write the amount on the line.

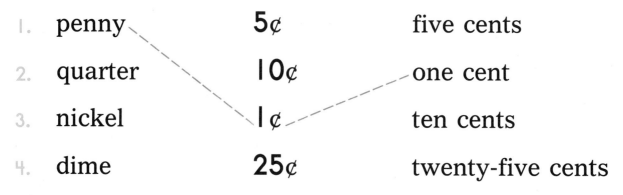

1. penny   **5¢**   five cents

2. quarter   **10¢**   one cent

3. nickel   **1¢**   ten cents

4. dime   **25¢**   twenty-five cents

Language and Vocabulary Review

8

Read with the children:

What time of the day do you think it is?
What do you do in the morning?
What do you do in the afternoon?
What do you do at night?

TIME

THE CLOCK

A **clock** tells us the time.

Write the numbers on the clock.

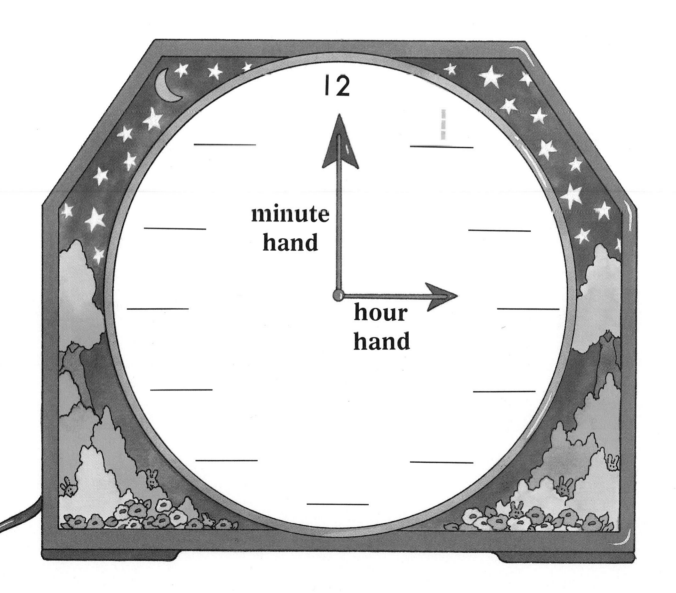

1. The minute hand is on the _____.

2. The hour hand is on the _____.

Identifying Minute and Hour Hands

HOUR

The clock tells us it is **4 o'clock.**

The minute hand is on the ___.

The hour hand is on the ___.

What time is it?

1.

_____ o'clock

_____ o'clock

_____ o'clock

2.

_____ o'clock

_____ o'clock

_____ o'clock

3.

_____ o'clock

_____ o'clock

_____ o'clock

Draw the hands to show the time.

4.

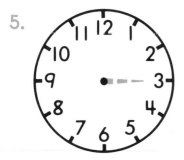

9 o'clock

6 o'clock

11 o'clock

5.

3 o'clock

7 o'clock

8 o'clock

☆ Show the time.

6. one hour **later**

7. one hour **earlier**

Telling Time to the Hour

HOUR

Both clocks tell us the time.

9 o'clock

9 o'clock

What time is it?

1.

| 3:00 | 10:00 | 6:00 |

<u>_3_</u> o'clock   _____ o'clock   _____ o'clock

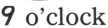

3:00

_____:_____   _____:_____   _____:_____

2.

| 12:00 | 4:00 | 1:00 |

_____ o'clock   _____ o'clock   _____ o'clock

_____:_____   _____:_____   _____:_____

3.

| 2:00 | 11:00 | 7:00 |

_____ o'clock   _____ o'clock   _____ o'clock

_____:_____   _____:_____   _____:_____

What time is it?

4.
_____ o'clock

_____ o'clock

4:00
_____ o'clock

_____:_____   _____:_____   _____:_____

5.
_____ o'clock

_____ o'clock

_____ o'clock

_____:_____   _____:_____   _____:_____

6. **12:00**
_____ o'clock

_____ o'clock

_____ o'clock

_____:_____   _____:_____   _____:_____

Is it more than two hours?
Ring yes or no.

7. From 1:00 to 4:00   yes   no

8. From 8:00 to 9:00   yes   no

9. From 2:00 to 7:00   yes   no

Telling Time to the Hour

NAME _____

HALF-HOUR

two o'clock
2:00

two thirty
2:30

BOAT RIDES ARE
EVERY HALF HOUR

What time is it?

1.

9:00   9:30

2.

___:___   ___:___

3.

___:___   ___:___

4.

___:___   ___:___

5.

___:___   ___:___

6.

___:___   ___:___

Telling Time to the Half-Hour

Draw the hands to show the time.

7.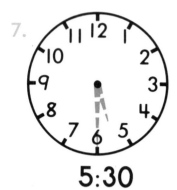
5:30

4:30

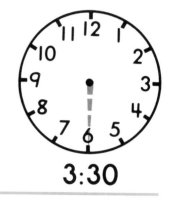
3:30

8.
6:30

8:30

2:30

9. Rico went to the store at **8:00**.
Show what time he went to the store.

10. Jill met her friends at **2:00**.
Show what time she met her friends.

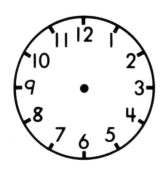

Telling Time to the Half-Hour

HALF-HOUR
Both clocks tell us the time.

twelve thirty
12:30

Ring the clock with the correct time.

1. 9:30

2. 6:30

3. 4:30

4. 8:30

Match.

5.

10:30

2:30

9:30

12:30

3:30

6.

4:30

11:30

1:30

7:30

6:30

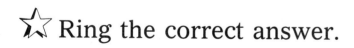

Ring the correct answer.

7. Your school bus comes at **8:00**.
You get to the bus stop at **7:30**.

Are you   early?   late?   on time?

Telling Time to the Half-Hour

HOUR AND HALF-HOUR

1:00

What time is it?

1.

_____ : _____ _____ : _____ _____ : _____ _____ : _____

2.

_____ : _____ _____ : _____ _____ : _____ _____ : _____

3.

_____ : _____ _____ : _____ _____ : _____ _____ : _____

Draw the hands to show the time.

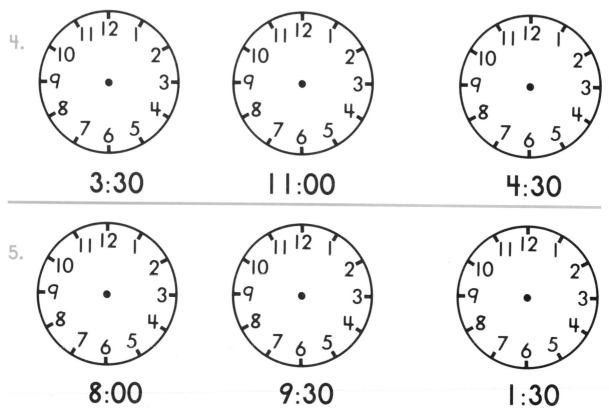

4.

3:30   11:00   4:30

5.

8:00   9:30   1:30

(pages 195–206)

CHECKPOINT 1

What time is it?

| : | : | : |

Extra practice on page 373

Telling Time to the Hour and Half-Hour

PROBLEM SOLVING

Bob had breakfast at **7:00**.
He got to school one hour later.
What time did he get to school?

_8_ _____ o'clock

Solve.

1.

Janet started painting at **3:00**.
She finished two hours later.
What time did she finish?

_____ o'clock

2.

Gina went to the store at **2:00**.
She got home one hour later.
What time did she get home?

_____ o'clock

3.

Ricardo started reading at **5:00**.
He read for two hours.
What time did he finish?

_____ o'clock

Elapsed Time

Solve.

4. Susan started playing the piano at 10:00.
She finished one hour later.
What time did she finish?

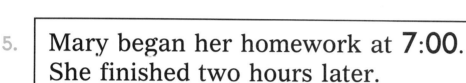

_____ o'clock

5. Mary began her homework at 7:00.
She finished two hours later.
What time did she finish?

_____ o'clock

6. Kim left home at 8:00.
She returned three hours later.
What time did she get back?

_____ o'clock

7. Jason started playing baseball at 3:00.
He stopped playing at 6:00.
How long did he play?

_____ hours

Problem Solving

NAME _____

DAYS OF THE WEEK

February						
Sunday	Monday	Tuesday	Wednesday	Thursday	Friday	Saturday
1	2	3	4	5	6	7
8	9	10	11	12	13	14
15	16	17	18	19	20	21
22	23	24	25	26	27	28

1. How many days are in a week? _____

Ring the day of the week that comes just after

2.	Friday	Wednesday	Saturday	Sunday
3.	Wednesday	Tuesday	Friday	Thursday
4.	Saturday	Sunday	Monday	Friday

Ring the day of the week that comes just before

5.	Monday	Tuesday	Sunday	Wednesday
6.	Tuesday	Wednesday	Sunday	Monday
7.	Sunday	Saturday	Monday	Tuesday

Identifying Days of the Week; Calendar

two hundred nine 209

8. Write the missing numbers on the calendar.

February						
Sunday	Monday	Tuesday	Wednesday	Thursday	Friday	Saturday
1	2		4	5	6	
		10	11			14
	16	17		19	20	21
22			25	26		28

9. How many days are in this month? _____

Ring the correct day.

10. February 6   Friday   Saturday

11. February 15   Saturday   Sunday

12. February 18   Wednesday   Thursday

Think of the number of days.
Is it less than two days? Circle yes or no.

13. Between Monday and Tuesday   yes   no

14. Between Tuesday and Saturday   yes   no

Identifying Days of the Week; Calendar

NAME _____

MONTHS OF THE YEAR

January	first
February	second
March	third
April	fourth
May	fifth
June	sixth
July	seventh
August	eighth
September	ninth
October	tenth
November	eleventh
December	twelfth

Complete.

1. January is the

   first

   _____

   month of the year.

2. March is the

   _____

   month of the year.

3. May is the

   _____

   month of the year.

4. August is the

   _____

   month of the year.

5. December is the

   _____

   month of the year.

Identifying Months of the Year

Ring the month that comes just after

6.	January	March	(February)	September
7.	March	January	February	April
8.	May	June	July	April
9.	June	May	July	August
10.	September	December	October	August

11. What is the month of your birthday?

_____

12. What month is it now? _____

13. What is the name of the next month?

_____

14. Maria's birthday is in May.
John's birthday is three months later.

What month is John's birthday? _____

15. Tom's birthday is in July.
July is what month of the year?

_____

Identifying Months of the Year

PROBLEM SOLVING

HOURS SPENT

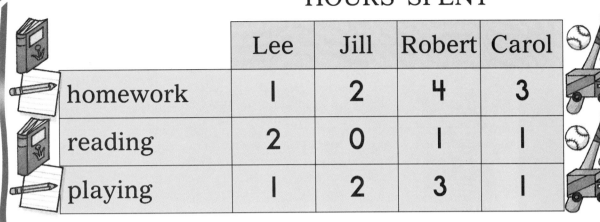

	Lee	Jill	Robert	Carol
homework	1	2	4	3
reading	2	0	1	1
playing	1	2	3	1

Write the number of hours.

1. How many hours does Carol spend

   on homework? __3__ hours

2. How many hours does Jill spend

   on homework? ____ hours

3. How many hours for both? ____ hours

4. How many hours does Lee read? ____ hours

5. How many hours does Robert read? ____ hour

6. How many hours for both? ____ hours

7. How many hours does Jill play? ____ hours

8. How many hours does Robert play? ____ hours

9. How many hours for both? ____ hours

TIMES WE EAT

	Lee	Jill	Robert	Carol
breakfast	8:00	6:30	7:00	7:00
lunch	1:00	11:30	12:00	12:30
dinner	6:00	5:30	6:30	6:00

Write the time.

10. When does Lee eat breakfast? _____:_____

11. When does Robert eat lunch? _____:_____

12. When does Jill eat lunch? _____:_____

13. When does Carol eat dinner? _____:_____

(pages 207–214)

CHECKPOINT 2 Write the number.

1. Mary left home at **9**:00.
   She returned home **3** hours later.
   When did she get home? [:]

Ring the day that comes just after Tuesday.

2. | Monday | Wednesday | Sunday |

Ring the fourth month of the year.

3. | May | March | April |

Extra practice on page 373

Problem Solving

CHAPTER 8 TEST

What time is it?

What time is it?

1.

_____ o'clock

2.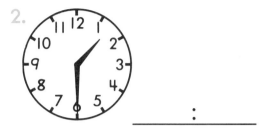

_____ : _____

Solve.

3. Debbie went for a bike ride at **3:00**.
She finished riding two hours later.
What time did she finish?   _____ o'clock

Ring the one that comes just before.

4.	Thursday	Friday	Tuesday	Wednesday
5.	July	March	June	August

Solve.

TIMES

	Kim	Dusty
leave home for school	8:30	8:00
come home from school	4:00	4:30

6. When does Kim leave for school? _____ : _____

7. When does Dusty come home? _____ : _____

8. Who leaves for school at **8:00**? _____

Extra practice on page 374

MATHEMATICS and SOCIAL STUDIES

This chart shows the number of president's birthdays in each month.

Month	Birthdays
January	4
February	4
March	4
April	4
May	2
June	0
July	3
August	3
September	1
October	6
November	5
December	3

Write the number of birthdays.

1. January ___   March ___   August ___

2. November ___   May ___   April ___

3. December ___   July ___   September ___

4. Which month has the most birthdays? _____

Mathematics and Social Studies

Enrichment

Show the time. Then write the time.

1.    one hour earlier   one hour later

4 o'clock   **6** o'clock

2. 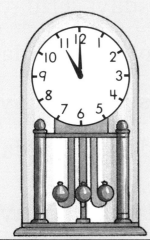   two hours earlier   two hours later

 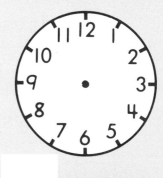

_____ o'clock   _____ o'clock

3.    four hours earlier   four hours later

_____ o'clock   _____ o'clock

Sunday Monday Tuesday Wednesday Thursday Friday Saturday

Wednesday is **2** days *after* Monday.
Wednesday is **2** days *before* Friday.
Wednesday is *between* Tuesday and Thursday.

Ring the day.

1. **2** days after Tuesday	(Thursday)	Friday
2. **3** days after Thursday	Friday	Sunday
3. **1** day before Saturday	Thursday	Friday
4. **4** days before Friday	Monday	Sunday
5. Between Thursday and Saturday	Sunday	Friday
6. Between Monday and Wednesday	Tuesday	Thursday

7. **Ring the days of the weekend.**

Sunday   Monday   Tuesday   Wednesday

Thursday   Friday   Saturday

Enrichment: Days Before, After and Between

NAME _____

 CUMULATIVE REVIEW

Fill in the ◯ for the correct answer.

Add.

1. 6 + 4	2. 3 + 6	3. 2 + 8
4 6 10	3 10 9	9 10 6
Ⓐ Ⓑ Ⓒ	Ⓐ Ⓑ Ⓒ	Ⓐ Ⓑ Ⓒ

4. 4 +4	5. 7 +1	6. 1 +9
8 0 10	8 9 6	8 9 10
Ⓐ Ⓑ Ⓒ	Ⓐ Ⓑ Ⓒ	Ⓐ Ⓑ Ⓒ

Subtract.

7. 7 − 4	8. 8 − 2	9. 10 − 5
2 3 5	6 10 8	6 5 7
Ⓐ Ⓑ Ⓒ	Ⓐ Ⓑ Ⓒ	Ⓐ Ⓑ Ⓒ

10. 9 −4	11. 10 − 7	12. 9 −3
4 6 5	4 3 5	3 6 9
Ⓐ Ⓑ Ⓒ	Ⓐ Ⓑ Ⓒ	Ⓐ Ⓑ Ⓒ

Choose the numbers in order.

13. 40, 41, 42, _?_, _?_, _?_, _?_, _?_, 48, 49

    Ⓐ 42, 44, 47, 46, 45

    Ⓑ 43, 44, 45, 46, 47

    Ⓒ 41, 43, 46, 44, 47

Choose the numbers that continue the pattern.

14. 4, 5, 6, 4, 5, 6, 4, _?_, _?_, _?_, _?_

    Ⓐ 6, 4, 5, 6, 4

    Ⓑ 6, 7, 8, 6, 7

    Ⓒ 5, 6, 4, 5, 6

LANGUAGE and VOCABULARY REVIEW

Ring the answer.

1. A year has ___ months.   10 ⑫

2. There are ___ days in one week.   7 8

3. November is the ___ month of the year.

         eleventh   ninth

4. Sunday comes just before ___.

        Saturday   Monday

COMPUTER
LITERACY

Ring the tool.

1.

2.

3.

4.

5.

6.

Ring what a computer can also do.

1.

2.

3.

4.

5.

6.

7.

8.

Functions of a Computer

9

Read with the children:

How many blue blocks
do you see?
How many red blocks?
How many green blocks?
How many yellow
blocks?
How many blocks in all?

ADDITION AND SUBTRACTION
FACTS THROUGH 12

ADDING THROUGH 11

$8 + 2 =$ __10__ $9 + 2 =$ __11__

Add.

1.

$7 + 3 =$ _____

2.

$8 + 3 =$ _____

3.

$6 + 4 =$ _____

4.

$7 + 4 =$ _____

5. $6 + 5 =$ _____ $6 + 4 =$ _____ $6 + 3 =$ _____

6. $0 + 9 =$ _____ $1 + 9 =$ _____ $2 + 9 =$ _____

7. $2 + 9 =$ _____ $2 + 8 =$ _____ $2 + 7 =$ _____

Addition Facts through 11

ADDING THROUGH 11

$$\begin{array}{r} 6 \\ +5 \\ \hline \end{array}$$

Add.

1.
$$\begin{array}{r} 7 \\ +3 \\ \hline \end{array}$$

2.
$$\begin{array}{r} 8 \\ +3 \\ \hline \end{array}$$

3.
$$\begin{array}{r} 8 \\ +2 \\ \hline \end{array}$$

4.
$$\begin{array}{r} 9 \\ +2 \\ \hline \end{array}$$

5.
$$\begin{array}{r} 9 \\ +0 \\ \hline \end{array}$$
$$\begin{array}{r} 9 \\ +1 \\ \hline \end{array}$$
$$\begin{array}{r} 9 \\ +2 \\ \hline \end{array}$$
$$\begin{array}{r} 6 \\ +5 \\ \hline \end{array}$$
$$\begin{array}{r} 6 \\ +4 \\ \hline \end{array}$$
$$\begin{array}{r} 6 \\ +3 \\ \hline \end{array}$$

6.
$$\begin{array}{r} 7 \\ +1 \\ \hline \end{array}$$
$$\begin{array}{r} 7 \\ +2 \\ \hline \end{array}$$
$$\begin{array}{r} 7 \\ +3 \\ \hline \end{array}$$
$$\begin{array}{r} 8 \\ +1 \\ \hline \end{array}$$
$$\begin{array}{r} 8 \\ +2 \\ \hline \end{array}$$
$$\begin{array}{r} 8 \\ +3 \\ \hline \end{array}$$

Add.

7.
3	7	2	9	4	6
+8	+3	+9	+0	+7	+4

8.
2	3	4	7	5	6
+8	+7	+6	+4	+5	+5

9.
9	9	1	8	2	9
+1	+2	+9	+3	+6	+0

10.
8	1	7	8	5	3
+2	+7	+0	+0	+6	+2

11.
3	6	2	3	9	2
+5	+2	+5	+6	+2	+7

12. Joe caught **7** fish.
May caught **4** fish.
How many fish
in all?

7 + 4 = _____ fish

13. Linda caught **6** fish.
May caught **4** fish.
How many fish
in all?

6 + 4 = _____ fish

Addition Facts through 11

ADDING THROUGH 12

$$5 + 7 = \underline{12}$$

$$7 + 5 = \underline{12}$$

Add.

1.

$$3 + 9 = \underline{\hphantom{00}}$$

$$9 + 3 = \underline{\hphantom{00}}$$

2.

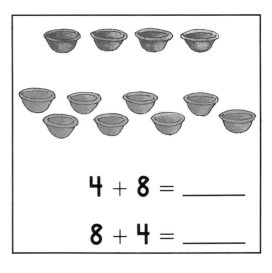

$$4 + 8 = \underline{\hphantom{00}}$$

$$8 + 4 = \underline{\hphantom{00}}$$

3.

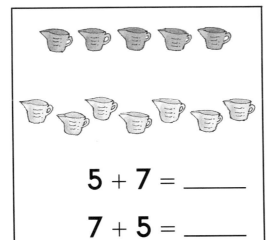

$$5 + 7 = \underline{\hphantom{00}}$$

$$7 + 5 = \underline{\hphantom{00}}$$

4.

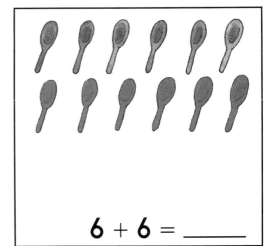

$$6 + 6 = \underline{\hphantom{00}}$$

5. $6 + 4 = \underline{\hphantom{00}}$ $6 + 5 = \underline{\hphantom{00}}$ $6 + 6 = \underline{\hphantom{00}}$

6. $7 + 5 = \underline{\hphantom{00}}$ $7 + 4 = \underline{\hphantom{00}}$ $7 + 3 = \underline{\hphantom{00}}$

Add.

7. $8 + 2 =$ _____ $8 + 3 =$ _____ $4 + 8 =$ _____

8. $6 + 1 =$ _____ $3 + 9 =$ _____ $4 + 3 =$ _____

9. $7 + 3 =$ _____ $7 + 5 =$ _____ $8 + 4 =$ _____

10. $8 + 1 =$ _____ $8 + 3 =$ _____ $7 + 4 =$ _____

11. $9 + 3 =$ _____ $5 + 7 =$ _____ $9 + 1 =$ _____

12. $4 + 8 =$ _____ $6 + 6 =$ _____ $4 + 6 =$ _____

13. $5 + 5 =$ _____ $2 + 9 =$ _____ $6 + 3 =$ _____

14. $3 + 2 =$ _____ $5 + 7 =$ _____ $8 + 3 =$ _____

⭐ Write the missing number.

15. $2 + 9 = 8 +$ _3_   16. $9 + 3 = 7 +$ _____

17. $5 +$ _____ $= 6 + 6$ 18. _____ $+ 8 = 6 + 5$

19. $3 + 5 = 2 +$ _____   20. $4 + 8 =$ _____ $+ 9$

Addition Facts through 12

ADDING THROUGH 12

$$\begin{array}{r} 8 \\ +4 \\ \hline 12 \end{array} \qquad \begin{array}{r} 4 \\ +8 \\ \hline 12 \end{array}$$

Add.

1.

$$\begin{array}{r} 7 \\ +5 \\ \hline \end{array} \qquad \begin{array}{r} 5 \\ +7 \\ \hline \end{array}$$

2.

$$\begin{array}{r} 9 \\ +3 \\ \hline \end{array} \qquad \begin{array}{r} 3 \\ +9 \\ \hline \end{array}$$

3.

$$\begin{array}{r} 8 \\ +4 \\ \hline \end{array} \qquad \begin{array}{r} 4 \\ +8 \\ \hline \end{array}$$

4.

$$\begin{array}{r} 6 \\ +6 \\ \hline \end{array}$$

5.

$$\begin{array}{r} 5 \\ +4 \\ \hline \end{array} \qquad \begin{array}{r} 6 \\ +4 \\ \hline \end{array} \qquad \begin{array}{r} 7 \\ +4 \\ \hline \end{array} \qquad \begin{array}{r} 6 \\ +4 \\ \hline \end{array} \qquad \begin{array}{r} 7 \\ +4 \\ \hline \end{array} \qquad \begin{array}{r} 8 \\ +4 \\ \hline \end{array}$$

6.

$$\begin{array}{r} 9 \\ +3 \\ \hline \end{array} \qquad \begin{array}{r} 8 \\ +3 \\ \hline \end{array} \qquad \begin{array}{r} 7 \\ +3 \\ \hline \end{array} \qquad \begin{array}{r} 8 \\ +3 \\ \hline \end{array} \qquad \begin{array}{r} 7 \\ +3 \\ \hline \end{array} \qquad \begin{array}{r} 6 \\ +3 \\ \hline \end{array}$$

7. Add.
Color.
10 ◼ 11 ◻ 12 ◼

$$\begin{array}{r}4\\+7\\\hline\end{array}\qquad\begin{array}{r}9\\+3\\\hline\end{array}\qquad\begin{array}{r}6\\+4\\\hline\end{array}\qquad\begin{array}{r}7\\+4\\\hline\end{array}\qquad\begin{array}{r}8\\+4\\\hline\end{array}\qquad\begin{array}{r}6\\+5\\\hline\end{array}$$

$$\begin{array}{r}4\\+8\\\hline\end{array}\qquad\begin{array}{r}2\\+9\\\hline\end{array}\qquad\begin{array}{r}1\\+9\\\hline\end{array}\qquad\begin{array}{r}8\\+3\\\hline\end{array}\qquad\begin{array}{r}3\\+9\\\hline\end{array}$$

$$\begin{array}{r}7\\+5\\\hline\end{array}\qquad\begin{array}{r}8\\+2\\\hline\end{array}\qquad\begin{array}{r}6\\+6\\\hline\end{array}\qquad\begin{array}{r}3\\+8\\\hline\end{array}\qquad\begin{array}{r}8\\+4\\\hline\end{array}$$

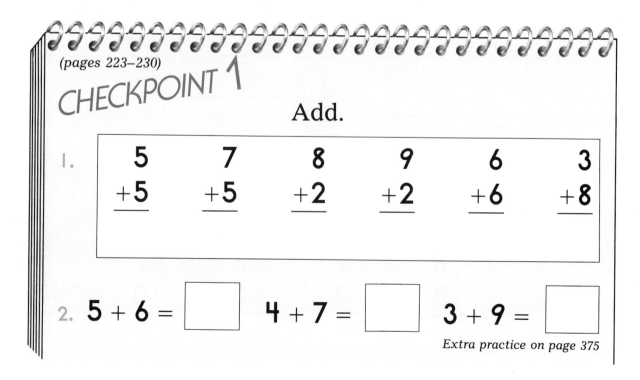

(pages 223–230)

CHECKPOINT 1

Add.

1.
$$\begin{array}{r}5\\+5\\\hline\end{array}\qquad\begin{array}{r}7\\+5\\\hline\end{array}\qquad\begin{array}{r}8\\+2\\\hline\end{array}\qquad\begin{array}{r}9\\+2\\\hline\end{array}\qquad\begin{array}{r}6\\+6\\\hline\end{array}\qquad\begin{array}{r}3\\+8\\\hline\end{array}$$

2. 5 + 6 = ☐   4 + 7 = ☐   3 + 9 = ☐

Extra practice on page 375

Addition Facts through 12

PROBLEM SOLVING

Sue wants **6** horns.

She has **3** horns.
How many more horns
does she need?

_3_____ horns

Draw pictures to show how many more
are needed. Then write the answer.

1. John needs **8** plates.

   He has **3** plates.
   How many more
   plates does he need?

   _____ plates

2. Maria needs **10** balloons.

   She has **4** balloons.
   How many more balloons
   does she need?

   _____ balloons

3. Diana wants **9** apples.

   She already has **4** apples.
   How many more
   does she need?

   _____ apples

Draw pictures to show how many more
are needed. Then write the answer.

4. Mrs. Thomas wants
   9 flowers.
   She has **7** flowers.
   How many more
   flowers does she need?

_____ flowers

5. Tim needs **9** hats.
   He already bought **3** hats.
   How many more hats
   should he buy?

_____ hats

6. Mr. Jones needs **10** cups.
   He has **3** cups.
   How many more cups
   does he need?

_____ cups

7. Pam wants **8** spoons.
   She has **4** spoons.
   How many more spoons
   does she need?

_____ spoons

Problem Solving

SUBTRACTING FROM 11

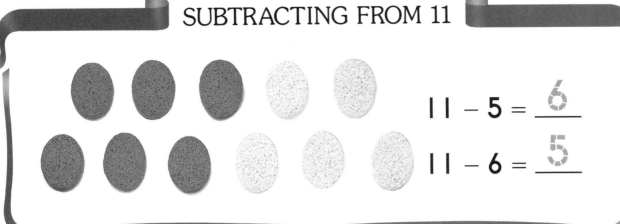

$11 - 5 = \underline{6}$

$11 - 6 = \underline{5}$

Subtract.

1.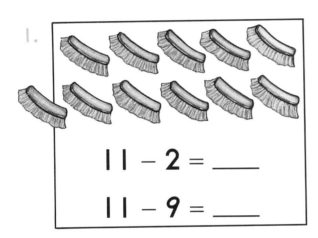

$11 - 2 = \underline{}$

$11 - 9 = \underline{}$

2.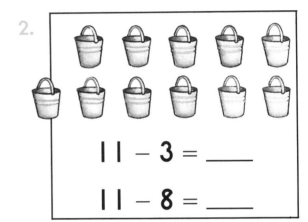

$11 - 3 = \underline{}$

$11 - 8 = \underline{}$

3.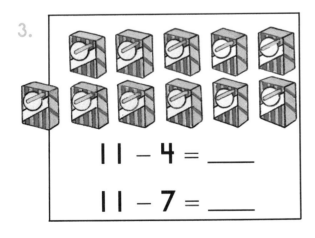

$11 - 4 = \underline{}$

$11 - 7 = \underline{}$

4.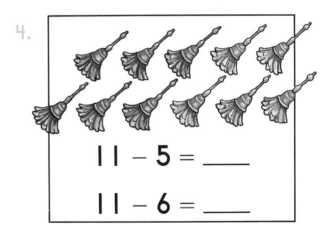

$11 - 5 = \underline{}$

$11 - 6 = \underline{}$

5. $11 - 6 = \underline{}$ $\quad$ $11 - 5 = \underline{}$ $\quad$ $11 - 4 = \underline{}$

6. $11 - 8 = \underline{}$ $\quad$ $11 - 7 = \underline{}$ $\quad$ $11 - 6 = \underline{}$

7. $11 - 2 = \underline{}$ $\quad$ $11 - 3 = \underline{}$ $\quad$ $11 - 4 = \underline{}$

Subtract.

8. $11 - 2 =$ _____ $\quad$ $11 - 5 =$ _____ $\quad$ $8 - 7 =$ _____

9. $11 - 7 =$ _____ $\quad$ $11 - 8 =$ _____ $\quad$ $11 - 6 =$ _____

10. $10 - 9 =$ _____ $\quad$ $10 - 2 =$ _____ $\quad$ $9 - 7 =$ _____

11. $6 - 2 =$ _____ $\quad$ $10 - 5 =$ _____ $\quad$ $8 - 5 =$ _____

12. $11 - 3 =$ _____ $\quad$ $11 - 4 =$ _____ $\quad$ $10 - 4 =$ _____

13. $9 - 9 =$ _____ $\quad$ $10 - 7 =$ _____ $\quad$ $9 - 7 =$ _____

14. $11 - 9 =$ _____ $\quad$ $10 - 3 =$ _____ $\quad$ $10 - 6 =$ _____

Think of the number.
Then write the number.

15. One more than **8** _____.

16. One less than **17** _____.

17. One less than **12** _____.

18. Three less than **56** _____.

19. Three more than **4** _____.

20. Four more than **37** _____.

21. Four less than **9** _____.

22. Two less than **28** _____.

SUBTRACTING FROM 11

$$11¢$$
$$- \ 3¢$$
$$\overline{8¢}$$

Subtract.

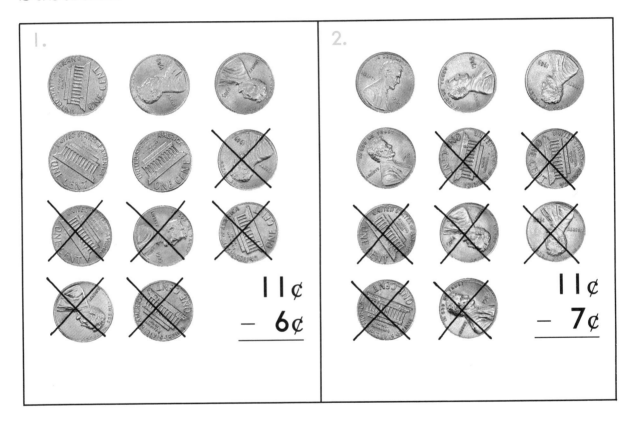

1.

$$11¢$$
$$- \ 6¢$$

2.

$$11¢$$
$$- \ 7¢$$

3.
$$11¢ \quad 11¢ \qquad 11¢ \quad 11¢ \qquad 11¢ \quad 11¢$$
$$- \ 2¢ \ - \ 9¢ \quad - \ 3¢ \ - \ 8¢ \quad - \ 6¢ \ - \ 5¢$$

4.
$$11¢ \quad 11¢ \qquad 11¢ \quad 11¢ \qquad 11¢ \quad 11¢$$
$$- \ 4¢ \ - \ 7¢ \quad - \ 6¢ \ - \ 5¢ \quad - \ 2¢ \ - \ 9¢$$

Subtract. Complete the table.

5.

−3	
11	8
10	
9	

6.

−6	
11	
9	
10	

7.

−5	
9	
10	
11	

8.

−7	
11	
9	
10	

9.

−8	
9	
10	
11	

10.

−9	
11	
10	
9	

Write + or − in the ☐.
Then add or subtract.

11. There are 11 children
on a bus. 5 get off the bus.
How many children
are still on the bus?

11 children
☐ 5 children
_____
children

12. There are 8 children
on a boat. 3 more children
get on. How many children
are now on the boat?

8 children
☐ 3 children
_____
children

Subtraction Facts through 11

SUBTRACTING FROM 12

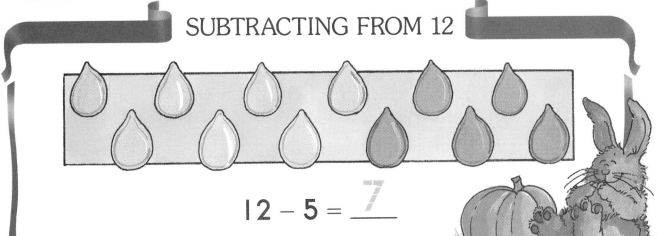

$12 - 5 = \underline{7}$

Subtract.

1.
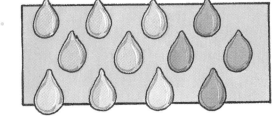

$12 - 3 = \underline{}$

$12 - 9 = \underline{}$

2.

$12 - 4 = \underline{}$

$12 - 8 = \underline{}$

3.
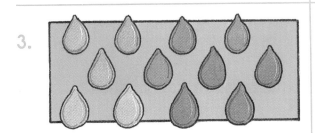

$12 - 7 = \underline{}$

$12 - 5 = \underline{}$

4.
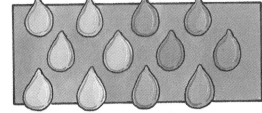

$12 - 6 = \underline{}$

5. $12 - 3 = \underline{}$ $12 - 4 = \underline{}$ $12 - 5 = \underline{}$

6. $12 - 9 = \underline{}$ $12 - 8 = \underline{}$ $12 - 7 = \underline{}$

7. $12 - 6 = \underline{}$ $12 - 7 = \underline{}$ $12 - 8 = \underline{}$

8. Subtract.

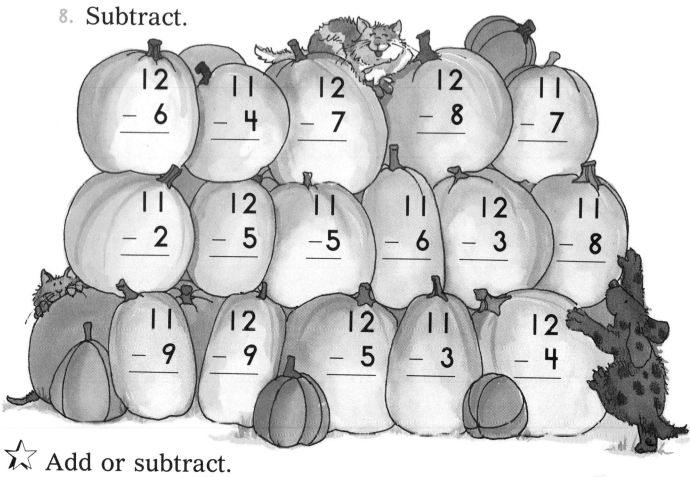

12 − 6	11 − 4	12 − 7	12 − 8	11 − 7

11 − 2	12 − 5	11 − 5	11 − 6	12 − 3	11 − 8

11 − 9	12 − 9	12 − 5	11 − 3	12 − 4

☆ Add or subtract.

9.

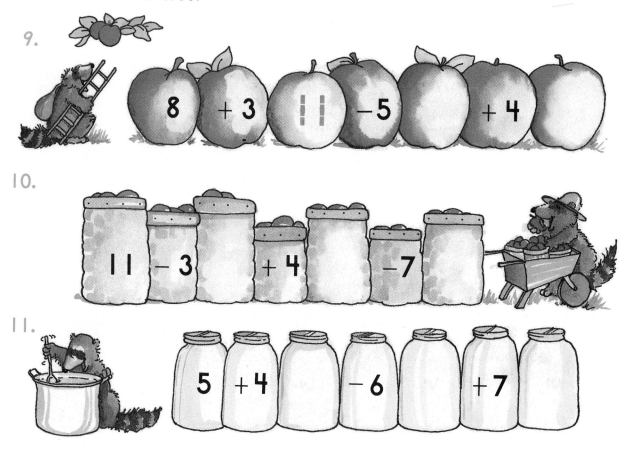

8 + 3 11 − 5 + 4

10.

11 − 3 + 4 − 7

11.

5 + 4 − 6 + 7

Subtraction Facts through 12

FACT FAMILIES

$$2 + 9 = \underline{11}$$

$$11 - 9 = \underline{2}$$

$$9 + 2 = \underline{11}$$

$$11 - 2 = \underline{9}$$

Add or subtract.

1. $5 + 6 = \underline{\hspace{1cm}}$

    $11 - 6 = \underline{\hspace{1cm}}$

    $6 + 5 = \underline{\hspace{1cm}}$

    $11 - 5 = \underline{\hspace{1cm}}$

2. $5 + 7 = \underline{\hspace{1cm}}$

    $12 - 7 = \underline{\hspace{1cm}}$

    $7 + 5 = \underline{\hspace{1cm}}$

    $12 - 5 = \underline{\hspace{1cm}}$

3. $3 + 9 = \underline{\hspace{1cm}}$

    $12 - 9 = \underline{\hspace{1cm}}$

    $9 + 3 = \underline{\hspace{1cm}}$

    $12 - 3 = \underline{\hspace{1cm}}$

4. $4 + 8 = \underline{\hspace{1cm}}$

    $12 - 8 = \underline{\hspace{1cm}}$

    $8 + 4 = \underline{\hspace{1cm}}$

    $12 - 4 = \underline{\hspace{1cm}}$

5. $4 + 7 = \underline{\hspace{1cm}}$

    $11 - 7 = \underline{\hspace{1cm}}$

    $7 + 4 = \underline{\hspace{1cm}}$

    $11 - 4 = \underline{\hspace{1cm}}$

6. $3 + 8 = \underline{\hspace{1cm}}$

    $11 - 8 = \underline{\hspace{1cm}}$

    $8 + 3 = \underline{\hspace{1cm}}$

    $11 - 3 = \underline{\hspace{1cm}}$

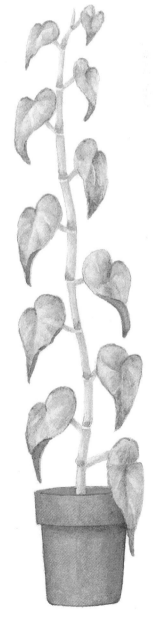

Add or subtract.

7.
$$\begin{array}{r} 11 \\ -\ 4 \\ \hline \end{array}$$
$$\begin{array}{r} 12 \\ -\ 8 \\ \hline \end{array}$$
$$\begin{array}{r} 4 \\ +8 \\ \hline \end{array}$$
$$\begin{array}{r} 8 \\ +3 \\ \hline \end{array}$$
$$\begin{array}{r} 9 \\ +3 \\ \hline \end{array}$$
$$\begin{array}{r} 11 \\ -\ 6 \\ \hline \end{array}$$

8.
$$\begin{array}{r} 3 \\ +9 \\ \hline \end{array}$$
$$\begin{array}{r} 12 \\ -\ 6 \\ \hline \end{array}$$
$$\begin{array}{r} 4 \\ +7 \\ \hline \end{array}$$
$$\begin{array}{r} 9 \\ +2 \\ \hline \end{array}$$
$$\begin{array}{r} 6 \\ +5 \\ \hline \end{array}$$
$$\begin{array}{r} 9 \\ -2 \\ \hline \end{array}$$

9.
$$\begin{array}{r} 5 \\ +6 \\ \hline \end{array}$$
$$\begin{array}{r} 8 \\ +4 \\ \hline \end{array}$$
$$\begin{array}{r} 11 \\ -\ 2 \\ \hline \end{array}$$
$$\begin{array}{r} 12 \\ -\ 5 \\ \hline \end{array}$$
$$\begin{array}{r} 7 \\ +4 \\ \hline \end{array}$$
$$\begin{array}{r} 11 \\ -\ 8 \\ \hline \end{array}$$

10.
$$\begin{array}{r} 12 \\ -\ 4 \\ \hline \end{array}$$
$$\begin{array}{r} 2 \\ +9 \\ \hline \end{array}$$
$$\begin{array}{r} 12 \\ -\ 9 \\ \hline \end{array}$$
$$\begin{array}{r} 11 \\ -\ 7 \\ \hline \end{array}$$
$$\begin{array}{r} 5 \\ +7 \\ \hline \end{array}$$
$$\begin{array}{r} 4 \\ +6 \\ \hline \end{array}$$

11.
$$\begin{array}{r} 12 \\ -\ 5 \\ \hline \end{array}$$
$$\begin{array}{r} 5 \\ +6 \\ \hline \end{array}$$
$$\begin{array}{r} 6 \\ +3 \\ \hline \end{array}$$
$$\begin{array}{r} 12 \\ -\ 7 \\ \hline \end{array}$$
$$\begin{array}{r} 4 \\ +3 \\ \hline \end{array}$$
$$\begin{array}{r} 11 \\ -\ 6 \\ \hline \end{array}$$

Think of the number.
Then write the number.

12. Two more than **35** _____

13. One less than **29** _____

14. Four more than **73** _____

15. Two less than **68** _____

16. Two less than **56** _____

Fact Families

PROBLEM SOLVING

7 bears are sleeping
5 bears are eating
How many bears in all?

$$
\begin{array}{r}
7 \\
+\ 5 \\
\hline
12
\end{array}
$$ bears

Solve.

1. There are 11 rabbits.
   Then **5** run away.
   How many rabbits
   are there now?

   rabbits

2. **6** squirrels are in the tree.
   6 are on the ground.
   How many squirrels
   are there?

   squirrels

3. **8** birds are on a rock.
   Then **5** fly away.
   How many birds are
   now on the rock?

   birds

Choosing the Operation

Solve.

4. A squirrel has 11 acorns.
It eats 7 of them.
How many acorns
does it have now?

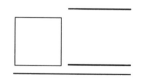

acorns

5. There are 7 deer
in the meadow.
4 more deer join them.
Now how many deer
are there?

deer

Copyright © 1987 by Houghton Mifflin Company. All rights reserved. Printed in U.S.A.

(pages 231–242)

CHECKPOINT 2

Subtract.

1.
$$11 - 5 \qquad 12 - 6 \qquad 11 - 2$$

2. $12 - 5 = \boxed{}$ $11 - 8 = \boxed{}$

Write + or − in the $\boxed{}$.
Then write the answer.

3. Debbie has 6 marbles.
Sue has 5 marbles.
How many marbles in all?

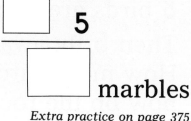

$$\boxed{}\ \begin{array}{r} 6 \\ 5 \\ \hline \end{array}$$

$\boxed{}$ marbles

Extra practice on page 375

Problem Solving

CHAPTER 9 TEST

Add.

1. $\begin{array}{r} 3 \\ +9 \\ \hline \end{array}$ $\begin{array}{r} 7 \\ +5 \\ \hline \end{array}$ $\begin{array}{r} 3 \\ +8 \\ \hline \end{array}$ $\begin{array}{r} 2 \\ +9 \\ \hline \end{array}$ $\begin{array}{r} 6 \\ +5 \\ \hline \end{array}$ $\begin{array}{r} 4 \\ +8 \\ \hline \end{array}$

Draw pictures to show how many more are needed. Then write the answer.

2. Ann wants **7** trees.
    She has planted **2** trees.
    How many more does she need?   _____ trees

Subtract.

3. $\begin{array}{r} 11 \\ -7 \\ \hline \end{array}$ $\begin{array}{r} 12 \\ -4 \\ \hline \end{array}$ $\begin{array}{r} 11 \\ -3 \\ \hline \end{array}$ $\begin{array}{r} 12 \\ -6 \\ \hline \end{array}$ $\begin{array}{r} 11 \\ -5 \\ \hline \end{array}$ $\begin{array}{r} 12 \\ -8 \\ \hline \end{array}$

Solve.

4. Allen has **6** pens.
    He buys **5** more pens.
    How many does he have now?

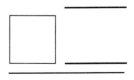

Extra practice on page 376

pens

MATHEMATICS and READING

A letter carrier delivers letters in order.
The letters are ordered beginning with the
lowest number on a street.
Help put the letters in order. Match.

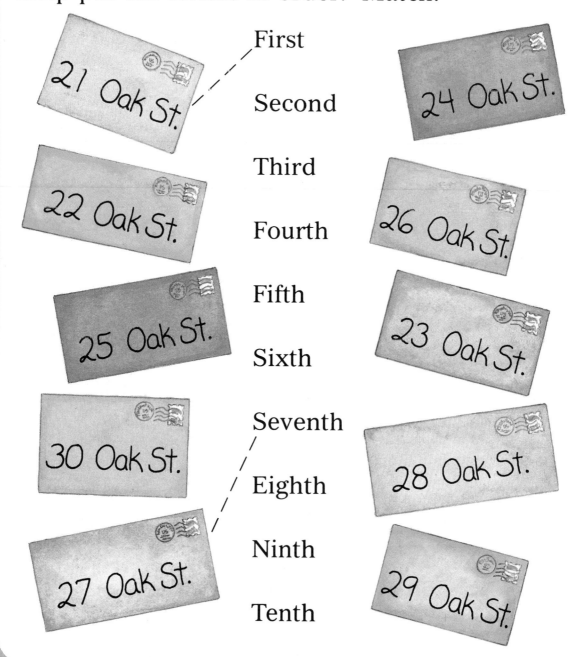

First

21 Oak St.

Second

24 Oak St.

Third

22 Oak St.

Fourth

26 Oak St.

Fifth

25 Oak St.

Sixth

23 Oak St.

Seventh

30 Oak St.

Eighth

28 Oak St.

27 Oak St.

Ninth

29 Oak St.

Tenth

Mathematics and Reading

Enrichment

You can check
subtraction
by adding.

$$\begin{array}{r} 8 \\ -2 \\ \hline 6 \end{array} \qquad \begin{array}{r} 6 \\ +2 \\ \hline 8 \end{array}$$

Subtract. Check by adding.

1. $\begin{array}{r} 6 \\ -3 \\ \hline \end{array}$ $\begin{array}{r} 3 \\ +3 \\ \hline \end{array}$ 2. $\begin{array}{r} 7 \\ -4 \\ \hline \end{array}$ $\begin{array}{r} 3 \\ +4 \\ \hline \end{array}$

3. $\begin{array}{r} 9 \\ -3 \\ \hline \end{array}$ $+$ 4. $\begin{array}{r} 8 \\ -2 \\ \hline \end{array}$ $+$

5. $\begin{array}{r} 12 \\ -5 \\ \hline \end{array}$ $+$ 6. $\begin{array}{r} 10 \\ -6 \\ \hline \end{array}$ $+$

7. $\begin{array}{r} 11 \\ -4 \\ \hline \end{array}$ $+$ 8. $\begin{array}{r} 12 \\ -8 \\ \hline \end{array}$ $+$

Ring the sum if it is incorrect. Then write the correct sum.

9. $5 + 3 = $ ⟨9⟩

8

___

10. $6 + 6 = 12$

___

11. $9 + 3 = 11$

___

12. $2 + 8 = 11$

___

13. $7 + 5 = 12$

___

14. $3 + 8 = 11$

___

15. $4 + 5 = 10$

___

16. $5 + 6 = 11$

___

17. $4 + 7 = 12$

___

18. $3 + 9 = 11$

___

Enrichment: Checking Addition

CUMULATIVE REVIEW

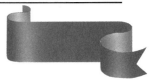

Fill in the ⬭ for the correct answer.

Choose the amount.

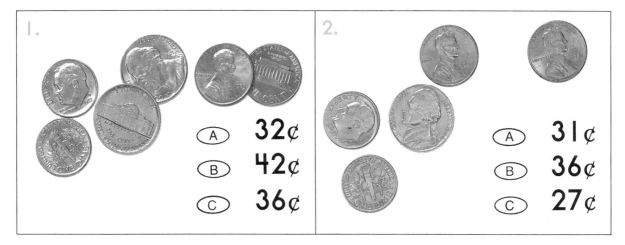

1.

- Ⓐ 32¢
- Ⓑ 42¢
- Ⓒ 36¢

2.

- Ⓐ 31¢
- Ⓑ 36¢
- Ⓒ 27¢

Choose the amount.

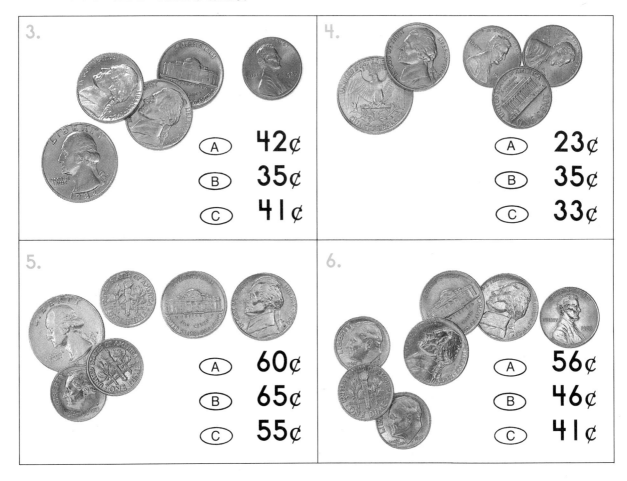

3.

- Ⓐ 42¢
- Ⓑ 35¢
- Ⓒ 41¢

4.

- Ⓐ 23¢
- Ⓑ 35¢
- Ⓒ 33¢

5.

- Ⓐ 60¢
- Ⓑ 65¢
- Ⓒ 55¢

6.

- Ⓐ 56¢
- Ⓑ 46¢
- Ⓒ 41¢

Choose the numbers that continue the pattern.

7. 30, 32, 34, ___?___, ___?___, ___?___, ___?___, ___?___

    Ⓐ 35, 36, 37, 38, 39

    Ⓑ 36, 38, 40, 42, 44

    Ⓒ 44, 54, 64, 74, 84

8. 18, 28, 38, ___?___, ___?___, ___?___

40, 42, 44	39, 41, 43	48, 58, 68
Ⓐ	Ⓑ	Ⓒ

9. 3, 2, 2, 3, 2, 2, 3, ___?___, ___?___, ___?___, ___?___, ___?___

2, 2, 3, 2, 2	3, 3, 2, 3, 3	2, 3, 2, 3, 2
Ⓐ	Ⓑ	Ⓒ

LANGUAGE and VOCABULARY REVIEW

Ring the sentence if it is correct.

1. To add means to find out how many are left.

2. In $9 - 3 = 6$, 6 is the difference.

3. To subtract means to find how many in all.

4. To solve a problem means to find an answer.

Language and Vocabulary Review

Read with the children:

The rider wants to know how high the horse jumped. Can you think of the different ways to measure how high the horse jumped?

10

MEASUREMENT

LONGER AND SHORTER

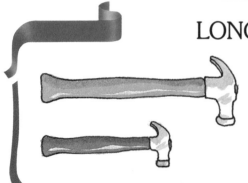 The  is **longer.**

The is **shorter.**

Ring the object that is longer.

1.

2.

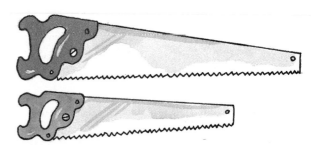

3.

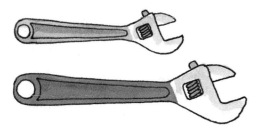

4.

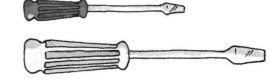

Ring the object that is shorter.

5.

6.

7.

8.

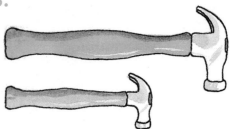

Comparing Lengths

MEASURING LENGTH

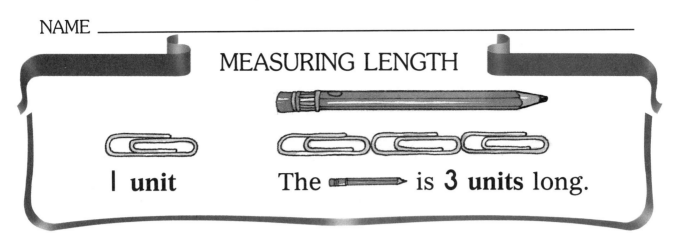

I unit   The is **3 units** long.

How long is each object?

1. 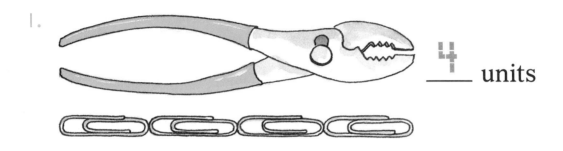 ____ units

2. 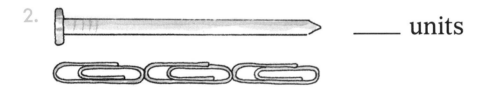 ____ units

3. 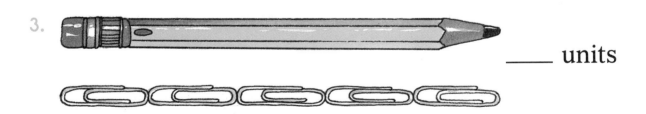 ____ units

4. 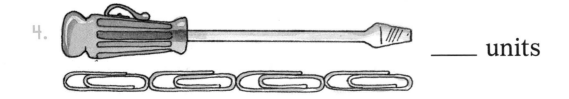 ____ units

How long is each object?

5.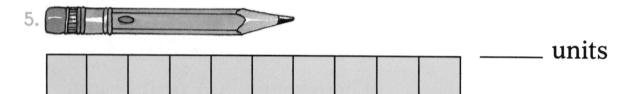

_____ units

6.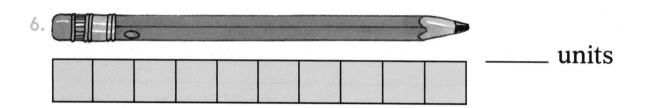

_____ units

7.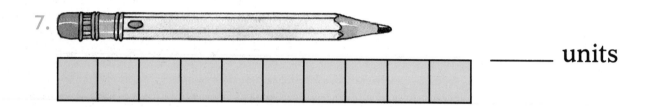

_____ units

8.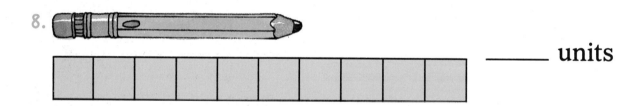

_____ units

9. Tina's desk is **37** ⌐⌐ long.

   Sue's desk is **46** ⌐⌐ long.

   Whose desk is longer? _____

10. Bill has a pencil **7** ⌐⌐ long.

    His other pencil is **4** ⌐⌐ long.

    How long are both pencils? _____

Measuring Length with Informal Units

CENTIMETER

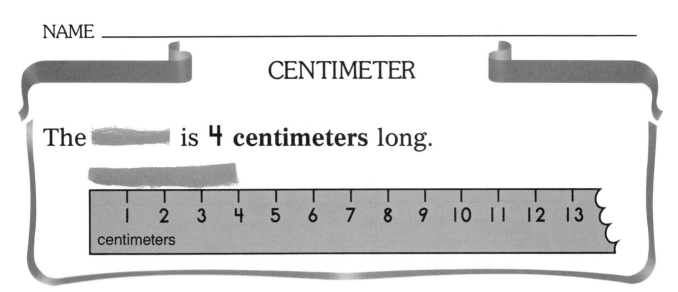

The ▬▬▬ is **4 centimeters** long.

How long is the object?

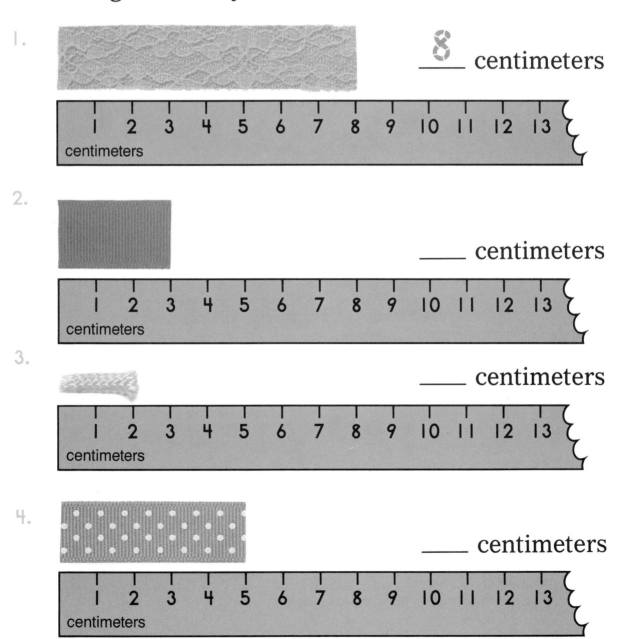

1. _8_ centimeters

2. ____ centimeters

3. ____ centimeters

4. ____ centimeters

Measure the object with your centimeter ruler.

5.  _____ centimeters

6.  _____ centimeters

7.  _____ centimeters

8.  _____ centimeters

9.  _____ centimeters

Is the object longer than **3** centimeters?
Ring yes or no.

10. 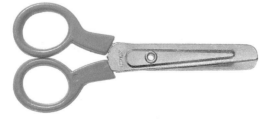 yes   no

11. yes   no

Centimeter

MORE AND LESS

The holds

more than the .

The 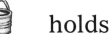 holds

less than the .

Ring the object that holds more.

1.

2.

3.

Ring the object that holds less.

4.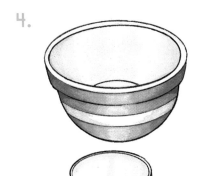

5.

6.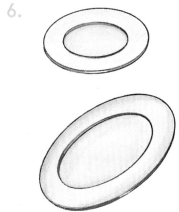

Identifying More and Less

Ring the object that holds more.
✓ the object that holds less.

7.

8.

9.

10.

11.

12.

⭐ Ring the object that holds the **most.**
✓ the object that holds the **least.**

13.

14.

15.

16.

Identifying More and Less

LITER

I liter   The mug holds **less** than a liter.   The pail holds **more** than a liter.

Does it hold more or less than a liter?

1.

more

(less)

2.

more

less

3.

more

less

4.

more

less

5.

more

less

6.

more

less

Ring the objects that hold more than a liter.
✓ the objects that hold less than a liter.

7.

8.

9.

10.

11.

12.

13.

14.

15.

16.

17.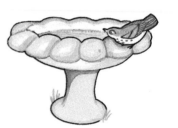

18. Sara made **4** liters of juice for the party.
Al brought **3** more liters of juice.
How many liters in all?

_____ liters

19. Ching put **3** liters of water
in the tub. The tub holds
10 liters. How many liters
does he need to fill the tub?

_____ liters

Liter

HEAVIER AND LIGHTER

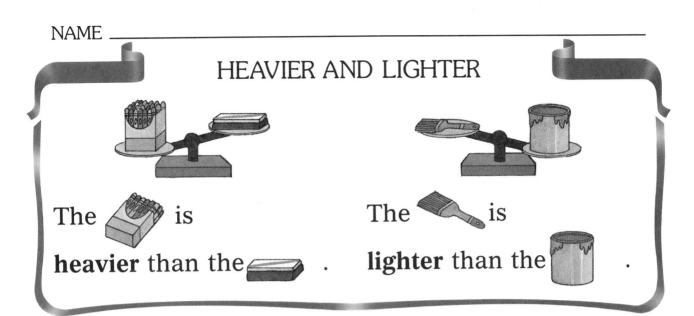

The 🔋 is

heavier than the ▭ .

The 🖌 is

lighter than the 🪣 .

Ring the object that is heavier.

1.

2.

3.

4.

Ring the object that is lighter.

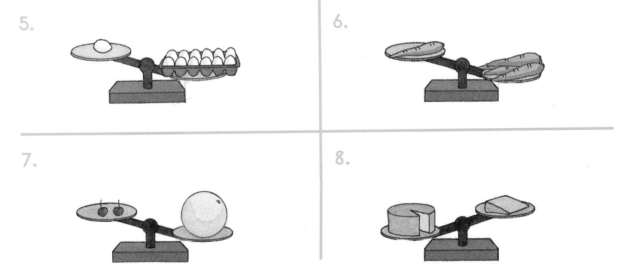

5.

6.

7.

8.

Ring the object that is heavier.
✓ the object that is lighter.

9.

10.

11.

12.

13.

14.

15.

16.

☆ Ring the **heaviest.** ✓ the **lightest.**

17.

18.

19.

20.

Identifying Heavier and Lighter

KILOGRAM

The fruit is
| **kilogram.**

Write the number of kilograms.

1.

___ kilograms

2.

___ kilogram

3.
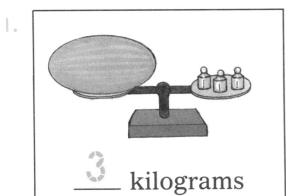

___ kilograms

4.

___ kilograms

5.

___ kilograms

6.

___ kilograms

Write the number of kilograms.

7.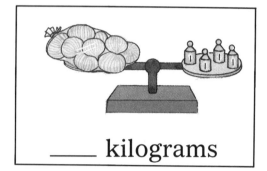

_____ kilograms

8.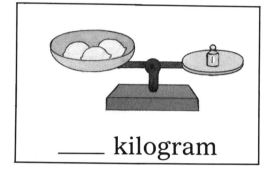

_____ kilogram

9.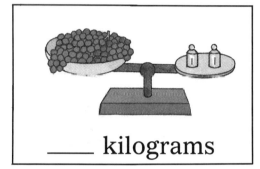

_____ kilograms

10.

_____ kilograms

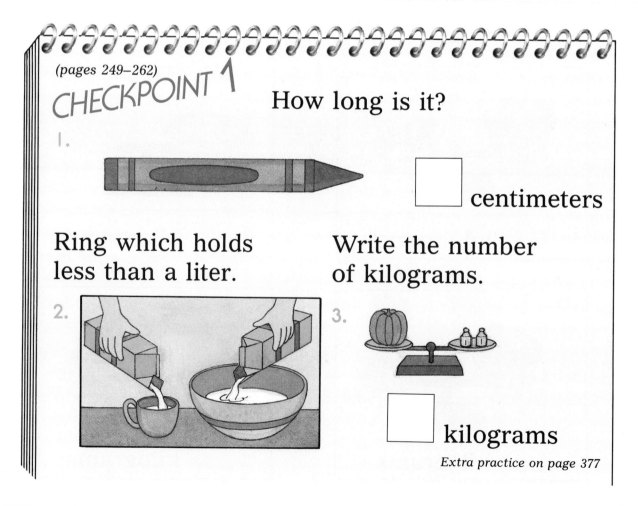

(pages 249–262)

CHECKPOINT 1   How long is it?

1.

☐ centimeters

Ring which holds less than a liter.

Write the number of kilograms.

2.

3.

☐ kilograms

Extra practice on page 377

Kilogram

PROBLEM SOLVING

BEACH ITEMS

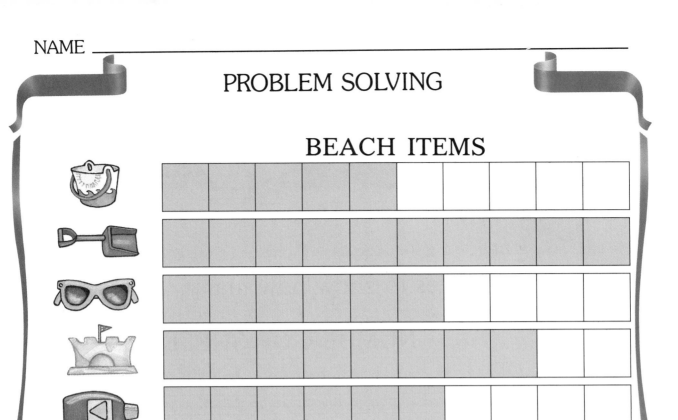

| | 0 | 1 | 2 | 3 | 4 | 5 | 6 | 7 | 8 | 9 | 10 |

Write the number.

1. How many  ? __10__

2. How many ? ____

3. How many ? ____

4. How many more than ? ____

5. How many more than ? ____

6. How many fewer than ? ____

7. Color the boxes to show how many.

NUMBER OF SHELLS

0 1 2 3 4 5 6 7 8 9 10

Write the number.

8. How many ? ___   **9.** How many ? ___

10. How many ? ___   **11.** How many ? ___

12. How many more than ? ___

13. How many more than ? ___

Problem Solving

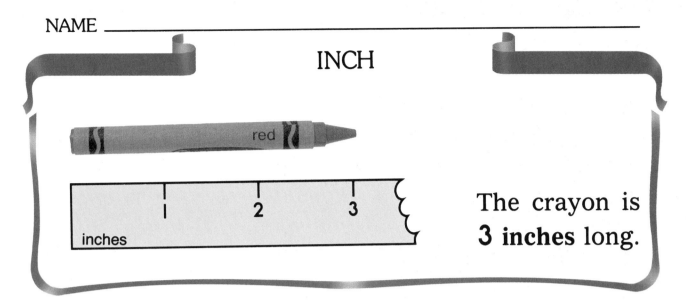

INCH

The crayon is **3 inches** long.

How long is each object?

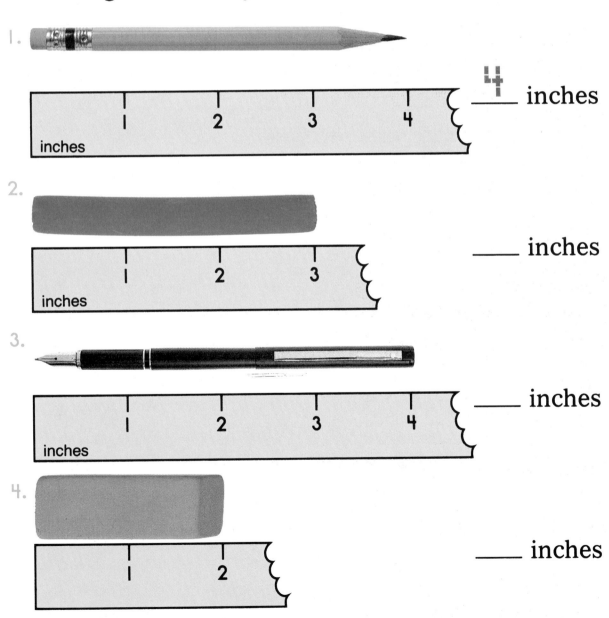

1. _4_ inches

2. ____ inches

3. ____ inches

4. ____ inches

Measure each object with your inch ruler.

5.  _____ inches

6.  _____ inches

7.  _____ inches

8.  _____ inches

9.  _____ inches

10. Sue's ═══► is **7** inches long.

Her ◼◼══► is **5** inches long.

How many inches in all? _____ inches

11. Pedro measured his ✂ .

It was **5** inches long.

How long are **3** ✂ ? _____ inches

Inch

CUP, PINT, AND QUART

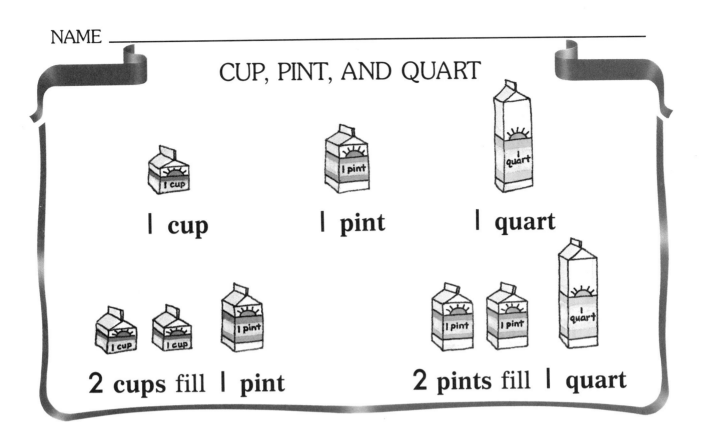

| cup | pint | quart |

2 cups fill **1 pint**   **2 pints** fill **1 quart**

Color the number you can fill.

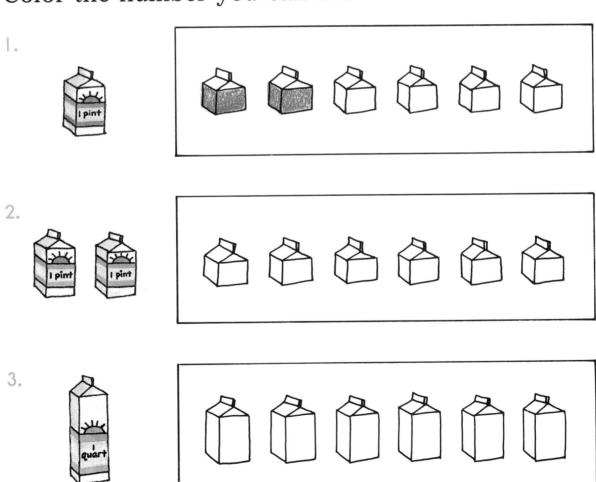

1.

2.

3.

Color the number you can fill.

4.

5.

6.

7.

Write the number.

8. **2** cups fill ___ **1** pint   **4** pints fill ___ quarts

9. **2** pints fill ___ quart   **8** cups fill ___ pints

10. **4** cups fill ___ pints   **8** cups fill ___ quarts

Cup, Pint, and Quart

NAME _____

POUND

The book weighs
1 pound.

Write the number of pounds.

1.

__2__ pounds

2.

_____ pounds

3.

_____ pounds

4.

_____ pounds

5.

_____ pounds

6.

_____ pounds

Write the number of pounds.

7.

_____ pounds

8.

_____ pounds

9.

_____ pounds

10.

_____ pounds

11.

_____ pound

12.

_____ pounds

Think of the answer.

Is it more than 10? Ring yes or no.

13. **8 + 4**   (yes)   no   **5 + 6**   yes   no

14. **11 + 4**   yes   no   **6 + 3**   yes   no

15. **10 + 2**   yes   no   **4 + 7**   yes   no

Pound

PROBLEM SOLVING

Use a ▭ to find out how **long** the rope is.

Use a ⚖ to find out how much the berries **weigh.**

Use a ▱ to find out how much the vase **holds.**

Ring the one you would use.

1. You want to know the cost of grapes.
   They are sold by the pound.

   You would use  .

2. You are making a hat.
   You need paper **10** inches long.

   You would use  .

3. There will be **8** children at the party.
   How many quarts of punch will you need?

   You would use  .

Ring the one you would use.

4. Each card is **4** inches long. How many pieces of paper will you need?

You would use

5. You are making soup. You need a pint of water. You would use

(pages 263–272)

CHECKPOINT 2

1.

Write the number of pounds.

☐ pounds

Color how many can be filled.

2.

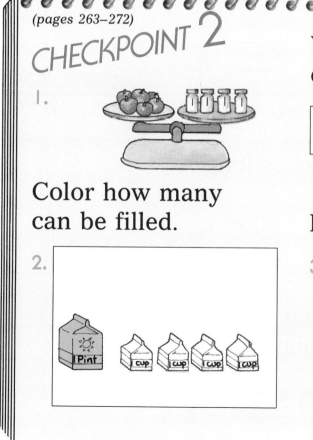

How long is it?

3.

☐ inches

Extra practice on page 377

Problem Solving

CHAPTER 10 TEST

Ring which holds more?

1.

How many?

2.

How many?

3.

____ kilograms

____ pounds

How long?

4.

____ centimeters

5.

____ inches

Write the number.   CRAYONS

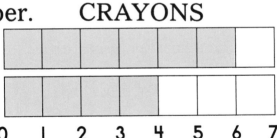

0   1   2   3   4   5   6   7

6. How many more ▰▰▰▷ than ▰▰▷ ? ____

Color the number you can fill.

7.

Extra practice on page 378

MATHEMATICS and SCIENCE

You use a **thermometer** to find temperature.
You measure temperature by **degrees.**
This thermometer reads **20** degrees.

Write the temperature.

1. _____ degrees

2. _____ degrees

3. _____ degrees

4. Match.

Mathematics and Health

Enrichment

You use a **centimeter** to measure small objects.

You use a **meter** to measure large objects.

A meter is
100 centimeters.

Which is the better measure to use?
Ring meter or centimeter.

1.

meter   centimeter

2.

meter   centimeter

3.

meter   centimeter

4.

meter   centimeter

Which is the better measure to use?
Ring meter or centimeter.

5.

meter   centimeter

6.

meter   centimeter

7.

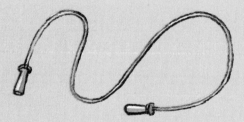

meter   centimeter

8.

meter   centimeter

9.

meter   centimeter

10.

meter   centimeter

11.

meter   centimeter

12.

meter   centimeter

Meter

NAME _____

 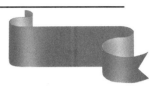
Fill in the ◯ for the correct answer.

Choose the number of tens and ones.

1.	57	2.	93
	Ⓐ **5** tens **5** ones		Ⓐ **3** tens **9** ones
	Ⓑ **7** tens **5** ones		Ⓑ **9** tens **3** ones
	Ⓒ **5** tens **7** ones		Ⓒ **3** tens **3** ones

Choose the missing numbers.

3.

33, __?__, __?__, __?__, 37

33, 34, 35	34, 35, 36	34, 37, 38
Ⓐ	Ⓑ	Ⓒ

Choose the number that is greater.

4.	42 54	Ⓐ 24 Ⓑ 42 Ⓒ 54	5.	87 85	Ⓐ 87 Ⓑ 58 Ⓒ 85

Choose the number that is less.

6.	13 11	Ⓐ 13 Ⓑ 11 Ⓒ 31	7.	26 27	Ⓐ 26 Ⓑ 62 Ⓒ 27

Use the chart to solve.

CIRCUS TIMES

	Mon.	Tues.	Wed.
Circus begins	1:00	3:30	8:00
Circus ends	3:00	5:30	10:00

8. What time does the circus begin on Wednesday?

  Ⓐ 1:00   Ⓑ 10:00   Ⓒ 8:00

9. On what day does the circus end at 5:30?

  Ⓐ Monday   Ⓑ Tuesday   Ⓒ Wednesday

LANGUAGE and VOCABULARY REVIEW

Ring the answer.

1. A __?__ holds less than a pint.

   quart   (cup)

2. The car is __?__ than the bus.

   heavier   lighter

3. A __?__ shows inches.

   ruler   scale

4. The book is 1 __?__.

   liter   kilogram

Language and Vocabulary Review

11

Read with the children:

Suppose you want to buy walnuts for **53**¢ and peanuts for **21**¢. How many dimes and pennies is that in all?

ADDITION AND SUBTRACTION TWO DIGIT NUMBERS

ADDING TENS

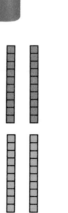

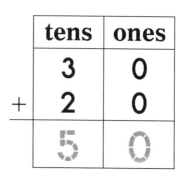

3 tens
+2 tens
_____
5 tens

tens	ones
3	0
+ 2	0
5	0

Add. 1.

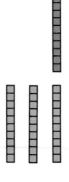

1 tens
+3 tens
_____
tens

tens	ones
1	0
+ 3	0

2.

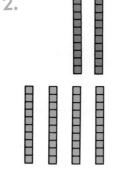

2 tens
+4 tens
_____
tens

tens	ones
2	0
+ 4	0

3. 3 tens   30
  +2 tens   +20
  _____   _____
  tens

4. 2 tens   20
  +5 tens   +50
  _____   _____
  tens

5. 4 tens   40
  +5 tens   +50
  _____   _____
  tens

6. 4 tens   40
  +4 tens   +40
  _____   _____
  tens

Adding Multiples of Ten

ADDING TWO DIGITS

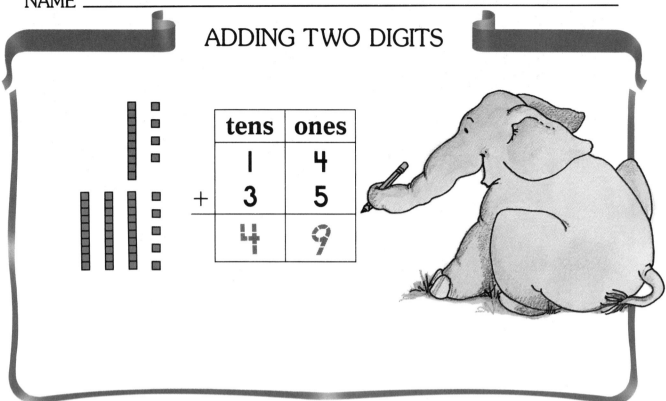

tens	ones
1	4
+ 3	5
4	9

Add.

1.

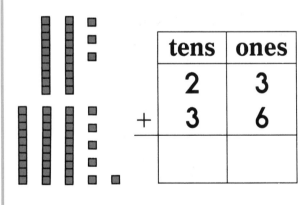

tens	ones
1	3
+ 2	1

2.

tens	ones
2	3
+ 3	6

3.

tens	ones
1	4
+ 2	5

4.

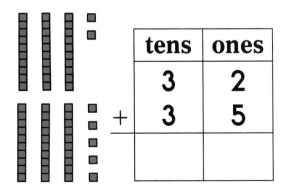

tens	ones
3	2
+ 3	5

Adding Two-Digit Numbers

Add.

5.

tens	ones
3	2
+ 4	3

tens	ones
3	5
+ 2	4

tens	ones
6	2
+ 2	3

6.

tens	ones
3	4
+ 3	4

tens	ones
2	6
+ 1	2

tens	ones
5	1
+ 4	1

7.

tens	ones
3	7
+ 2	2

tens	ones
5	3
+ 2	2

tens	ones
1	4
+ 1	5

Think.
$$30 + 20 = 50$$
$$30 + 22 = 52$$

8. $20 + 20 = 40$
$20 + 21 = \underline{\hspace{1cm}}$

9. $30 + 40 = 70$
$30 + 47 = \underline{\hspace{1cm}}$

10. $10 + 40 = 50$
$10 + 46 = \underline{\hspace{1cm}}$

11. $30 + 30 = 60$
$30 + 35 = \underline{\hspace{1cm}}$

Adding Two-Digit Numbers

ADDING TWO DIGITS

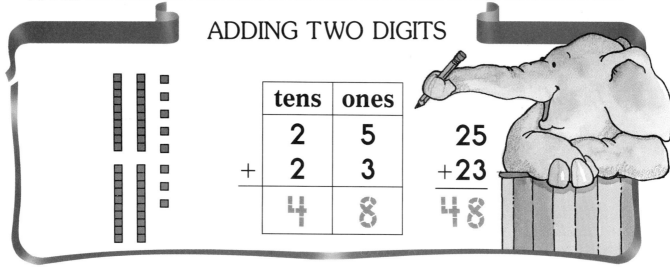

tens	ones
2	5
+ 2	3
4	8

25
+23
48

Add.

1.

tens	ones
2	3
+ 1	5

23
+15

2.

tens	ones
3	2
+ 2	4

32
+24

3.

tens	ones
3	4
+ 3	4

34
+34

4.

tens	ones
1	5
+ 4	2

15
+42

5.
```
 36    71    78    32    41    52
+52   +20   +21   +16   +35   +36
```

6.
```
 75    48    52    78    32    61
+13   +21   +30   +20   +67   +34
```

Add.

7.
23	11	61	24	57	32
+15	+57	+26	+32	+31	+47

8.
43	59	64	26	50	43
+46	+40	+25	+70	+37	+25

9.
12	29	43	65	56	82
+47	+50	+21	+31	+31	+17

10.
32	81	40	31	61	37
+67	+12	+52	+14	+27	+21

11.
23	45	52	26	42	36
+61	+12	+37	+50	+25	+51

Write the numbers.

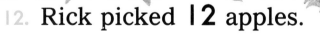

12. Rick picked **12** apples.

John picked **32** apples.

How many in all?

```
 12
+32
____
```

apples

Adding Two-Digit Numbers

ADDING TWO DIGITS

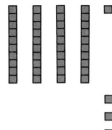

tens	ones
4	1
+	6
4	7

  4 1
+   6
-----
  4 7

Add.

1.

tens	ones
2	2
+	7

  2 2
+   7

2.

tens	ones
	3
+ 7	5

    3
+ 7 5

3.

tens	ones
3	4
+	5

  3 4
+   5

4.

tens	ones
6	8
+	1

  6 8
+   1

5.

36	25	67	4	32	42
+ 3	+ 2	+ 2	+45	+ 6	+ 5

6.

17	5	72	82	26	91
+ 2	+53	+ 6	+ 4	+ 3	+ 5

Add.

7.
31	92	63	96	64	4
+ 7	+ 4	+22	+ 2	+33	+81

8.
43	85	74	3	45	37
+ 3	+12	+ 5	+22	+ 1	+ 2

9.
56	22	2	36	32	33
+ 3	+77	+17	+52	+ 6	+ 5

10.
51	42	57	22	4	14
+32	+ 7	+30	+ 6	+35	+ 2

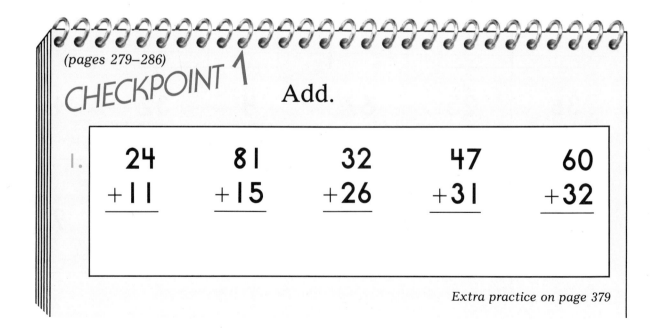

(pages 279–286)

CHECKPOINT 1   Add.

1.
24	81	32	47	60
+11	+15	+26	+31	+32

Extra practice on page 379

Adding a One-Digit and a Two-Digit Number

PROBLEM SOLVING

Write the numbers. Then solve.

1. George bought a mop
   and a duster. How much
   did he spend?

$$50¢$$
$$+42¢$$
$$92¢$$

2. Mrs. Smith needs a duster
   and soap. How much
   would they both cost?

3. Nancy wants to buy a broom
   and soap. How much
   money does she need?

4. Mr. Garcia bought a bucket
   and a broom. How much
   did he spend?

Write the numbers. Then solve.

5. Mrs. Smith needs to buy
a fish and a bear. How much
will both cost?

$$\begin{array}{r}\underline{}\\+\underline{}\\\hline\end{array}$$

6. Roberta bought a duck
and a bear. How much
did she spend?

$$\begin{array}{r}\underline{}\\+\underline{}\\\hline\end{array}$$

7. Mr. Lee wants to buy a dog
and a fish. How much
money does he need?

$$\begin{array}{r}\underline{}\\+\underline{}\\\hline\end{array}$$

8. Eric has **75¢**.
Can he buy a cat and a bear?
Ring yes or no.

$$\begin{array}{r}\underline{}\\+\underline{}\\\hline\end{array}$$

yes   no

Problem Solving

SUBTRACTING TENS

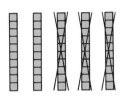

5 tens
−3 tens
2 tens

tens	ones
5	0
3	0
2	0

Subtract.

1.

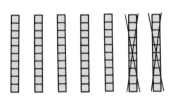

4 tens
−2 tens
___ tens

tens	ones
4	0
2	0

2.

7 tens
−2 tens
___ tens

tens	ones
7	0
2	0

3. 3 tens   30
   −1 tens   −10
   ___ tens

4. 8 tens   80
   −5 tens   −50
   ___ tens

5. 5 tens   50
   −2 tens   −20
   ___ tens

6. 9 tens   90
   −7 tens   −70
   ___ tens

Subtract.

7.
80	40	70	40	90	30
−40	−30	−30	−20	−70	−10

8.
50	30	70	80	50	40
−30	−10	−40	−60	−30	−20

9.
90	40	50	30	60	70
−50	−30	−20	−20	−30	−20

10.
40	60	70	30	90	80
−30	−20	−40	−30	−60	−50

Write + or − in the ☐ .
Then add or subtract.

11. The Smith family drove
74 miles on Monday.
They drove **23** miles on Tuesday.
How many miles did they drive?

```
   74
☐  23
─────
```

miles

Subtracting Multiples of Ten

SUBTRACTING TWO DIGITS

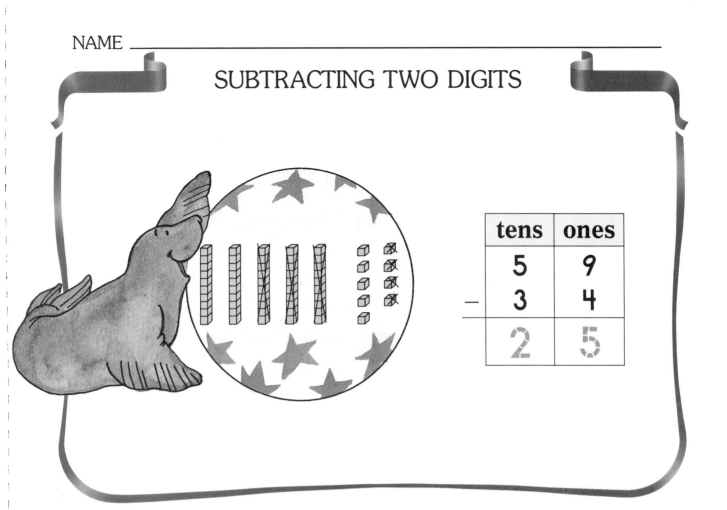

tens	ones
5	9
− 3	4
2	5

Subtract.

1.

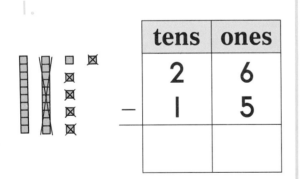

tens	ones
2	6
− 1	5

2.

tens	ones
3	7
− 2	4

3.

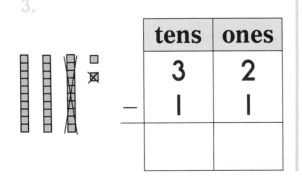

tens	ones
3	2
− 1	1

4.

tens	ones
4	6
− 2	3

Subtracting Two-Digit Numbers

Subtract.

5.

tens	ones
7	3
− 3	1

tens	ones
5	9
− 1	4

tens	ones
6	8
− 4	5

6.

tens	ones
3	6
− 2	4

tens	ones
4	5
− 2	3

tens	ones
5	7
− 3	2

7.

tens	ones
5	9
− 2	7

tens	ones
8	7
− 6	3

tens	ones
7	9
− 1	2

Think.

$$50 - 20 = 30$$

$$52 - 20 = 32$$

8. $40 - 10 = 30$

$42 - 10 = \underline{\hphantom{00}}$

10. $70 - 30 = 40$

$77 - 30 = \underline{\hphantom{00}}$

9. $60 - 40 = 20$

$65 - 40 = \underline{\hphantom{00}}$

11. $50 - 20 = 30$

$51 - 20 = \underline{\hphantom{00}}$

Subtracting Two-Digit Numbers

SUBTRACTING TWO DIGITS

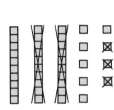

tens	ones
3	9
− 2	3
1	6

39
−23
16

Subtract.

1.

tens	ones
7	8
− 5	3

78
−53

2.

tens	ones
8	6
− 2	5

86
−25

3.

tens	ones
6	8
− 2	5

68
−25

4.

tens	ones
4	7
− 1	3

47
−13

5.
$$52 \quad 37 \quad 68 \quad 96 \quad 78 \quad 85$$
$$-21 \quad -10 \quad -32 \quad -43 \quad -37 \quad -21$$

6.
$$72 \quad 98 \quad 21 \quad 67 \quad 78 \quad 95$$
$$-51 \quad -32 \quad -10 \quad -35 \quad -32 \quad -21$$

Subtract.

7.
$$
\begin{array}{r} 95 \\ -22 \\ \hline \end{array}
\qquad
\begin{array}{r} 79 \\ -27 \\ \hline \end{array}
\qquad
\begin{array}{r} 85 \\ -31 \\ \hline \end{array}
\qquad
\begin{array}{r} 46 \\ -10 \\ \hline \end{array}
\qquad
\begin{array}{r} 98 \\ -63 \\ \hline \end{array}
\qquad
\begin{array}{r} 87 \\ -25 \\ \hline \end{array}
$$

8.
$$
\begin{array}{r} 99 \\ -21 \\ \hline \end{array}
\qquad
\begin{array}{r} 79 \\ -48 \\ \hline \end{array}
\qquad
\begin{array}{r} 94 \\ -60 \\ \hline \end{array}
\qquad
\begin{array}{r} 37 \\ -24 \\ \hline \end{array}
\qquad
\begin{array}{r} 66 \\ -23 \\ \hline \end{array}
\qquad
\begin{array}{r} 68 \\ -35 \\ \hline \end{array}
$$

9.
$$
\begin{array}{r} 86 \\ -24 \\ \hline \end{array}
\qquad
\begin{array}{r} 64 \\ -42 \\ \hline \end{array}
\qquad
\begin{array}{r} 54 \\ -30 \\ \hline \end{array}
\qquad
\begin{array}{r} 37 \\ -16 \\ \hline \end{array}
\qquad
\begin{array}{r} 78 \\ -46 \\ \hline \end{array}
\qquad
\begin{array}{r} 65 \\ -24 \\ \hline \end{array}
$$

10.
$$
\begin{array}{r} 97 \\ -32 \\ \hline \end{array}
\qquad
\begin{array}{r} 43 \\ -32 \\ \hline \end{array}
\qquad
\begin{array}{r} 89 \\ -31 \\ \hline \end{array}
\qquad
\begin{array}{r} 85 \\ -62 \\ \hline \end{array}
\qquad
\begin{array}{r} 75 \\ -52 \\ \hline \end{array}
\qquad
\begin{array}{r} 57 \\ -43 \\ \hline \end{array}
$$

11.
$$
\begin{array}{r} 36 \\ -21 \\ \hline \end{array}
\qquad
\begin{array}{r} 55 \\ -31 \\ \hline \end{array}
\qquad
\begin{array}{r} 62 \\ -21 \\ \hline \end{array}
\qquad
\begin{array}{r} 98 \\ -81 \\ \hline \end{array}
\qquad
\begin{array}{r} 37 \\ -16 \\ \hline \end{array}
\qquad
\begin{array}{r} 89 \\ -63 \\ \hline \end{array}
$$

☆ Rewrite. Then add or subtract.

12. **56 − 24**　　13. **62 + 21**　　14. **36 + 23**

Subtracting Two-Digit Numbers

SUBTRACTING TWO DIGITS

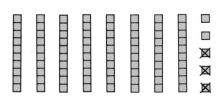

tens	ones
8	5
−	3
8	2

85
− 3
82

Subtract.

1.

tens	ones
2	9
−	8

29
− 8

2.

tens	ones
9	8
−	3

98
− 3

3.

tens	ones
7	6
−	5

76
− 5

4.

tens	ones
5	7
−	2

57
− 2

5.
```
  27      86      57      78      89      95
－  3    －  4    －  3    －  6    －72    －  3
```

6.
```
  96      37      68      19      28      87
－  2    －16    －  3    －  3    －  5    －  3
```

Subtract.

7.
$$\begin{array}{r} 49 \\ -\ 3 \\ \hline \end{array}$$
$$\begin{array}{r} 85 \\ -\ 1 \\ \hline \end{array}$$
$$\begin{array}{r} 56 \\ -\ 2 \\ \hline \end{array}$$
$$\begin{array}{r} 75 \\ -23 \\ \hline \end{array}$$
$$\begin{array}{r} 58 \\ -\ 6 \\ \hline \end{array}$$
$$\begin{array}{r} 26 \\ -\ 3 \\ \hline \end{array}$$

8.
$$\begin{array}{r} 97 \\ -\ 3 \\ \hline \end{array}$$
$$\begin{array}{r} 77 \\ -15 \\ \hline \end{array}$$
$$\begin{array}{r} 38 \\ -\ 5 \\ \hline \end{array}$$
$$\begin{array}{r} 64 \\ -\ 3 \\ \hline \end{array}$$
$$\begin{array}{r} 48 \\ -\ 2 \\ \hline \end{array}$$
$$\begin{array}{r} 89 \\ -55 \\ \hline \end{array}$$

9.
$$\begin{array}{r} 68 \\ -\ 7 \\ \hline \end{array}$$
$$\begin{array}{r} 56 \\ -14 \\ \hline \end{array}$$
$$\begin{array}{r} 37 \\ -\ 2 \\ \hline \end{array}$$
$$\begin{array}{r} 29 \\ -\ 3 \\ \hline \end{array}$$
$$\begin{array}{r} 68 \\ -37 \\ \hline \end{array}$$
$$\begin{array}{r} 95 \\ -\ 2 \\ \hline \end{array}$$

10.
$$\begin{array}{r} 92 \\ -11 \\ \hline \end{array}$$
$$\begin{array}{r} 55 \\ -\ 3 \\ \hline \end{array}$$
$$\begin{array}{r} 27 \\ -\ 2 \\ \hline \end{array}$$
$$\begin{array}{r} 38 \\ -16 \\ \hline \end{array}$$
$$\begin{array}{r} 46 \\ -\ 4 \\ \hline \end{array}$$
$$\begin{array}{r} 78 \\ -\ 5 \\ \hline \end{array}$$

Write + or − in the ☐.
Then add or subtract.

11. Maria had **55** balloons to sell.
She lost **3** balloons.
How many does she have now?

$$\begin{array}{r} 55 \\ \boxed{}\ 3 \\ \hline \end{array}$$

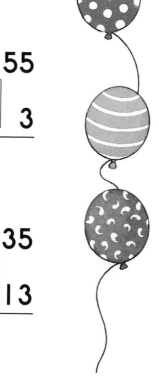

12. Jason had **35** marbles.
He bought **13** more marbles.
How many marbles
does he have now?

$$\begin{array}{r} 35 \\ \boxed{}\ 13 \\ \hline \end{array}$$

Subtracting Two-Digit Numbers.

ADD, SUBTRACT MONEY

48¢
−22¢
_____
26¢

Add or subtract.

1.

23¢
+11¢
_____

2.

66¢
−21¢
_____

3.

47¢
−12¢
_____

4.

35¢
+21¢
_____

Add or subtract.

5.
33¢	84¢	50¢	79¢	58¢
+36¢	−52¢	+40¢	− 3¢	−35¢

6.
53¢	39¢	98¢	34¢	46¢
+32¢	+20¢	−65¢	+53¢	+32¢

7.
67¢	69¢	23¢	74¢	40¢
−23¢	−35¢	+26¢	−42¢	+30¢

8.
59¢	32¢	34¢	13¢	55¢
−13¢	+47¢	+42¢	+41¢	+12¢

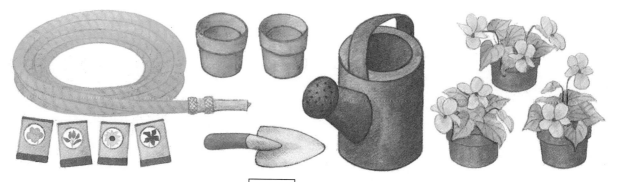

☆ Write numbers in the ☐ to make the sum or difference.

9.

	1	5		☐	☐		☐	☐		☐	☐
+	6	4	−	☐	☐	+	☐	☐	−	☐	☐
	7	9		6	8		4	6		3	2

Adding and Subtracting Money

PROBLEM SOLVING

Molly has **26¢**.
She spends **12¢**.
How much does she have left?

$$\begin{array}{r} 26¢ \\ -\ 12¢ \\ \hline 14¢ \end{array}$$

Write the numbers.
Then add or subtract.

1. Jeff has **25¢**.
   He gets **20¢** more.
   How much does he have in all?

2. Chris had **32¢**.
   He saves **46¢** more.
   How much does he have?

3. Barbara had **76¢**.
   She spends **45¢**.
   How much does she have left?

Write the numbers. Then add or subtract.

4. Bill had **53¢**.
   Then he saved **36¢**.
   How much does he have?

5. David had **46¢**.
   He gave **32¢** to Chris.
   How much does David have?

(pages 287–300)

CHECKPOINT 2

Write the number.
Then add or subtract.

1. Lupita had **45¢**. She gave
   21¢ to Jim. How much
   does she have now?

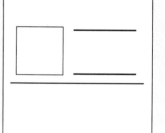

Subtract.

2.
89	67	79
−31	−26	−48

Add or subtract.

3.
52¢	75¢
+41¢	−40¢

Extra practice on page 379

Problem Solving

CHAPTER 11 TEST

Add.

1. | 35 | 26 | 50 | 37 | 56 | 17 |
    | +34 | +12 | +40 | +22 | +31 | +82 |

Write the number. Then solve.

2. Paul wants to buy marbles and jacks. How much money does he need?

Subtract.

3. | 58 | 46 | 70 | 79 | 45 | 68 |
    | −23 | −31 | −40 | −12 | −23 | −45 |

Add or subtract.

4. | 58¢ | 65¢ | 37¢ | 79¢ | 50¢ | 53¢ |
    | −35¢ | +32¢ | −12¢ | − 3¢ | +40¢ | +32¢ |

Write the numbers. Then add or subtract.

5. Kathy had **76**¢. She spent **34**¢. How much does she have now?

Extra Practice on page 380

MATHEMATICS and HEALTH

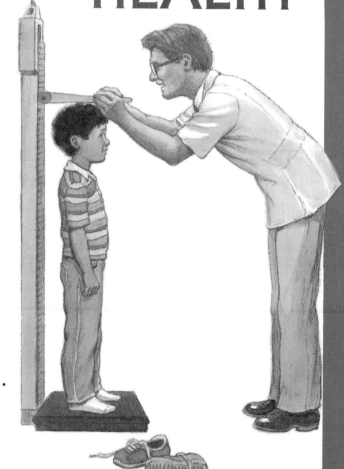

A nurse measures
your height.
He may use a
machine like this.

Write the number.

1. Eurico is **46** in. tall.
Last year he was
41 inches tall.
How much has he
grown in one year? _____ inches

2. Janet is **3** inches taller than Susan.
Susan is **44** inches.
How tall is Janet? _____ inches

3. **3** years ago Kate was **40** inches tall.
She has grown **6** inches.
How tall is she now? _____ inches

Enrichment

30 31 32 33 34 35 36 37 38 39 40

32 is nearer **30** than **40**.   **37** is nearer **40** than **30**.

30 is the ten nearest **32**.   **40** is the ten nearest **37**.

Write the ten nearest the number.

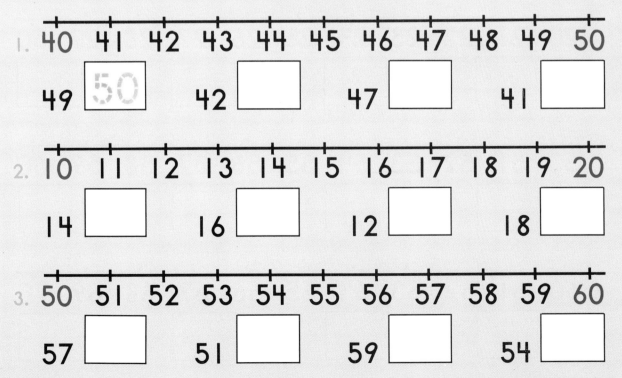

1. 40 41 42 43 44 45 46 47 48 49 50

49 50   42 ☐   47 ☐   41 ☐

2. 10 11 12 13 14 15 16 17 18 19 20

14 ☐   16 ☐   12 ☐   18 ☐

3. 50 51 52 53 54 55 56 57 58 59 60

57 ☐   51 ☐   59 ☐   54 ☐

When we find the nearest ten
of a number, that number is
rounded.

22, rounded to the nearest ten, is **20**.
28, rounded to the nearest ten, is **30**.

Round to the nearest ten.

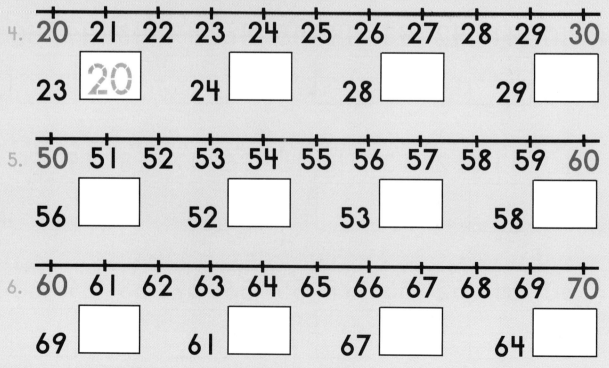

4. 20 21 22 23 24 25 26 27 28 29 30

23 [20]   24 [ ]   28 [ ]   29 [ ]

5. 50 51 52 53 54 55 56 57 58 59 60

56 [ ]   52 [ ]   53 [ ]   58 [ ]

6. 60 61 62 63 64 65 66 67 68 69 70

69 [ ]   61 [ ]   67 [ ]   64 [ ]

Enrichment: Rounding

 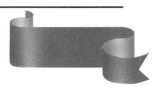

CUMULATIVE REVIEW

Fill in the ⬭ for the correct answer.

Choose the correct example.

1.	Jane had **5¢**. She spent **3¢**. How much does she have now?	Ⓐ **5¢ + 3¢** Ⓑ **3¢ + 5¢** Ⓒ **5¢ − 3¢**
2.	Michael had **4¢**. He saved **5¢** more. How much does he have now?	Ⓐ **4¢ + 5¢** Ⓑ **5¢ − 4¢** Ⓒ **9¢ − 5¢**

Solve.

3. Anita has **6** pennies.
She needs **9** pennies.
How many more pennies
does she need?

Ⓐ

Ⓑ

Ⓒ

Add or subtract.

4. **9 + 3**	5. **7 + 4**	6. **6 + 6**
10 11 12	11 10 12	11 12 10
Ⓐ Ⓑ Ⓒ	Ⓐ Ⓑ Ⓒ	Ⓐ Ⓑ Ⓒ
7. **11 − 3**	8. **12 − 8**	9. **11 − 7**
7 8 6	4 5 6	3 5 4
Ⓐ Ⓑ Ⓒ	Ⓐ Ⓑ Ⓒ	Ⓐ Ⓑ Ⓒ

How long?

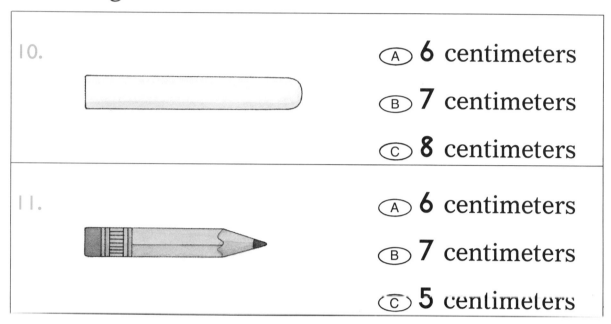

10.   Ⓐ **6** centimeters

         Ⓑ **7** centimeters

         Ⓒ **8** centimeters

11.   Ⓐ **6** centimeters

         Ⓑ **7** centimeters

         Ⓒ **5** centimeters

LANGUAGE and VOCABULARY REVIEW

Match

1. heavy      2. longer   

    light      shorter

3. ruler      4. kilograms   

    scale      centimeters

    cup   

Language and Vocabulary Review

COMPUTER
LITERACY

Number the story in order.

1.

2.

Follow the steps to draw the picture.

3.

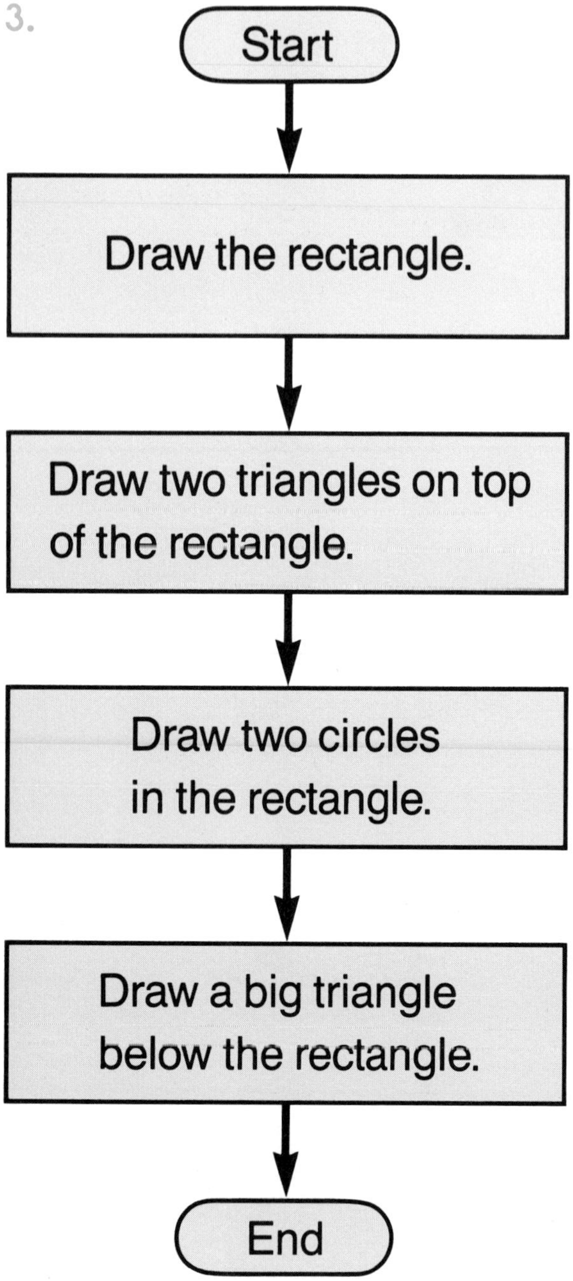

Start

↓

Draw the rectangle.

↓

Draw two triangles on top of the rectangle.

↓

Draw two circles in the rectangle.

↓

Draw a big triangle below the rectangle.

↓

End

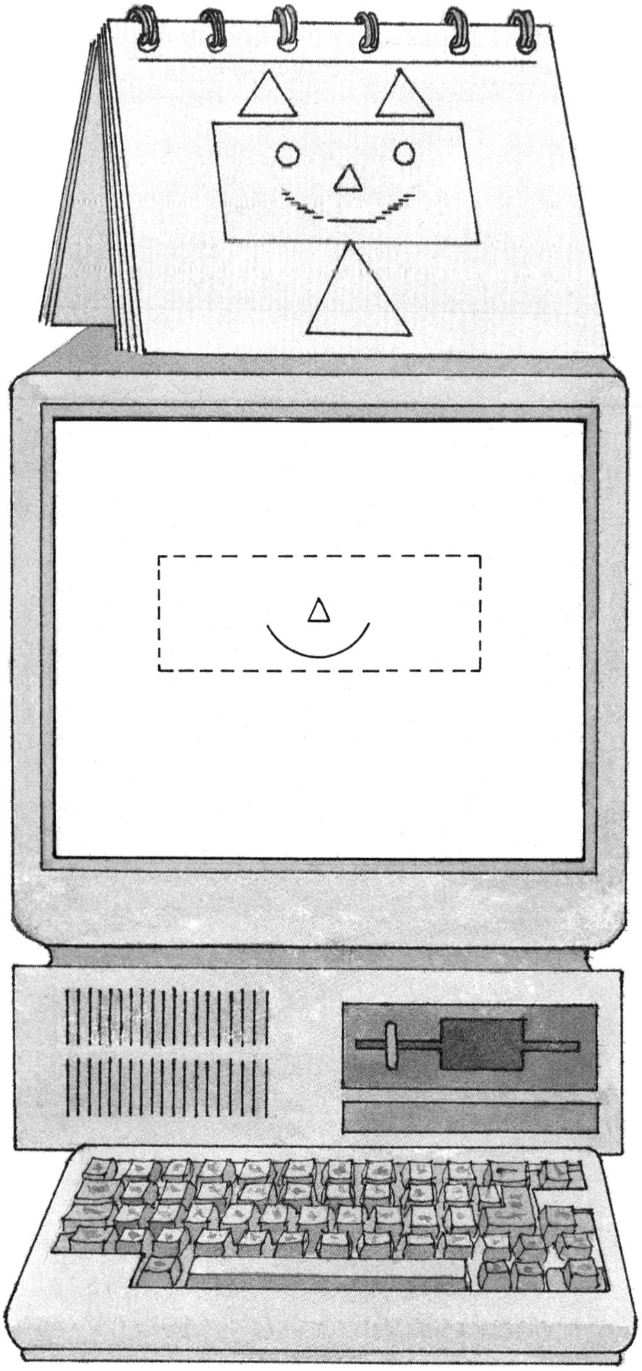

Flowcharting

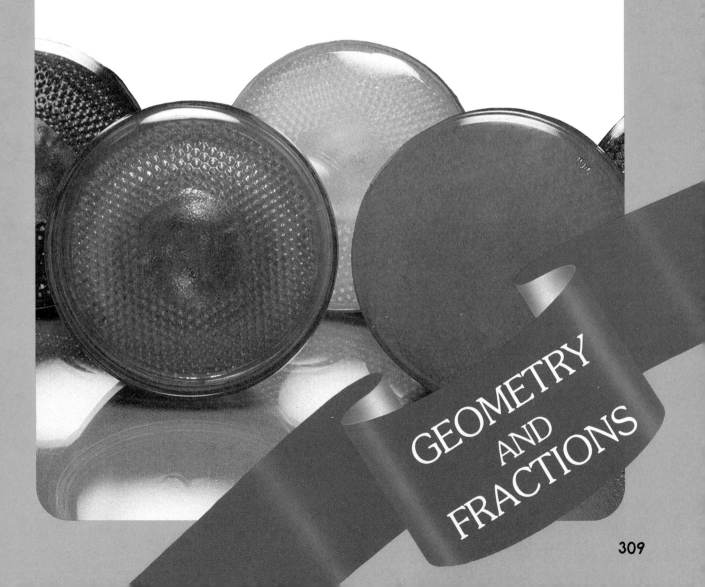

Read with the children:

What is the shape of the
red lights?
Could the yellow light
be a circle?
What other shapes can
you find in your
classroom?

12

GEOMETRY
AND
FRACTIONS

TRIANGLE AND RECTANGLE

This is a **triangle**.
It has 3 sides.

This is a **rectangle**.
It has 4 sides.

1. Color triangles ▣ .

2. Color rectangles ▢ .

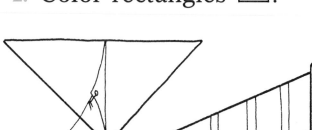

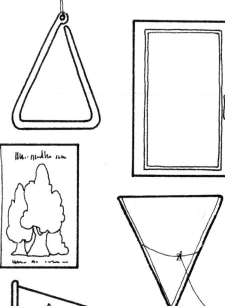

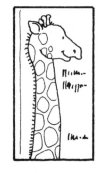

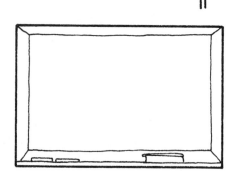

3. How many triangles? ____

4. How many rectangles? ____

Identifying Triangle and Rectangle

CIRCLE AND SQUARE

This is a **circle**.
It has no sides.

This is a **square**.
It has **4** sides.
The sides are
the same length.

1. Ring the circles.

2. ✔ the squares.

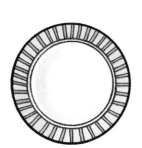

3. How many circles? ____

4. How many squares? ____

5. Color circles 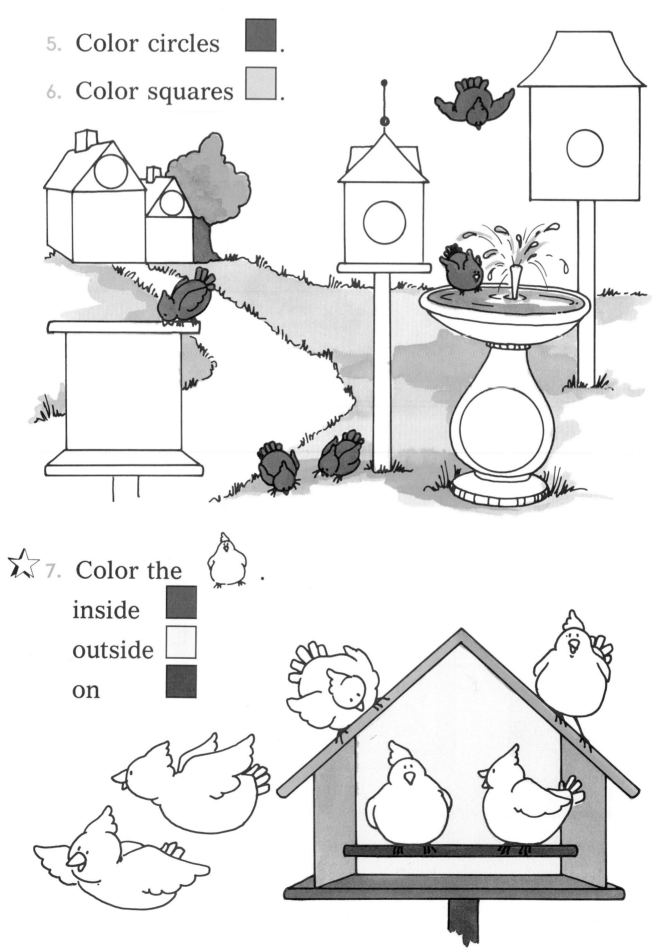.
6. Color squares .

7. Color the .
inside
outside
on

Identifying Circle and Square

ONE THIRD

There are **3** equal parts.
I part is green.

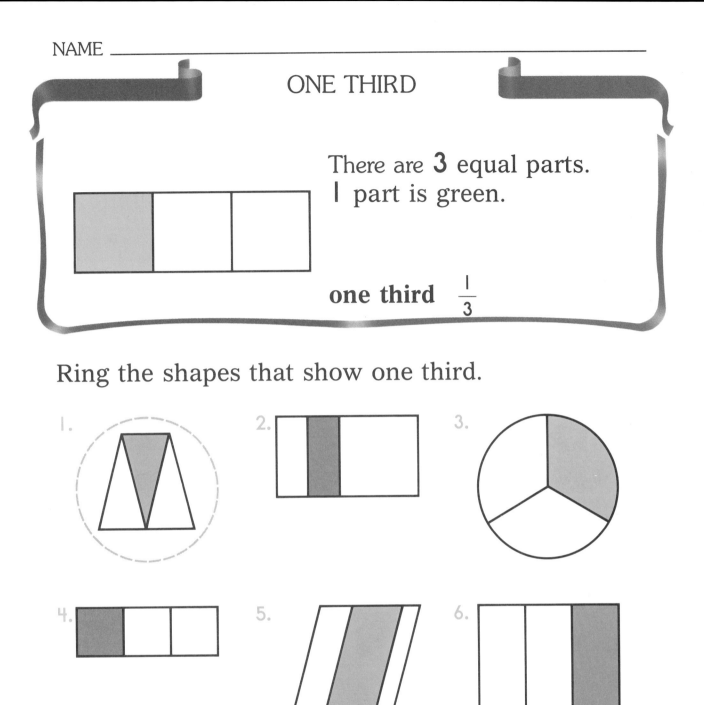

one third $\frac{1}{3}$

Ring the shapes that show one third.

1.
2.
3.

4.
5.
6.

7.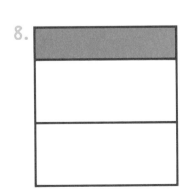
8.
9.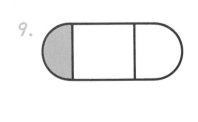

Ring $\frac{1}{2}$ or $\frac{1}{3}$.

10. $\frac{1}{2}$ $\left(\frac{1}{3}\right)$	11. $\frac{1}{2}$ $\frac{1}{3}$	12. $\frac{1}{2}$ $\frac{1}{3}$
13. $\frac{1}{2}$ $\frac{1}{3}$	14. $\frac{1}{2}$ $\frac{1}{3}$	15. $\frac{1}{2}$ $\frac{1}{3}$
16. $\frac{1}{2}$ $\frac{1}{3}$	17. $\frac{1}{2}$ $\frac{1}{3}$	18. $\frac{1}{2}$ $\frac{1}{3}$

Ring the answer.

19. Sarah had half of a glass of milk.
Juan had a third of a glass of milk.
Who had more milk?

Sarah   Juan

Identifying One Third

ONE FOURTH

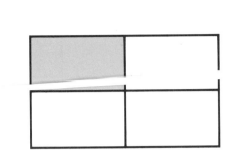

There are **4** equal parts.
I part is blue.

one fourth $\frac{1}{4}$

Ring the shapes that show one fourth.

1.
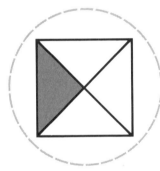

2.
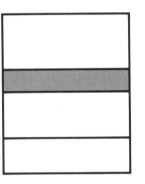

3.
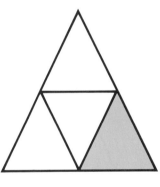

4.
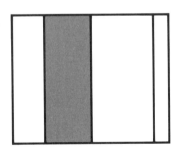

5.
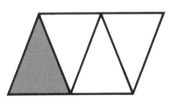

6.
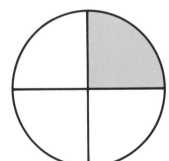

7.
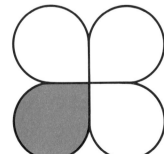

8.
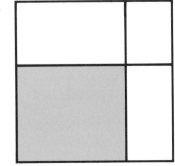

9.
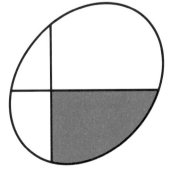

Ring $\frac{1}{2}$, $\frac{1}{3}$, or $\frac{1}{4}$.

10.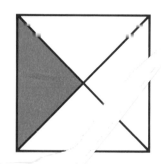

$\frac{1}{2}$ $\frac{1}{3}$ $\boxed{\frac{1}{4}}$

11.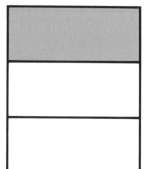

$\frac{1}{2}$ $\frac{1}{3}$ $\frac{1}{4}$

12.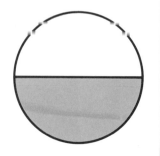

$\frac{1}{2}$ $\frac{1}{3}$ $\frac{1}{4}$

13.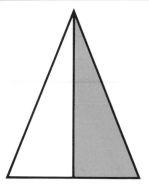

$\frac{1}{2}$ $\frac{1}{3}$ $\frac{1}{4}$

14.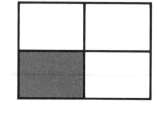

$\frac{1}{2}$ $\frac{1}{3}$ $\frac{1}{4}$

15.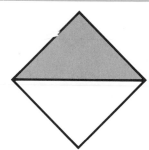

$\frac{1}{2}$ $\frac{1}{3}$ $\frac{1}{4}$

☆ Write the fraction for the shaded part.

16.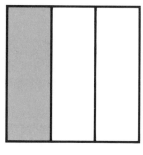

_____

17.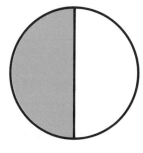

_____

18.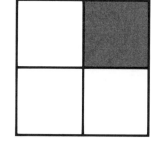

_____

Identifying One Fourth

PROBLEM SOLVING

Tina can buy either
carrots or squash.
She does not want to
buy squash.

What does she want to buy?

carrots _____

1. Jane was **6** years old
two years ago.
How old is she now?

_____

2. Micki is not as tall
as James.
She is taller than Amy.
Who is the shortest?

_____

3. Carl is **10** years old.
Susan is **4** years younger
than Carl.
How old is Susan?

_____

Logical Reasoning

4. Jim has **5¢** more than Rick.
Rick has **6¢**.
How much money does Jim have? _____

5. Amanda is two years older than Alex.
Alex is **8** years old.
How old is Amanda? _____

6. Think of this number.
It is greater than **18** and less than **27**.
There is no **2** in this number.
What is the number? _____

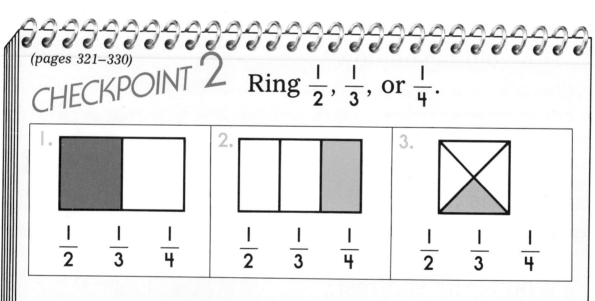

(pages 321–330)

CHECKPOINT 2 Ring $\frac{1}{2}$, $\frac{1}{3}$, or $\frac{1}{4}$.

1.
$\frac{1}{2}$ $\frac{1}{3}$ $\frac{1}{4}$

2.
$\frac{1}{2}$ $\frac{1}{3}$ $\frac{1}{4}$

3.
$\frac{1}{2}$ $\frac{1}{3}$ $\frac{1}{4}$

Write the answer.

4. Juan has two hats.
They are blue and red.
He is not wearing the blue hat.
What color hat is he wearing?

Extra practice on page 379

Problem Solving

CHAPTER 12 TEST

Color.

1. triangle

   rectangle ▢

Color.

2. cylinder

   cone ▢

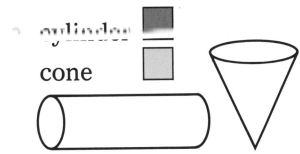

Write the number.

FRUIT

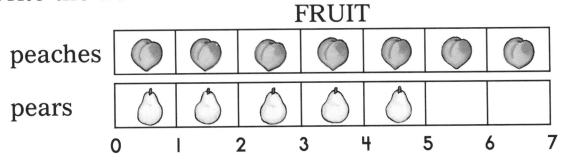

peaches

pears

0   1   2   3   4   5   6   7

3. How many peaches?

____ peaches

4. How many pears?

____ pears

Ring $\frac{1}{2}$, $\frac{1}{3}$, or $\frac{1}{4}$.

5.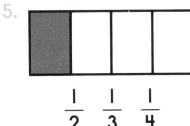

$\frac{1}{2}$ $\frac{1}{3}$ $\frac{1}{4}$

6.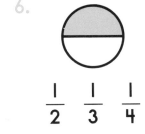

$\frac{1}{2}$ $\frac{1}{3}$ $\frac{1}{4}$

7.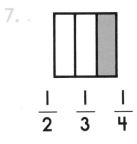

$\frac{1}{2}$ $\frac{1}{3}$ $\frac{1}{4}$

Write the number.

8. Sue was 4 years old three years ago.

   How old is she now? _____

Extra practice on page 380

MATHEMATICS and SOCIAL STUDIES

You may have seen these signs.
Do you know what they mean?

A

B

C

D

Read the clues. Write the letter that matches.

1. I am a circle.
   I mark train tracks.
   When you see me,
   you slow down and
   look both ways.
   What letter am I?

   ____

2. I am a square.
   You look for me
   when you are on
   your bike.
   I mark a safe place
   to ride.
   What letter am I?

   ____

3. I have **3** circles.
   They are lights.
   The red light means
   "Stop."
   What letter am I?

   ____

4. I am a square.
   You see me in
   parking lots.
   I am there to
   help people.
   What letter am I?

   ____

Enrichment

One half of **4**
is **2**

One third of **9**
is **3**

One fourth of
4 is **1**

Color one half.

1.

2.

3.

4.

Color one third.

5.

6.
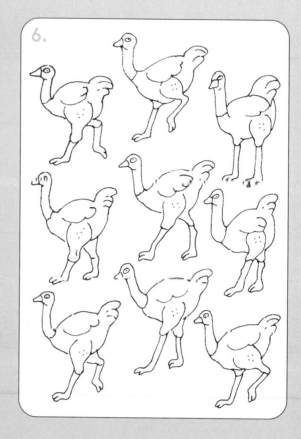

Color one fourth.

7.
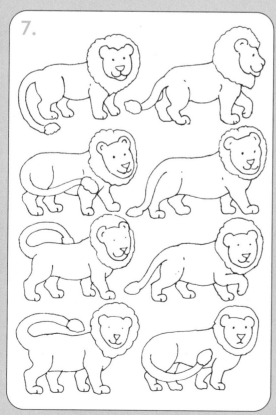

8.
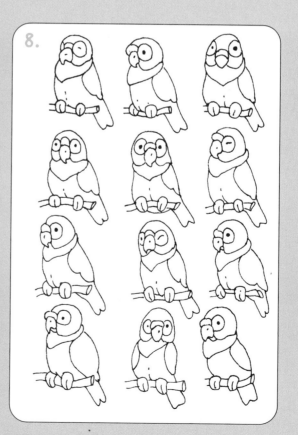

Enrichment: Fractions and Sets

CUMULATIVE REVIEW

Fill in the ⬭ for the correct answer.

What is the amount?

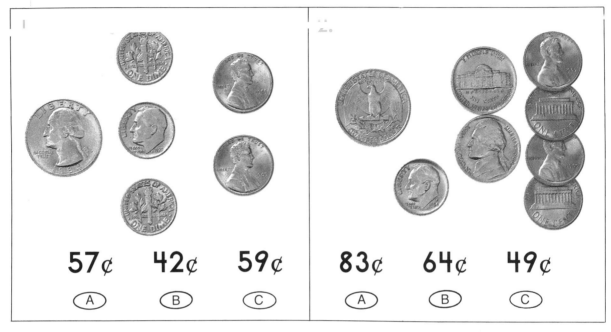

1.			2.		
57¢	42¢	59¢	83¢	64¢	49¢
(A)	(B)	(C)	(A)	(B)	(C)

What time is it?

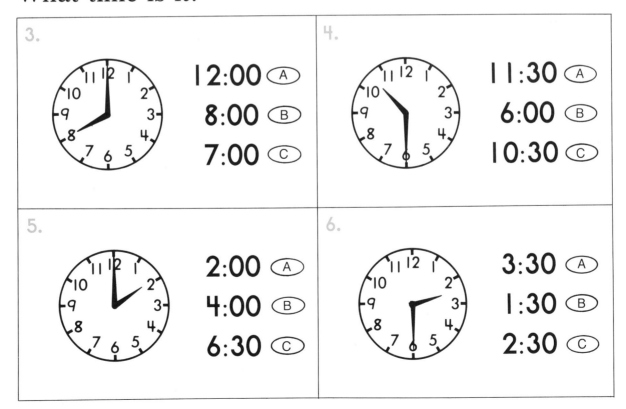

3.
12:00 (A)
8:00 (B)
7:00 (C)

4.
11:30 (A)
6:00 (B)
10:30 (C)

5.
2:00 (A)
4:00 (B)
6:30 (C)

6.
3:30 (A)
1:30 (B)
2:30 (C)

How much?

7. Bill has **35¢**. He saved **23¢** more. How much does he have in all?	8. Janet has **87¢**. She lost **52¢**. How much does she have now?
48¢ **63¢** **58¢** Ⓐ Ⓑ Ⓒ	**28¢** **35¢** **47¢** Ⓐ Ⓑ Ⓒ

LANGUAGE and VOCABULARY REVIEW

Write the word.

ruler   scale   cup

1. Tom used a _____ to find how long.

2. Alan weighed lemons on a _____.

3. Lee used a _____ to fill a pint.

4. A _____ can show how many inches.

5. A _____ can show how many pounds.

        Language and Vocabulary Review

Read with the children:

How many children are getting on the bus? If there are **6** more children already on the bus, how many children are there in all?

13

ADDITION AND SUBTRACTION FACTS THROUGH 18

ADDING THROUGH 15

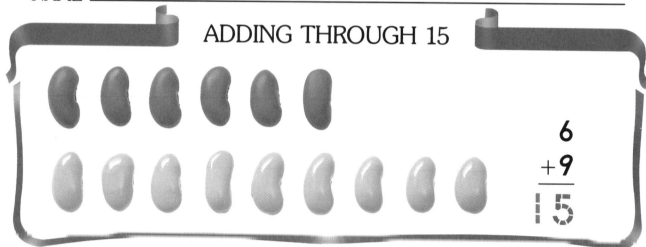

$$\begin{array}{r} 6 \\ +9 \\ \hline 15 \end{array}$$

Add.

1.
$$\begin{array}{r} 8 \\ +7 \\ \hline \end{array}$$

2.
$$\begin{array}{r} 5 \\ +8 \\ \hline \end{array}$$

3.
$$\begin{array}{r} 6 \\ +8 \\ \hline \end{array}$$

4.
$$\begin{array}{r} 7 \\ +6 \\ \hline \end{array}$$

5.
$$\begin{array}{r} 7 \\ +7 \\ \hline \end{array} \qquad \begin{array}{r} 9 \\ +6 \\ \hline \end{array} \qquad \begin{array}{r} 8 \\ +6 \\ \hline \end{array} \qquad \begin{array}{r} 7 \\ +8 \\ \hline \end{array} \qquad \begin{array}{r} 9 \\ +4 \\ \hline \end{array} \qquad \begin{array}{r} 5 \\ +9 \\ \hline \end{array}$$

6.
$$\begin{array}{r} 4 \\ +9 \\ \hline \end{array} \qquad \begin{array}{r} 6 \\ +7 \\ \hline \end{array} \qquad \begin{array}{r} 9 \\ +5 \\ \hline \end{array} \qquad \begin{array}{r} 8 \\ +5 \\ \hline \end{array} \qquad \begin{array}{r} 6 \\ +9 \\ \hline \end{array} \qquad \begin{array}{r} 8 \\ +6 \\ \hline \end{array}$$

Addition Facts through 15

ADDING THROUGH 18

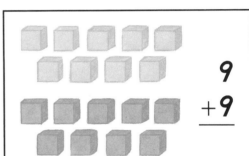

$$\begin{array}{r} 9 \\ +7 \\ \hline 16 \end{array}$$

Add.

1.

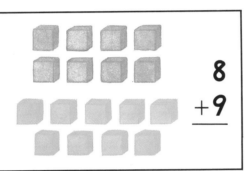

$$\begin{array}{r} 8 \\ +9 \\ \hline \end{array}$$

2.

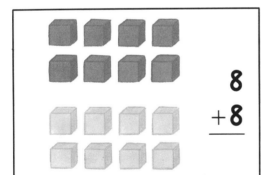

$$\begin{array}{r} 9 \\ +9 \\ \hline \end{array}$$

3.

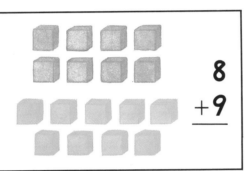

$$\begin{array}{r} 8 \\ +8 \\ \hline \end{array}$$

4.

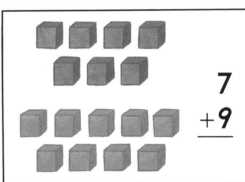

$$\begin{array}{r} 7 \\ +9 \\ \hline \end{array}$$

5.

| $\begin{array}{r} 7 \\ +9 \\ \hline \end{array}$ | $\begin{array}{r} 8 \\ +9 \\ \hline \end{array}$ | $\begin{array}{r} 9 \\ +9 \\ \hline \end{array}$ | $\begin{array}{r} 9 \\ +8 \\ \hline \end{array}$ | $\begin{array}{r} 8 \\ +8 \\ \hline \end{array}$ | $\begin{array}{r} 7 \\ +8 \\ \hline \end{array}$ |

6.

| $\begin{array}{r} 7 \\ +7 \\ \hline \end{array}$ | $\begin{array}{r} 8 \\ +7 \\ \hline \end{array}$ | $\begin{array}{r} 9 \\ +7 \\ \hline \end{array}$ | $\begin{array}{r} 5 \\ +8 \\ \hline \end{array}$ | $\begin{array}{r} 6 \\ +8 \\ \hline \end{array}$ | $\begin{array}{r} 7 \\ +8 \\ \hline \end{array}$ |

Add.

7.
   5   7   8   9   6   7
  +9   +8   +6   +9   +7   +7

8.
   6   8   9   9   6   7
  +9   +7   +5   +7   +8   +6

9.
   4   9   4   7   8   6
  +9   +6   +8   +5   +9   +4

10.
   5   9   6   8   7   9
  +8   +4   +6   +5   +9   +8

11.
   4   8   7   3   9   7
  +9   +8   +9   +8   +6   +8

6 + 6

  6
+6
12

6 + 7 is one more.

  6
+7
13

Add.

12. 8   8   13. 7   7   14. 5   5
    +8   +9   +7   +8   +5   +6

Addition Facts through 18

PROBLEM SOLVING

Ryan bought **4** tickets.
Paul bought **5** tickets.
Ann bought **3** tickets.
Together they bought

12 tickets.

Solve.

1. Melanie had **3** rides on the slide.
Sue had **4** rides.
John had **6** rides.
Together they had

_____ rides.

2. Jamie won **5** animals.
Matthew won **3** boats.
Jeanne won **4** clowns.
Together they won

_____ prizes.

3. There are **4** red cars.
There are **3** yellow cars.
There are **7** green cars.
Together there are

_____ cars.

Solve.

4. Jack sold **6** cups of juice.
Andrea sold **3** cups of juice.
Penny sold **9** cups of juice.
Together they sold

_____ cups of juice.

5. Luis won **2** blue ribbons.
Susan won **3** blue ribbons.
Will won **5** blue ribbons.
Together they won

_____ blue ribbons.

6. The Andersons showed
2 cows, **4** goats,
and **7** lambs.
Together they showed

_____ animals.

7. Terry saw **6** white horses.
Tom saw **3** black horses.
Raoul saw **7** brown horses.
Together they saw

_____ horses.

Problem Solving

SUBTRACTING FROM 15

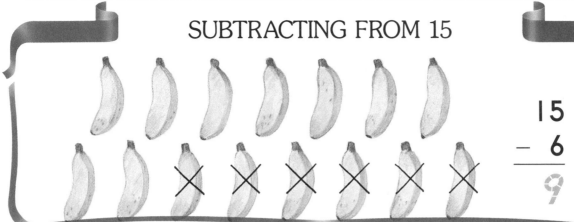

$$
\begin{array}{r}
15 \\
-\ 6 \\
\hline
9
\end{array}
$$

Subtract.

1.
$$
\begin{array}{r}
14 \\
-\ 7 \\
\hline
\end{array}
$$

2.
$$
\begin{array}{r}
13 \\
-\ 4 \\
\hline
\end{array}
$$

3.
$$
\begin{array}{r}
15 \\
-\ 7 \\
\hline
\end{array}
$$

4.
$$
\begin{array}{r}
14 \\
-\ 9 \\
\hline
\end{array}
$$

5.
$$
\begin{array}{r}
15 \\
-\ 9 \\
\hline
\end{array}
\qquad
\begin{array}{r}
15 \\
-\ 8 \\
\hline
\end{array}
\qquad
\begin{array}{r}
15 \\
-\ 7 \\
\hline
\end{array}
\qquad
\begin{array}{r}
14 \\
-\ 6 \\
\hline
\end{array}
\qquad
\begin{array}{r}
14 \\
-\ 7 \\
\hline
\end{array}
\qquad
\begin{array}{r}
14 \\
-\ 8 \\
\hline
\end{array}
$$

6.
$$
\begin{array}{r}
13 \\
-\ 4 \\
\hline
\end{array}
\qquad
\begin{array}{r}
13 \\
-\ 5 \\
\hline
\end{array}
\qquad
\begin{array}{r}
13 \\
-\ 6 \\
\hline
\end{array}
\qquad
\begin{array}{r}
15 \\
-\ 9 \\
\hline
\end{array}
\qquad
\begin{array}{r}
15 \\
-\ 8 \\
\hline
\end{array}
\qquad
\begin{array}{r}
15 \\
-7 \\
\hline
\end{array}
$$

Subtract.

7.
$$15 - 6$$ $$14 - 5$$ $$13 - 4$$ $$12 - 8$$ $$13 - 7$$ $$10 - 8$$

8.
$$14 - 9$$ $$13 - 8$$ $$11 - 9$$ $$10 - 5$$ $$13 - 6$$ $$15 - 8$$

9.
$$15 - 7$$ $$12 - 7$$ $$14 - 6$$ $$13 - 5$$ $$11 - 9$$ $$10 - 7$$

10.
$$12 - 8$$ $$13 - 9$$ $$14 - 8$$ $$12 - 6$$ $$14 - 7$$ $$15 - 9$$

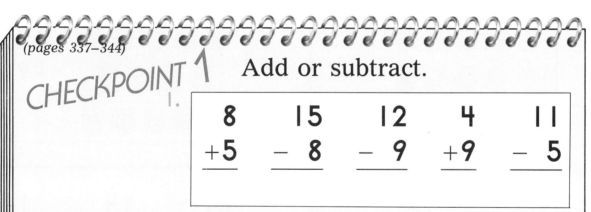

(pages 337–344)

CHECKPOINT 1

Add or subtract.

1.
$$8 + 5$$ $$15 - 8$$ $$12 - 9$$ $$4 + 9$$ $$11 - 5$$

Solve.

2. Jessica picked **4** red,
5 yellow, and **3** orange flowers.

She picked ☐ flowers in all.

Extra practice on page 383

Subtraction Facts through 15

SUBTRACTING FROM 18

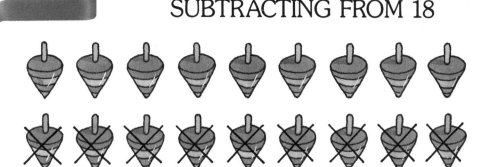

$$\begin{array}{r} 18 \\ -\ 9 \\ \hline 9 \end{array}$$

Subtract.

1.
$$\begin{array}{r} 17 \\ -\ 8 \\ \hline \end{array}$$

2.
$$\begin{array}{r} 16 \\ -\ 9 \\ \hline \end{array}$$

3.
$$\begin{array}{r} 18 \\ -\ 9 \\ \hline \end{array}$$

4.
$$\begin{array}{r} 16 \\ -\ 8 \\ \hline \end{array}$$

5.
$$\begin{array}{r} 17 \\ -\ 9 \\ \hline \end{array} \qquad \begin{array}{r} 16 \\ -\ 9 \\ \hline \end{array} \qquad \begin{array}{r} 15 \\ -\ 9 \\ \hline \end{array} \qquad \begin{array}{r} 15 \\ -\ 8 \\ \hline \end{array} \qquad \begin{array}{r} 16 \\ -\ 8 \\ \hline \end{array} \qquad \begin{array}{r} 17 \\ -\ 8 \\ \hline \end{array}$$

6.
$$\begin{array}{r} 16 \\ -\ 9 \\ \hline \end{array} \qquad \begin{array}{r} 17 \\ -\ 9 \\ \hline \end{array} \qquad \begin{array}{r} 18 \\ -\ 9 \\ \hline \end{array} \qquad \begin{array}{r} 16 \\ -\ 7 \\ \hline \end{array} \qquad \begin{array}{r} 16 \\ -\ 8 \\ \hline \end{array} \qquad \begin{array}{r} 16 \\ -9 \\ \hline \end{array}$$

7. Subtract.
Color.   6 ■   7 ■   8 ■   9 ■

14 − 6

17 − 8

17 − 9

15 − 9

16 − 7

15 − 6

15 − 7

18 − 9

16 − 7

14 − 7

16 − 9

17 − 8

15 − 8

16 − 8

14 − 8

14 − 5

☆ Write the missing number.

8.

5	8	□	6	□	□
+ □	+ □	+ 7	+ □	+ 9	+ 7
11	14	13	15	12	16

Subtraction Facts through 18

FACT FAMILIES

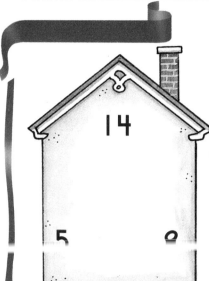

14

5   **9**

If you know $5 + 9 = \underline{14}$

Then you know $14 - 5 = \underline{9}$

$9 + 5 = \underline{14}$

$14 - 9 = \underline{5}$

Add or subtract.

1.   **7**   **15**   **8**

$7 + 8 = \underline{\hspace{1cm}}$

$15 - 8 = \underline{\hspace{1cm}}$

$8 + 7 = \underline{\hspace{1cm}}$

$15 - 7 = \underline{\hspace{1cm}}$

2.   **6**   **13**   **7**

$6 + 7 = \underline{\hspace{1cm}}$

$13 - 7 = \underline{\hspace{1cm}}$

$7 + 6 = \underline{\hspace{1cm}}$

$13 - 6 = \underline{\hspace{1cm}}$

3.   **6**   **14**   **8**

$6 + 8 = \underline{\hspace{1cm}}$

$14 - 8 = \underline{\hspace{1cm}}$

$8 + 6 = \underline{\hspace{1cm}}$

$14 - 6 = \underline{\hspace{1cm}}$

4.   **6**   **15**   **9**

$6 + 9 = \underline{\hspace{1cm}}$

$15 - 9 = \underline{\hspace{1cm}}$

$9 + 6 = \underline{\hspace{1cm}}$

$15 - 6 = \underline{\hspace{1cm}}$

Add or subtract.

5.

13
5   8

5 + 8 = _____

13 − 8 = _____

8 + 5 = _____

13 − 5 = _____

6.
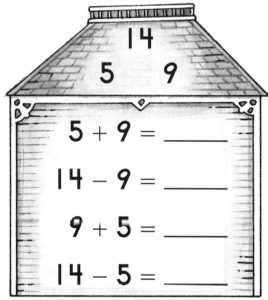

14
5   9

5 + 9 = _____

14 − 9 = _____

9 + 5 = _____

14 − 5 = _____

7.

13
4   9

4 + 9 = _____

13 − 9 = _____

9 + 4 = _____

13 − 4 = _____

8.

12
4   8

4 + 8 = _____

12 − 8 = _____

8 + 4 = _____

12 − 4 = _____

Add or subtract.

9. Mike had 14 balloons. He sold 8.

How many does he have left? _____ balloons

10. Janet walked 8 blocks to the store.
Then she walked 7 blocks to the park.

How many blocks did she walk? _____ blocks

Fact Families through 15

FACT FAMILIES

9   8   17

$$8 + 9 = 17 \qquad 17 - 9 = 8$$
$$9 + 8 = 17 \qquad 17 - 8 = 9$$

Complete the fact families. Then add or subtract.

1.
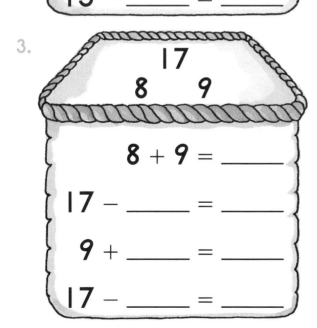

15
7   8

$7 + 8 = \underline{\hspace{1cm}}$

$15 - \underline{\hspace{1cm}} = \underline{\hspace{1cm}}$

$8 + \underline{\hspace{1cm}} = \underline{\hspace{1cm}}$

$15 - \underline{\hspace{1cm}} = \underline{\hspace{1cm}}$

2.
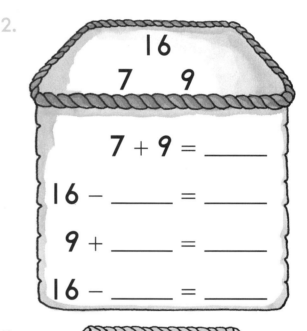

16
7   9

$7 + 9 = \underline{\hspace{1cm}}$

$16 - \underline{\hspace{1cm}} = \underline{\hspace{1cm}}$

$9 + \underline{\hspace{1cm}} = \underline{\hspace{1cm}}$

$16 - \underline{\hspace{1cm}} = \underline{\hspace{1cm}}$

3.

17
8   9

$8 + 9 = \underline{\hspace{1cm}}$

$17 - \underline{\hspace{1cm}} = \underline{\hspace{1cm}}$

$9 + \underline{\hspace{1cm}} = \underline{\hspace{1cm}}$

$17 - \underline{\hspace{1cm}} = \underline{\hspace{1cm}}$

4.

15
6   9

$6 + 9 = \underline{\hspace{1cm}}$

$15 - \underline{\hspace{1cm}} = \underline{\hspace{1cm}}$

$9 + \underline{\hspace{1cm}} = \underline{\hspace{1cm}}$

$15 - \underline{\hspace{1cm}} = \underline{\hspace{1cm}}$

Complete the fact families. Then add or subtract.

5. **7   16   9**

$7 + 9 =$ _____

$16 -$ _____ $=$ _____

$9 +$ _____ $=$ _____

$16 -$ _____ $=$ _____

6. **6   13   7**

$6 + 7 =$ _____

$13 -$ _____ $=$ _____

$7 +$ _____ $=$ _____

$13 -$ _____ $=$ _____

7. **7   15   8**

$7 + 8 =$ _____

$15 -$ _____ $=$ _____

$8 +$ _____ $=$ _____

$15 -$ _____ $=$ _____

8. **8   17   9**

$8 + 9 =$ _____

$17 -$ _____ $=$ _____

$9 +$ _____ $=$ _____

$17 -$ _____ $=$ _____

6 + 6

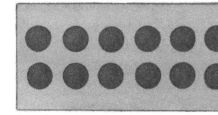

$$\begin{array}{r} 6 \\ +6 \\ \hline 12 \end{array}$$

6 + 5 is one less.

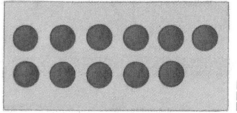

$$\begin{array}{r} 6 \\ +5 \\ \hline 11 \end{array}$$

Add.

9. $\begin{array}{r} 8 \\ +8 \\ \hline \end{array}$ $\begin{array}{r} 8 \\ +7 \\ \hline \end{array}$

10. $\begin{array}{r} 7 \\ +7 \\ \hline \end{array}$ $\begin{array}{r} 7 \\ +6 \\ \hline \end{array}$

11. $\begin{array}{r} 9 \\ +9 \\ \hline \end{array}$ $\begin{array}{r} 9 \\ +8 \\ \hline \end{array}$

Fact Families through 18

PROBLEM SOLVING

Write the numbers. Then add or subtract.

1. Nancy spends **8**¢ for a top.

   Anna spends **6**¢ for a doll.

   Together they spend ___14¢___.

   $$\begin{array}{r} 8¢ \\ +6¢ \\ \hline 14¢ \end{array}$$

2. Michael has **13**¢.
   He spends **6**¢ for a ball.

   How much does he have left? _____

3. Elizabeth spends **3**¢ for a book.
   She spends **9**¢ for a truck.

   How much does she spend? _____

4. Lindsay has **18**¢.
   He spends **9**¢ for a pencil.

   How much does he have now? _____

Write the numbers. Then add or subtract.

5. Robert buys three items. He spends
6¢ for a pencil, 3¢ for a pen,
and 7¢ for an eraser.

How much does he spend in all? _____

6. Christie has 12¢.
She spends 6¢ for a car.

How much does she have left? _____

7. Simon spends 8¢ for a jack-in-the-box.
Luke spends 8¢ for a stuffed animal.

Together they spend _____.

(pages 345–352)

CHECKPOINT 2

Subtract.

16	15	17	15	18
− 8	− 7	− 9	− 6	− 9

Solve.

2. Jason bought a notebook for 9¢
and a pencil for 6¢.
How much were both items?

Extra practice on page 383

Problem Solving

CHAPTER 13 TEST

Add.

1.
```
  7        6        8        5        9        7
 +6       +6       +7       +6       +4       +5
 ___      ___      ___      ___      ___      ___
```

Write the number.

2. Cindy won **3** red ribbons, **7** blue ribbons, and **4** yellow ribbons.

   How many ribbons did she win in all?

   _____ ribbons

Subtract.

3.
```
  14       16       15       12       13       17
 - 6      - 9      - 6      - 4      - 7      - 9
 ___      ___      ___      ___      ___      ___
```

Write the numbers. Then add or subtract.

4. Joe spent **8¢** for a ball.

   Lydia spent **6¢** for a bucket.

   How much did they spend together?

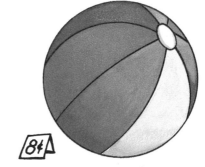

Extra practice on page 384

MATHEMATICS and PHYSICAL EDUCATION

The graph shows how many each first grade class won.

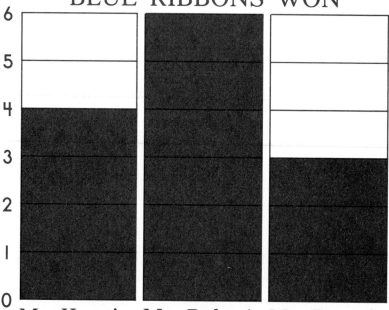

BLUE RIBBONS WON

Mr. Kane's class   Ms. Baker's class   Ms. Perez's class

1. How many did each class win?

Mr. Kane's ____ Ms. Baker's ____ Ms. Perez's ____

2. Ring the class that won the most .

   Mr. Kane's   Ms. Baker's   Ms. Perez's

3. How many ribbons
   did the classes win in all? ____

Enrichment

Write the number.

1.

2 + 2 = _____

2 groups of 2 = _____

2.

2 + 2 + 2 = _____

3 groups of 2 = _____

3.

3 + 3 = _____

2 groups of 3 = _____

4.

3 + 3 + 3 = _____

3 groups of 3 = _____

5.

4 + 4 = _____

2 groups of 4 = _____

6.

4 + 4 + 4 = _____

3 groups of 4 = _____

Write the number.

7.

$2 + 2 + 2 + 2 = $ _____

4 groups of $2 = $ _____

8.

$3 + 3 + 3 + 3 = $ _____

4 groups of $3 = $ _____

9.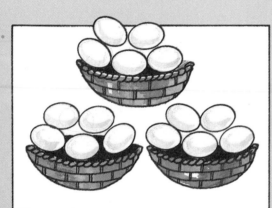

$5 + 5 + 5 = $ _____

3 groups of $5 = $ _____

10.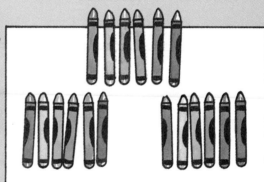

$6 + 6 + 6 = $ _____

3 groups of $6 = $ _____

11.

$3 + 3 + 3 + 3 + 3 = $ _____

5 groups of $3 = $ _____

Enrichment: Multiplication Readiness

NAME _____

 CUMULATIVE REVIEW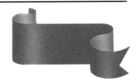

Fill in the ○ for the correct answer.

Add or subtract.

1.   84¢
  −33¢
	2. 13¢
	  +43¢
		3. 35¢
		  +22¢

48¢ 31¢ 37¢ ⓐ Ⓑ Ⓒ	56¢ 50¢ 46¢ ⓐ Ⓑ Ⓒ	33¢ 57¢ 48¢ ⓐ Ⓑ Ⓒ

How much?

4. Tom had **50¢**. He saved **26¢** more. How much does he have now? **78¢** **76¢** **34¢** ⓐ Ⓑ Ⓒ	5. Susan had **96¢**. She spent **73¢**. How much does she have left? **23¢** **59¢** **29¢** ⓐ Ⓑ Ⓒ

Which is the square?   Which is the cylinder?

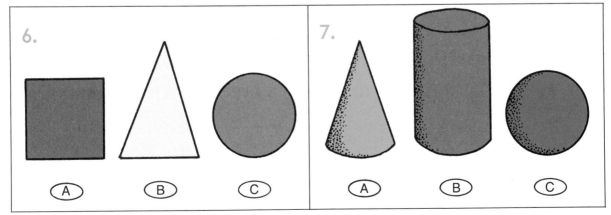

6. ⓐ   Ⓑ   Ⓒ   7. ⓐ   Ⓑ   Ⓒ

Which shows the shaded part?

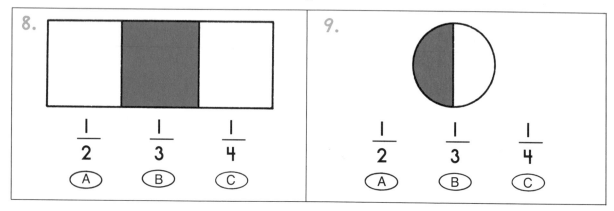

8.

$\frac{1}{2}$ (A) $\frac{1}{3}$ (B) $\frac{1}{4}$ (C)

9.

$\frac{1}{2}$ (A) $\frac{1}{3}$ (B) $\frac{1}{4}$ (C)

LANGUAGE and VOCABULARY REVIEW

Solve the riddle.
Write the word.

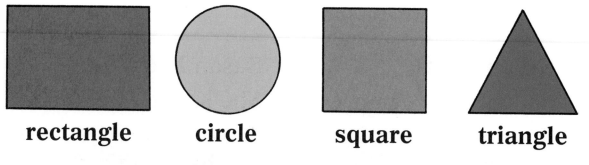

rectangle **circle** **square** **triangle**

1. I have four sides.
Each side is the
same length.

2. I have three sides.

_____

3. I have no sides.
I am a round shape.

4. I have four sides.
Two of the sides
are longer than
the other two.

_____

Language and Vocabulary Review

EXTRA PRACTICE

FOR USE AFTER CHECKPOINT 1

Write the number.

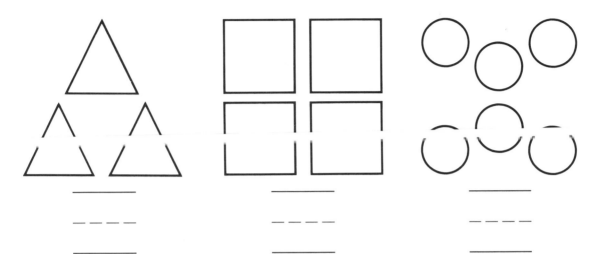

_____

- - - - -

_____

_____

- - - - -

_____

_____

- - - - -

_____

FOR USE AFTER CHECKPOINT 2

Write the number.

1.

_____ ¢

2.

_____ ¢

3.

1									10

Ring the .   ✓ the .

4.

Ring the number.

1.

   6 7 8   7 8 9   5 6 7

Write the number.

2.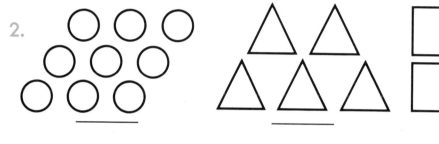

_____   _____   _____

_ _ _ _   _ _ _ _   _ _ _ _

_____   _____   _____

3.   4.

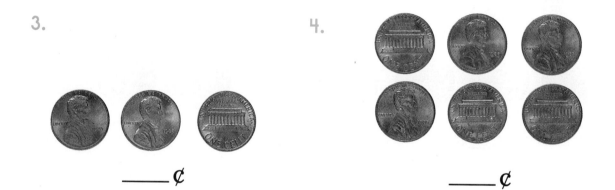

    ___ ¢   ___ ¢

5.

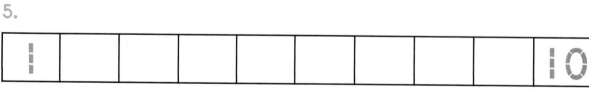

Ring the ⚾ .   ✔ the 🏏 .

6.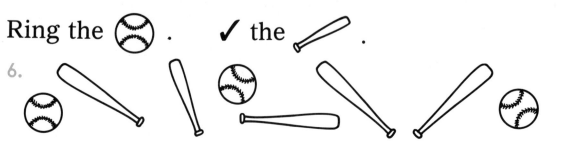

Chapter 1 Extra Practice

EXTRA PRACTICE

FOR USE AFTER CHECKPOINT 1

Add.

1. $2 + 1 =$ _____ $3 + 2 =$ _____ $4 + 2 =$ _____

2. $3 + 2 =$ _____ $4 + 3 =$ _____ $2 + 3 =$ _____

3. $2 + 2 =$ _____ $1 + 1 =$ _____ $5 + 2 =$ _____

4. $6 + 1 =$ _____ $5 + 1 =$ _____ $4 + 1 =$ _____

FOR USE AFTER CHECKPOINT 2

Add.

1.
$$\begin{array}{cc} 3 \\ +1 \\ \hline \end{array} \qquad \begin{array}{cc} 4 \\ +0 \\ \hline \end{array} \qquad \begin{array}{cc} 5 \\ +2 \\ \hline \end{array} \qquad \begin{array}{cc} 2 \\ +4 \\ \hline \end{array} \qquad \begin{array}{cc} 3 \\ +0 \\ \hline \end{array} \qquad \begin{array}{cc} 1 \\ +5 \\ \hline \end{array}$$

2. $0 + 3 =$ _____ $1 + 3 =$ _____ $2 + 0 =$ _____

3. $3 + 4 =$ _____ $3 + 2 =$ _____ $6 + 0 =$ _____

Write the number.

4.

_____ + _____ = _____ in all

Add.

1. $1 + 3 = \underline{\quad}$ $2 + 0 = \underline{\quad}$ $2 + 4 = \underline{\quad}$

2. $3 + 2 = \underline{\quad}$ $5 + 1 = \underline{\quad}$ $1 + 1 = \underline{\quad}$

3. $6 + 0 = \underline{\quad}$ $4 + 1 = \underline{\quad}$ $3 + 3 = \underline{\quad}$

4.
$$\begin{array}{cc} 5 \\ +0 \\ \hline \end{array} \quad \begin{array}{cc} 2 \\ +2 \\ \hline \end{array} \quad \begin{array}{cc} 1 \\ +2 \\ \hline \end{array} \quad \begin{array}{cc} 3 \\ +3 \\ \hline \end{array} \quad \begin{array}{cc} 1 \\ +5 \\ \hline \end{array} \quad \begin{array}{cc} 0 \\ +1 \\ \hline \end{array}$$

5.
$$\begin{array}{cc} 2 \\ +3 \\ \hline \end{array} \quad \begin{array}{cc} 4 \\ +0 \\ \hline \end{array} \quad \begin{array}{cc} 5 \\ +1 \\ \hline \end{array} \quad \begin{array}{cc} 2 \\ +1 \\ \hline \end{array} \quad \begin{array}{cc} 2 \\ +3 \\ \hline \end{array} \quad \begin{array}{cc} 4 \\ +2 \\ \hline \end{array}$$

6.
$$\begin{array}{cc} 6 \\ +0 \\ \hline \end{array} \quad \begin{array}{cc} 1 \\ +1 \\ \hline \end{array} \quad \begin{array}{cc} 4 \\ +1 \\ \hline \end{array} \quad \begin{array}{cc} 3 \\ +2 \\ \hline \end{array} \quad \begin{array}{cc} 5 \\ +0 \\ \hline \end{array} \quad \begin{array}{cc} 2 \\ +4 \\ \hline \end{array}$$

Write the number.

7.

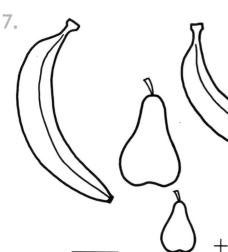

$\underline{\quad}$ $+ \underline{\quad}$ $= \underline{\quad}$ in all

Chapter 2 Extra Practice

EXTRA PRACTICE

CHAPTER 3

Add.

1. $5 + 4 =$ ____ $6 + 2 =$ ____ $3 + 6 =$ ____

2. $4 + 3 =$ ____ $7 + 1 =$ ____ $2 + 7 =$ ____

3.
$$\begin{array}{cc} 3 \\ +5 \\ \hline \end{array} \quad \begin{array}{cc} 4 \\ +4 \\ \hline \end{array} \quad \begin{array}{cc} 3 \\ +2 \\ \hline \end{array} \quad \begin{array}{cc} 9 \\ +0 \\ \hline \end{array} \quad \begin{array}{cc} 5 \\ +3 \\ \hline \end{array} \quad \begin{array}{cc} 0 \\ +8 \\ \hline \end{array}$$

Add.

1. $3 + 5 =$ ____ $3 + 7 =$ ____ $8 + 0 =$ ____

2.
$$\begin{array}{cc} 4 \\ +6 \\ \hline \end{array} \quad \begin{array}{cc} 1 \\ +8 \\ \hline \end{array} \quad \begin{array}{cc} 9 \\ +0 \\ \hline \end{array} \quad \begin{array}{cc} 5 \\ +5 \\ \hline \end{array} \quad \begin{array}{cc} 3 \\ +5 \\ \hline \end{array} \quad \begin{array}{cc} 7 \\ +3 \\ \hline \end{array}$$

3.
$$\begin{array}{cc} 6 \\ 1 \\ +2 \\ \hline \end{array} \quad \begin{array}{cc} 1 \\ 3 \\ +4 \\ \hline \end{array} \quad \begin{array}{cc} 5 \\ 0 \\ +2 \\ \hline \end{array} \quad \begin{array}{cc} 1 \\ 7 \\ +2 \\ \hline \end{array} \quad \begin{array}{cc} 5 \\ 1 \\ +4 \\ \hline \end{array} \quad \begin{array}{cc} 5 \\ 1 \\ +3 \\ \hline \end{array}$$

How much in all? Write the numbers.

4.

____¢

+ ____¢

____¢

Add.

1. $4 + 3 =$ ___ $6 + 0 =$ ___ $3 + 2 =$ ___

2. $4 + 4 =$ ___ $5 + 4 =$ ___ $3 + 7 =$ ___

3.
$$\begin{array}{r} 4 \\ +5 \\ \hline \end{array} \qquad \begin{array}{r} 1 \\ 7 \\ \hline \end{array} \qquad \begin{array}{r} 8 \\ +2 \\ \hline \end{array} \qquad \begin{array}{r} 3 \\ 7 \\ \hline \end{array} \qquad \begin{array}{r} 4 \\ +4 \\ \hline \end{array} \qquad \begin{array}{r} 2 \\ +5 \\ \hline \end{array}$$

4.
$$\begin{array}{r} 1 \\ +9 \\ \hline \end{array} \qquad \begin{array}{r} 6 \\ +3 \\ \hline \end{array} \qquad \begin{array}{r} 2 \\ +6 \\ \hline \end{array} \qquad \begin{array}{r} 9 \\ +0 \\ \hline \end{array} \qquad \begin{array}{r} 9 \\ +1 \\ \hline \end{array} \qquad \begin{array}{r} 6 \\ +4 \\ \hline \end{array}$$

5.
$$\begin{array}{r} 4 \\ 1 \\ +5 \\ \hline \end{array} \qquad \begin{array}{r} 2 \\ 6 \\ +2 \\ \hline \end{array} \qquad \begin{array}{r} 3 \\ 1 \\ +2 \\ \hline \end{array} \qquad \begin{array}{r} 1 \\ 8 \\ +1 \\ \hline \end{array} \qquad \begin{array}{r} 3 \\ 4 \\ +2 \\ \hline \end{array} \qquad \begin{array}{r} 3 \\ 3 \\ +2 \\ \hline \end{array}$$

How much in all? Write the numbers.

6.

7.

___ ¢

+___ ¢

___ ¢

___ ¢

+___ ¢

___ ¢

EXTRA PRACTICE   CHAPTER 4

Subtract.

1. 4 – 2 = ____   6 – 3 = ____   2 – 1 = ____

2. 5 – 2 = ____   4 – 3 = ____   2 – 2 = ____

3. 3 – 2 = ____   6 – 3 = ____   3 – 1 = ____

4. 7 – 4 = ____   4 – 1 = ____   5 – 3 = ____

Subtract.

1.
4	6	5	4	7	5
−4	−1	−3	−1	−2	−0

2.
6	7	3	6	4	7
−5	−0	−3	−2	−0	−4

Write + or − in the ☐.
Then add or subtract.

 3.

How many are left?

7 ☐ 2 = ____

Subtract.

1. 3 – 2 = ___   5 – 4 = ___   7 – 4 = ___

2. 4 – 1 = ___   1 – 0 = ___   6 – 6 = ___

3. 6 – 0 = ___   5 – 1 = ___   7 – 2 = ___

4.
$$\begin{array}{cc} 3 \\ -1 \\ \hline \end{array} \quad \begin{array}{c} 5 \\ -3 \\ \hline \end{array} \quad \begin{array}{c} 6 \\ -3 \\ \hline \end{array} \quad \begin{array}{c} 7 \\ -0 \\ \hline \end{array} \quad \begin{array}{c} 7 \\ -1 \\ \hline \end{array} \quad \begin{array}{c} 3 \\ -2 \\ \hline \end{array}$$

5.
$$\begin{array}{c} 6 \\ -4 \\ \hline \end{array} \quad \begin{array}{c} 5 \\ -5 \\ \hline \end{array} \quad \begin{array}{c} 2 \\ -0 \\ \hline \end{array} \quad \begin{array}{c} 6 \\ -1 \\ \hline \end{array} \quad \begin{array}{c} 3 \\ -3 \\ \hline \end{array} \quad \begin{array}{c} 1 \\ -0 \\ \hline \end{array}$$

6.
$$\begin{array}{c} 4 \\ -2 \\ \hline \end{array} \quad \begin{array}{c} 6 \\ -5 \\ \hline \end{array} \quad \begin{array}{c} 5 \\ -2 \\ \hline \end{array} \quad \begin{array}{c} 3 \\ -0 \\ \hline \end{array} \quad \begin{array}{c} 2 \\ -1 \\ \hline \end{array} \quad \begin{array}{c} 4 \\ -3 \\ \hline \end{array}$$

Write + or – in the ☐.
Then add or subtract.

7.

How many in all?

5 ☐ 3 = ___

Chapter 4 Extra Practice

EXTRA PRACTICE   CHAPTER 5

Subtract.

1. $\begin{array}{r} 9 \\ -7 \\ \hline \end{array}$ $\begin{array}{r} 9 \\ -4 \\ \hline \end{array}$ $\begin{array}{r} 8 \\ -8 \\ \hline \end{array}$ $\begin{array}{r} 9 \\ -6 \\ \hline \end{array}$ $\begin{array}{r} 7 \\ -4 \\ \hline \end{array}$ $\begin{array}{r} 9 \\ -3 \\ \hline \end{array}$

2. $\begin{array}{r} 7 \\ -0 \\ \hline \end{array}$ $\begin{array}{r} 8 \\ -5 \\ \hline \end{array}$ $\begin{array}{r} 7 \\ -2 \\ \hline \end{array}$ $\begin{array}{r} 8 \\ -4 \\ \hline \end{array}$ $\begin{array}{r} 7 \\ -7 \\ \hline \end{array}$ $\begin{array}{r} 6 \\ -0 \\ \hline \end{array}$

Subtract.

1. $\begin{array}{r} 10 \\ -\ 4 \\ \hline \end{array}$ $\begin{array}{r} 9 \\ -1 \\ \hline \end{array}$ $\begin{array}{r} 10 \\ -\ 0 \\ \hline \end{array}$ $\begin{array}{r} 6 \\ -1 \\ \hline \end{array}$ $\begin{array}{r} 10 \\ -\ 3 \\ \hline \end{array}$ $\begin{array}{r} 10 \\ -\ 6 \\ \hline \end{array}$

2. $\begin{array}{r} 8 \\ -4 \\ \hline \end{array}$ $\begin{array}{r} 9 \\ -6 \\ \hline \end{array}$ $\begin{array}{r} 10 \\ -\ 9 \\ \hline \end{array}$ $\begin{array}{r} 8 \\ -2 \\ \hline \end{array}$ $\begin{array}{r} 10 \\ -\ 5 \\ \hline \end{array}$ $\begin{array}{r} 10 \\ -\ 7 \\ \hline \end{array}$

Write + or − in the ☐.
Then add or subtract.

3. Mary has **8**¢.
   She spends **2**¢.

   ¢

4. Ron has **6**¢.
   He saves **4**¢.

   ¢

Subtract.

1.
```
  9      10      9      8      10      7
 -3     - 7    -9    -0    - 1    -5
```

2.
```
  7      8      9     10     10      8
 -2     -3    -4    - 8    - 0    -6
```

3.
```
  8      9     10      8      9     10
 -5     -5    - 4    -7    -6    - 6
```

4.
```
  9     10     10      9     10     10
 -3    - 3    - 9    -7    - 5    - 2
```

Ring the correct example.

5.

$7 + 2$

$7 - 2$

$5 + 2$

6.

$5 - 3$

$8 - 3$

$5 + 3$

    Chapter 5 Extra Practice

FOR USE AFTER CHECKPOINT 1

Write the number.

1.
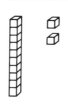

_____ ten _____ ones

_____

2.
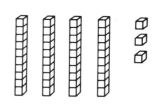

_____ tens _____ ones

_____

3.

32	33		35	

4.

78	79			82

FOR USE AFTER CHECKPOINT 2

Write the number.

FRUITS

0 1 2 3 4 5

1. _____

2. _____

Ring the third car.

3.

Ring the number that is greater.

4. **29**   5. **74**   6. **71**   7. **43**

    36   **68**   **83**   **42**

Write the number.

1. 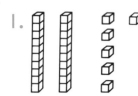   2. 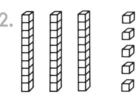   3.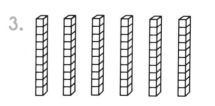

___ tens ___ ones   _____   _____

Write the missing numbers.

4.

22			26

5.

63			67

Write the number.

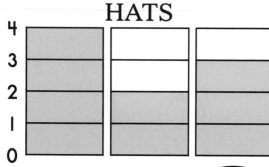

6. How many 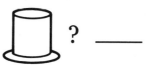 ? ____

7. How many ? ____

8. How many ? ____

Ring the number that is greater.

9. **44**   **41**   **25**   **30**   **86**   **79**

Ring the number that is less.

10. **16**   **19**   **37**   **40**   **93**   **57**

Ring the fourth letter.   11. A   B   C   D   E

Count by twos.   12. **2, 4,** ____, ____, ____

EXTRA PRACTICE   CHAPTER **7**

Count by fives.

1.

5	10				

Write the amount.

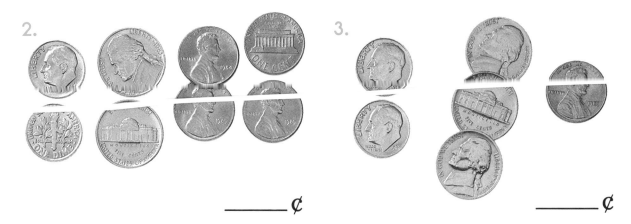

2.   3.

_____ ¢   _____ ¢

Write the amount.

1.

_____ ¢

2.

_____ ¢

3.

_____ ¢

4.

_____ ¢

Continue the number pattern.

5. **8, 10, 12,** _____, _____, _____, _____

6. **27, 37, 47,** _____, _____, _____, _____

Count by fives.

1. **5, 10, _____, _____**

2. **35, 40, _____, _____**

Write the amount.

3.

_____ ¢

4.

_____ ¢

5.

_____ ¢

6.

_____ ¢

7.

_____ ¢

8.

_____ ¢

Continue the number pattern.

9. **24, 26, 28, _____, _____, _____, 36**

10. **2, 5, 5, 2, 5, 5, 2, _____, _____, _____**

11. **45, 50, 55, _____, _____, _____**

     Chapter 7 Extra Practice

EXTRA PRACTICE   CHAPTER 8

FOR USE AFTER CHECKPOINT 1

What time is it?

_____ o'clock   _____ : _____   _____ o'clock

FOR USE AFTER CHECKPOINT 2

Solve.

1. Carlos went to play baseball at 1:00.
   He played for **3** hours.
   What time did he stop playing?   ____ o'clock

Ring the fourth month of the year.

2.   March   April   May

Write the time.

TIMES

	recess	lunch
Bill's class	10:00	12:00
Cathy's class	10:30	1:00

3. When does Bill's class
   have recess?   _____ : _____

4. When does Cathy's class
   have lunch?   _____ : _____

What time is it?

1.

_____ o'clock   _____ o'clock   _____ : _____

Solve.

2. Anne started reading at **7:00**.
   She read for **2** hours.
   What time did she finish?   _____ o'clock

Ring the day that comes just after.

3. Friday | Sunday   Thursday   Saturday

Ring the eighth month of the year.

4.   July   August   September

Solve.

THINGS WE COLLECTED

	Kim	Robert
shells	7	9
rocks	8	6

5. Who collected **7** shells? _____

6. Who collected **6** rocks? _____

EXTRA PRACTICE   CHAPTER 9

Add.

1.
$$\begin{array}{r} 4 \\ +7 \\ \hline \end{array} \qquad \begin{array}{r} 3 \\ +6 \\ \hline \end{array} \qquad \begin{array}{r} 2 \\ +9 \\ \hline \end{array} \qquad \begin{array}{r} 5 \\ +6 \\ \hline \end{array} \qquad \begin{array}{r} 3 \\ +7 \\ \hline \end{array} \qquad \begin{array}{r} 8 \\ +3 \\ \hline \end{array}$$

2.
$$\begin{array}{r} 5 \\ +5 \\ \hline \end{array} \qquad \begin{array}{r} 9 \\ +2 \\ \hline \end{array} \qquad \begin{array}{r} 6 \\ +4 \\ \hline \end{array} \qquad \begin{array}{r} 6 \\ +5 \\ \hline \end{array} \qquad \begin{array}{r} 9 \\ +3 \\ \hline \end{array} \qquad \begin{array}{r} 5 \\ +7 \\ \hline \end{array}$$

Draw as many more as needed.
Then write the answer.

1. Dina needs 10 jars. She has 5 jars.
   How many more does she need?

   ___ jars

Subtract.

2.
$$\begin{array}{r} 12 \\ - 6 \\ \hline \end{array} \qquad \begin{array}{r} 12 \\ - 4 \\ \hline \end{array} \qquad \begin{array}{r} 11 \\ - 4 \\ \hline \end{array} \qquad \begin{array}{r} 12 \\ - 7 \\ \hline \end{array} \qquad \begin{array}{r} 11 \\ - 2 \\ \hline \end{array} \qquad \begin{array}{r} 12 \\ - 3 \\ \hline \end{array}$$

Solve.

3. Bob has 7 blue ribbons.

   He wins 5 more.

   How many does he
   have now?

   blue ribbons

Add.

1.
7	5	7	3	3	2
+3	+5	+5	+8	+9	+9

Subtract.

2.
11	11	12	10	11	11
− 3	− 7	− 5	− 7	− 6	− 8

Draw as many more as needed.
Then write the answer.

3. Bob needs 10 stamps. He has 6 stamps.
   How many more does he need?

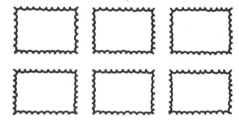

_____ stamps

Solve.

4. Joan has 12 eggs. She uses 7.
   How many are left?

eggs

EXTRA PRACTICE   CHAPTER 10

How long is it?

1.

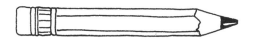

_____ centimeters

_____ centimeters

Ring the one that holds less than a liter.

2.

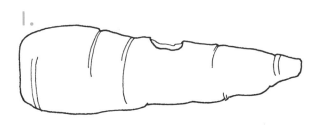

Write the number of kilograms.

3.

_____ kilograms

How long is it?

1.

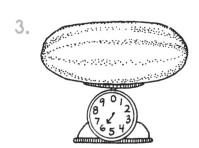

_____ inches

Color how many can be filled.

2.

Write the number of pounds.

3.

_____ pounds

How long?

1.

____ centimeters

2.

____ inches

How much?

3.

____ kilograms

4.

____ pounds

Write the number.

SHOES

5. How many ? ____

6. How many ? ____

7. How many ? ____

Ring the one that holds more than a liter.

8.

Color the number you can fill.

9.

EXTRA PRACTICE CHAPTER 11

FOR USE AFTER CHECKPOINT 1

Add.

1.
30	20	32	50	12	40
+10	+40	+64	+20	+82	+25

FOR USE AFTER CHECKPOINT 2

Subtract.

1.
80	57	86	79	68	29
−10	−22	−12	− 5	−15	− 3

Add or subtract.

2.
95¢	54¢	38¢	44¢	85¢
−24¢	+33¢	−26¢	+21¢	−41¢
¢	¢	¢	¢	¢

Write the numbers. Then add or subtract.

3. Bill wants to buy a car and a boat. How much are both?

4. Pat has **43¢**. She earned **35¢** more. How much does she have now?

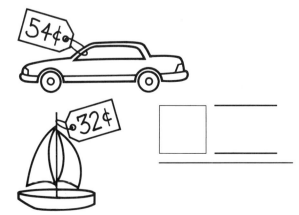

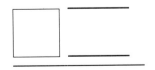

Add.

1.	70	17	43	51	44	26
	+20	+12	+46	+14	+ 4	+23

Subtract.

2.	80	98	76	67	99	82
	−70	−72	−55	− 6	−19	−41

Add or subtract.

3.	35¢	48¢	77¢	74¢	97¢
	+14¢	−26¢	+20¢	−31¢	−21¢

Write the numbers.
Then add or subtract.

4. Brian has **69**¢.
   He spends **47**¢.
   How much does
   he have left?

5. Ginny wants to buy
   an apple and
   an orange.
   How much are both?

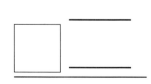

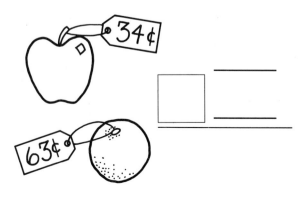

EXTRA PRACTICE   CHAPTER 12

Color the shapes.

1. cube

   cylinder

   cone

   sphere

2. triangle

   circle

   rectangle

   square

Write the number.

SHAPES

circle

square

0 1 2 3 4 5

3. How many circles? ____

4. How many squares? ____

Ring the shape.

1.

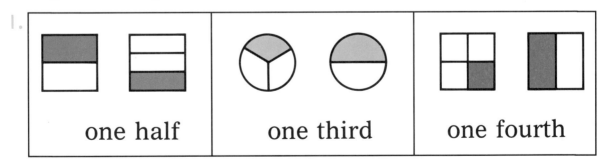

| one half | one third | one fourth |

Solve.

2. Tom has **6** more marbles than Bill.
   Bill has **4** marbles.
   How many marbles
   does Tom have?   ____ marbles

1. Ring the circle.
   ✓ the triangle.
   X the square.

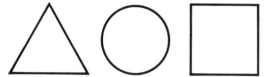

2. Ring the sphere.
   ✓ the cube.
   X the cone.

Write the number.

SHADES... SHAPES

triangle
rectangle

0 1 2 3 4 5

3. How many triangles? _____

4. How many rectangles? _____

Write the number of equal parts.

5.

___   ___   ___   ___

Ring the shape that shows one half.

Ring the shape that shows one third.

6.

7.

Solve.

8. John has an apple and an orange.
   His favorite is not the orange.
   What is his favorite? _____

Chapter 12 Extra Practice

EXTRA PRACTICE   CHAPTER 13

Add or subtract.

1.
$$\begin{array}{r} 9 \\ +5 \\ \hline \end{array} \qquad \begin{array}{r} 7 \\ +6 \\ \hline \end{array} \qquad \begin{array}{r} 8 \\ +7 \\ \hline \end{array} \qquad \begin{array}{r} 4 \\ +9 \\ \hline \end{array} \qquad \begin{array}{r} 6 \\ +8 \\ \hline \end{array} \qquad \begin{array}{r} 9 \\ +6 \\ \hline \end{array}$$

2.
$$\begin{array}{r} 14 \\ -8 \\ \hline \end{array} \qquad \begin{array}{r} 13 \\ -9 \\ \hline \end{array} \qquad \begin{array}{r} 15 \\ -9 \\ \hline \end{array} \qquad \begin{array}{r} 13 \\ -6 \\ \hline \end{array} \qquad \begin{array}{r} 14 \\ -8 \\ \hline \end{array} \qquad \begin{array}{r} 12 \\ -7 \\ \hline \end{array}$$

Solve.

3. Michael bought **3** red, **6** blue, and **5** yellow cars.
   How many did he have in all?   _____ cars

Subtract.

1.
$$\begin{array}{r} 14 \\ -9 \\ \hline \end{array} \qquad \begin{array}{r} 17 \\ -9 \\ \hline \end{array} \qquad \begin{array}{r} 16 \\ -8 \\ \hline \end{array} \qquad \begin{array}{r} 13 \\ -6 \\ \hline \end{array} \qquad \begin{array}{r} 16 \\ -9 \\ \hline \end{array} \qquad \begin{array}{r} 17 \\ -8 \\ \hline \end{array}$$

2.
$$\begin{array}{r} 15 \\ -6 \\ \hline \end{array} \qquad \begin{array}{r} 18 \\ -9 \\ \hline \end{array} \qquad \begin{array}{r} 16 \\ -7 \\ \hline \end{array} \qquad \begin{array}{r} 15 \\ -7 \\ \hline \end{array} \qquad \begin{array}{r} 14 \\ -6 \\ \hline \end{array} \qquad \begin{array}{r} 18 \\ -9 \\ \hline \end{array}$$

Write the numbers.
Then add or subtract.

3. Carlos has **17**¢.

   He buys a toy for **9**¢.

   How much does he have now?

Add or subtract.

1.
$$\begin{array}{r} 6 \\ +9 \\ \hline \end{array}$$
$$\begin{array}{r} 9 \\ +4 \\ \hline \end{array}$$
$$\begin{array}{r} 7 \\ +7 \\ \hline \end{array}$$
$$\begin{array}{r} 8 \\ +6 \\ \hline \end{array}$$
$$\begin{array}{r} 5 \\ +9 \\ \hline \end{array}$$
$$\begin{array}{r} 8 \\ +4 \\ \hline \end{array}$$

2.
$$\begin{array}{r} 8 \\ +7 \\ \hline \end{array}$$
$$\begin{array}{r} 6 \\ +6 \\ \hline \end{array}$$
$$\begin{array}{r} 8 \\ +9 \\ \hline \end{array}$$
$$\begin{array}{r} 7 \\ +8 \\ \hline \end{array}$$
$$\begin{array}{r} 5 \\ +8 \\ \hline \end{array}$$
$$\begin{array}{r} 8 \\ +8 \\ \hline \end{array}$$

3.
$$\begin{array}{r} 9 \\ +9 \\ \hline \end{array}$$
$$\begin{array}{r} 7 \\ +9 \\ \hline \end{array}$$
$$\begin{array}{r} 6 \\ +8 \\ \hline \end{array}$$
$$\begin{array}{r} 14 \\ -8 \\ \hline \end{array}$$
$$\begin{array}{r} 13 \\ -9 \\ \hline \end{array}$$
$$\begin{array}{r} 15 \\ -9 \\ \hline \end{array}$$

4.
$$\begin{array}{r} 13 \\ -8 \\ \hline \end{array}$$
$$\begin{array}{r} 18 \\ -9 \\ \hline \end{array}$$
$$\begin{array}{r} 16 \\ -8 \\ \hline \end{array}$$
$$\begin{array}{r} 14 \\ -9 \\ \hline \end{array}$$
$$\begin{array}{r} 17 \\ -8 \\ \hline \end{array}$$
$$\begin{array}{r} 16 \\ -7 \\ \hline \end{array}$$

5.
$$\begin{array}{r} 15 \\ -7 \\ \hline \end{array}$$
$$\begin{array}{r} 13 \\ -4 \\ \hline \end{array}$$
$$\begin{array}{r} 14 \\ -5 \\ \hline \end{array}$$
$$\begin{array}{r} 15 \\ -6 \\ \hline \end{array}$$
$$\begin{array}{r} 16 \\ -9 \\ \hline \end{array}$$
$$\begin{array}{r} 17 \\ -9 \\ \hline \end{array}$$

Solve.

6. Jamie has **6** red, **5** yellow, and **3** blue
balloons. How many balloons does he have?

_____ balloons

7. Doris has **18**¢.
She spends **9**¢.
How much does she have left? _____¢

    Chapter 13 Extra Practice

USING YOUR CALCULATOR

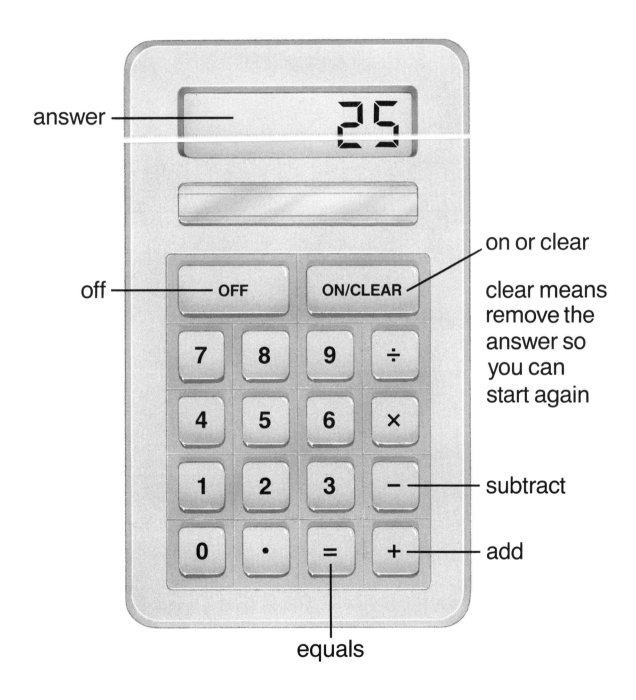

answer

off

on or clear

clear means remove the answer so you can start again

subtract

add

equals

NAME

CALCULATOR ACTIVITIES

CHAPTER 1

Match.

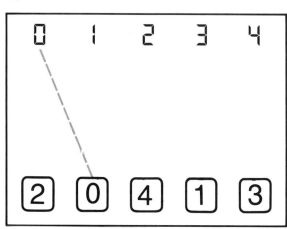

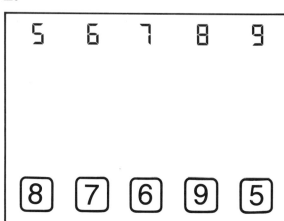

CHAPTER 2

To add **5** + **2** on a calculator you do this.

Press [C] .

Press [5] [+] [2] [=]

Your calculator will show ▷ ⟨ 7 ⟩

Add.

1. [4] [+] [2] [=] ___

2. [2] [+] [5] [=] ___

3. [4] [+] [1] [+] [1] [=] ___

4. [2] [+] [1] [+] [3] [=] ___

Calculator Activities

CALCULATOR ACTIVITIES

CHAPTER 3

Write the number to complete the number sentence.
Use your calculator to help check your answers.

1. ⬜ + ⬜ + ⬜ = 9

2. ⬜ + ⬜ + ⬜ = 8

3. ⬜ + ⬜ + ⬜ = 10

CHAPTER 4

$$4 + 2 = 6 \Rightarrow 6 - 2 = 4$$

4 ➕ 2 🟰 **6** ➖ 2 🟰 **4**

Add and subtract on your calculator.

1. 5 ➕ 4 🟰 ___ ➖ 4 🟰 ___

2. 3 ➕ 5 🟰 ___ ➖ 5 🟰 ___

CALCULATOR ACTIVITIES

CHAPTER 5

How many ⌈2⌉ can we subtract from 4?

⌈4⌉ ⌈−⌉ ⌈2⌉ ⌈=⌉ 〔 2 〕 ⌈−⌉ ⌈2⌉ ⌈=⌉ 〔 0 〕

We can subtract 2 ⌈2⌉ .

1. How many ⌈2⌉ can you subtract from 10? ____

2. How many ⌈3⌉ can you subtract from 9? ____

CHAPTER 6

Count by 10 on your calculator.

1. Press ⌈C⌉ .

   Press ⌈1⌉ ⌈0⌉ ⇨ 10

   Press ⌈+⌉ ⌈1⌉ ⌈0⌉ ⌈=⌉ ⇨ 20

   Press ⌈+⌉ ⌈1⌉ ⌈0⌉ ⌈=⌉ ⇨ 30

What number comes next? 10, 20, 30, 40, ____

2. Press ⌈C⌉ .

   Press ⌈4⌉ ⇨ 4

   Press ⌈+⌉ ⌈1⌉ ⌈0⌉ ⌈=⌉ ⇨ 14

What number comes next? 4, 14, 24, ____, ____,

CALCULATOR ACTIVITIES

CHAPTER 7

Your calculator writes money without the ¢ sign.

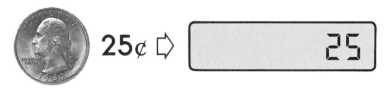

25¢ ▷ | 25

Use your calculator to find the amount.

1.
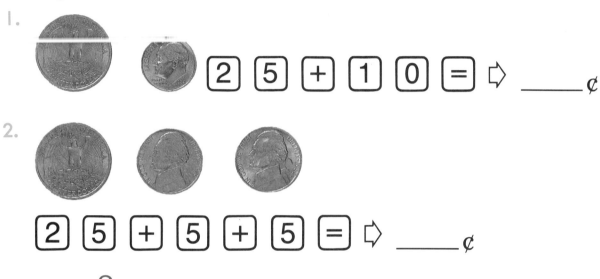

[2] [5] [+] [1] [0] [=] ▷ _____ ¢

2.

[2] [5] [+] [5] [+] [5] [=] ▷ _____ ¢

CHAPTER 8

Find how long the trip takes. Use your calculator.

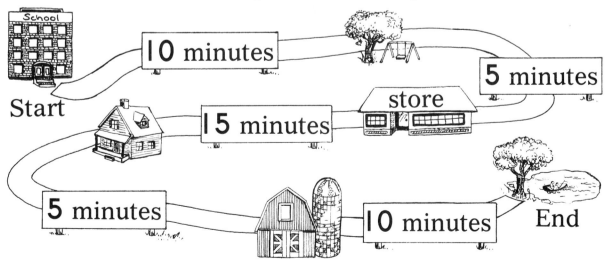

School

10 minutes

5 minutes

Start

15 minutes

store

5 minutes

10 minutes

End

_____ minutes

CHAPTER 9

Use your calculator to add or subtract.

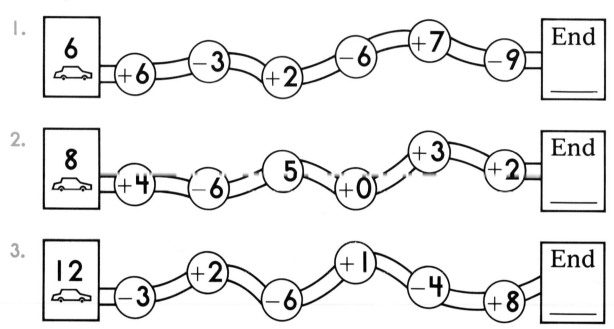

1. 6 🚗 +6 −3 +2 −6 +7 −9 End ____

2. 8 🚗 +4 −6 5 +0 +3 +2 End ____

3. 12 🚗 −3 +2 −6 +1 −4 +8 End ____

CHAPTER 10

Measure to find how long.
Then use your calculator to find
how many centimeters in all.

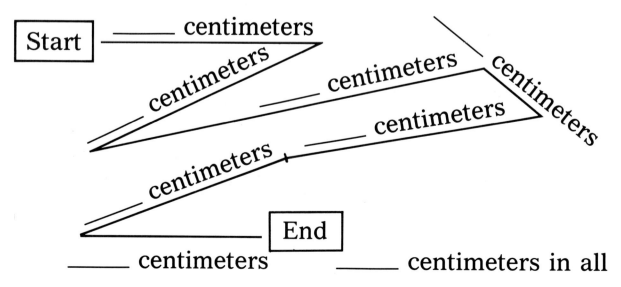

Start ____ centimeters
____ centimeters
____ centimeters
____ centimeters
____ centimeters
End
____ centimeters   ____ centimeters in all

CALCULATOR ACTIVITIES

CHAPTER **11**

Which way does the car go?
Color the path.

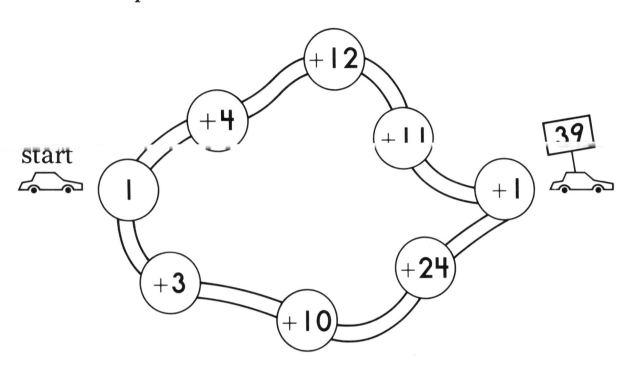

CHAPTER **12**

Find the missing number under the ⭐.

1. $14 + 5 = 19$

2. $3 + = 28$

3. $ - 12 = 11$

4. $ + 10 = 35$

5. $36 - = 21$

6. $23 + = 36$

Calculator Activities

CHAPTER 13

Can you find the sum 10 by adding twos?
Your calculator can help.

2 + 2 + 2 + 2 + 2 + ⇨ [10]

You add 5 twos.

1. Add without using your calculator.

6 + 3 = _____		5 + 4 = _____		8 + 1 = _____	
6 +8	9 + 8 = _____	8 +8	7 +4	5 +5	11 − 4
	7 + 5 = _____				
	4 + 3 = _____				
7 +6	9 +4	15 − 8	5 + 8 = _____	10 − 3	6 +5
			15 − 6 = _____		
			14 − 9 = _____		
16 − 9 = _____		18 − 9 = _____		7 + 8 = _____	

2. Use your calculator to find the sums
that can be made by adding twos.
Color those boxes red.

3. What is the message? _____

Calculator Activities

CHAPTER **1**   PROBLEM SOLVING ACTIVITIES

Cut out pictures from a magazine.
Paste them on this page.
Show **1** dog, **2** children, and **3** trees.

Tell a story about your page to a partner.

Use counters to show different ways to make **7**. Here is one way.

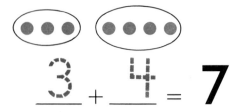

$$\underline{3} + \underline{4} = \textbf{7}$$

Draw counters to show your work.
Write the number sentence.

1.

_____ + _____ = **7**

2.

_____ + _____ = **7**

3.

_____ + _____ = **7**

4.

_____ + _____ = **7**

CHAPTER 3   PROBLEM SOLVING ACTIVITIES

Use punchout pennies
Show how to make the sum.
Draw pennies in the boxes to show your work.
Write the number sentence.

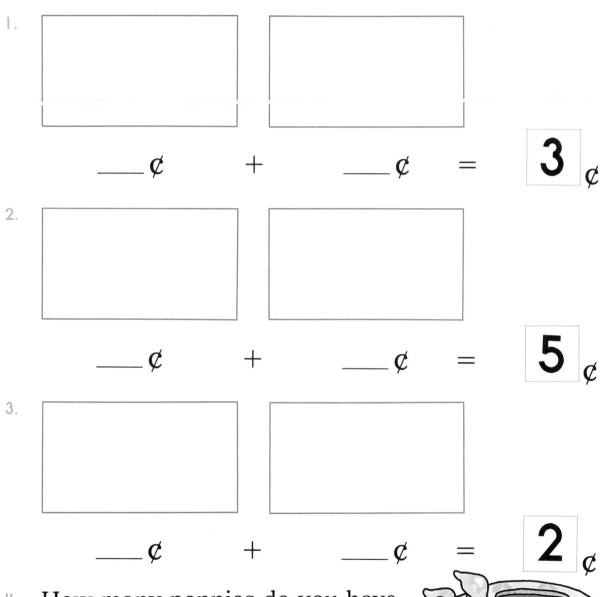

1.

___ ¢   +   ___ ¢   =   **3** ¢

2.

___ ¢   +   ___ ¢   =   **5** ¢

3.

___ ¢   +   ___ ¢   =   **2** ¢

4. How many pennies do you have
   for the bank? Tell a partner
   how you found the answer. Did
   your partner use a different way?   _____ ¢

Mike catches 10 fish at the fair.
Draw an X on each fish that he catches.

Complete.

1. Mike catches ____  .

    There are ____ left.   **7** − ____ = ____

2. Mike catches ____  .

    There are ____ left.   ____ − ____ = ____

3. Mike catches ____ 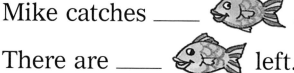 .

    There are ____ 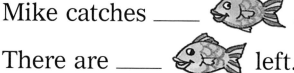 left.   ____ − ____ = ____

Your partner writes the subtraction sentence to show your story.

Work with a partner. Take turns.
Use the picture to tell a subtraction story.

_____ − _____ = _____   _____ − _____ = _____

Share your subtraction sentences with another group. What do you notice?

Play this number game with a partner.
Make **2** sets of cards like this:

| 0 | 1 | 2 | 3 | 4 | 5 | 6 | 7 | 8 | 9 |

Mix the cards in a pile.
Each of you takes **5** cards.
Think of a number clue like this one:

> I am thinking of
> a number. It has
> 3 tens and 8 ones.

Tell your partner your clue.
Can your partner use his or her
cards to show the number?
If yes, your partner scores 1 point.
Each of you takes a turn.

Mix the cards again.
Take **5** new cards.
See who can score 10 points first!

CHAPTER 7   PROBLEM SOLVING ACTIVITIES

This is the money that you can spend.
Use punchout coins.

Cut out the pictures below.
What would you like to buy?
Paste the pictures in the box.

Do you have any money left over? _____

How much? _____

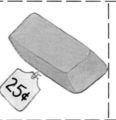

Write the time.

MY DAY

I get up at _____:_____ .

I go to school at _____:_____ .

I eat lunch at _____:_____ .

I come home at _____:_____ .

I eat dinner at _____:_____ .

I go to bed at _____:_____ .

Now work with a partner.
Compare your days.
Ring the times that are the same.

Write number sentences to show the
sum or difference.
Draw balloons to show your number sentence.

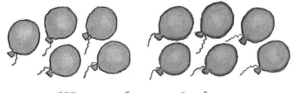

$5 + 6 = 11$

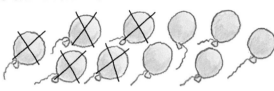

$10 - 5 = 5$

1. [ ]

2. [ ]

___ + ___ = 10

___ − ___ = 7

Now draw pictures for a partner.
Let your partner write the number sentence.

3. [ ]

4. [ ]

___ − ___ = ___

___ + ___ = ___

Cut out the unit stick at the bottom of the page.
Find these objects in your classroom.
Measure them with the unit stick.

1.  _____ units

2.  _____ units

3.  _____ units

4.  _____ units

5. _____ units

6. Share your work with a partner.
   Are your answers the same?

CHAPTER **11**   PROBLEM SOLVING ACTIVITIES

Use these circles to make spinners.
You need a pencil and paper clip.

Take turns with a partner.
Spin each spinner once.
Write the numbers you spin.
Add the two numbers.
Use this chart to find your score:

sum	0–20	21–40	41–60	61–80	81–100
points	1	2	3	4	5

See who scores **20** points first!
Now use one spinner for both spins.
Which spinner will you use? Why? Try it.

Color inside the rectangle blue.
Color inside the circle yellow.
Color inside the triangle red.

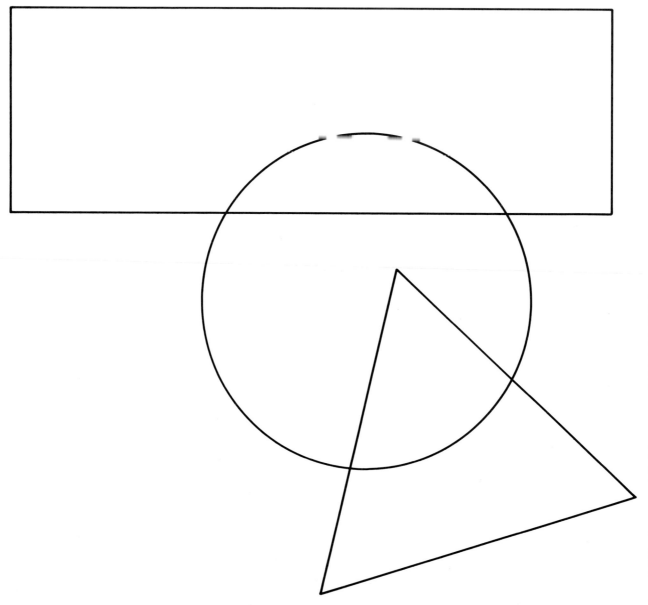

Talk with a partner. What happens
to the colors of the shapes?
Try this with other colors on a sheet of paper.

Use the clues to write number sentences.

1. I am an addition fact. One of my numbers is 6. What number sentence could I be?

_____

_____

_____

3. I am a subtraction fact. My first number is 15. What number sentence could I be?

_____

_____

_____

2. I am a subtraction fact. My answer is more than 5. What number sentence could I be?

_____

_____

_____

4. I am an addition fact. My sum is less than 17. What number sentence could I be?

_____

_____

Now work with a partner.
Make up some clues of your own.
Your partner writes the number sentences. Take turns.

_____

_____

_____

_____

PICTURE GLOSSARY

centimeter

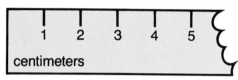

circle

cone

cube

cup

cylinder

difference

$$10 - 6 = 4$$

difference

dime

graph

FRUITS

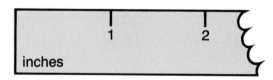

0 1 2 3 4

greater than

15 is **greater than** 12.

inch

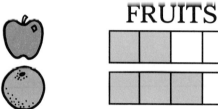

kilogram

less than

37 is **less than 63.**

Picture Glossary

liter

quart

nickel

quarter

one fourth

rectangle

one half

sphere

one third

square

penny

sum

$$2 + 7 = 9$$

⇧
sum

pint

pound

triangle